DATE DUE

JE 26 '97			
NO 25 '97			
AG 5 04			
OE 1 05			

DEMCO 38-296

Women Singing in the Snow

Women

Singing in the Snow

a cultural analysis of chicana literature

Tey Diana Rebolledo

The University of Arizona Press   Tucson / London

The preparation of this volume was made possible in part by a grant from the Division of Research Programs of the National Endowment for the Humanities, an independent federal agency, and by support from the Southwest Hispanic Research Institute and the University of New Mexico.

THE UNIVERSITY OF ARIZONA PRESS

Library of Congress Cataloging-in-Publication Data
Rebolledo, Tey Diana, 1937–
    Women singing in the snow : a cultural analysis of Chicana literature /
Tey Diana Rebolledo.
        p.   cm.
    Includes bibliographical references and index.
    ISBN 0-8165-1520-4 (alk. paper). — ISBN 0-8165-1546-8 (pbk. : alk.
paper)
        1. American literature — Mexican American authors — History and
criticism. 2. American literature — Women authors — History and criticism.
3. Women and literature — United States — History. 4. Mexican American
women — Intellectual life. 5. Mexican American women in literature.
6. Mexican Americans in literature. I. Title.
PS153.M4R43   1995
810.9′9287′0896872 — dc20   94-18740
                                                        CIP

British Cataloguing-in-Publication Data
A catalogue record for this book is available from the British Library.

For my sisters
Gloria Sandra Rebolledo Ingham
and
María de los Angeles López-Portillo Stiteler

Contents

Contents

Preface

She is a
woman singing
in the snow . . . We are her
echo. —Alma Luz Villanueva, "Siren" (*Life Span*)

The title *Women Singing in the Snow* may seem antithetical for a book about Chicana writers, who are traditionally associated with the Southwest and the desert. Those familiar with Chicana writing know, however, that Chicanas write about their experiences in Chicago, California, Texas — wherever they may be. Although there have been many attempts to silence Chicanas, they have continued singing, speaking, and writing.

Alma Luz Villanueva's magnificent image of a woman singing in the snow also conjures up the unexpected, the startling. Snow could stand for paper, as in Sandra Cisneros's description, "only a house quiet as snow . . . clean as paper before the poem" (*The House on Mango Street*, 100), wherein all creativity is at once contained but not always revealed. Thus the "blank page" can symbolize not only women's creative power but also their silence and silencing. It could refer to the chain of women who never told their stories, or the symbolic hardships of women trying to write without a room of their own — women writing in the face of a cold, inhospitable, and unreceptive climate. Yet the image can also be seen as a metaphor for the triumph of women who manage, finally, to sing in spite of it all.

This project started in another guise many years ago and resulted in a collection of many texts in *Infinite Divisions: An Anthology of Chicana Literature,* which I edited with Eliana Rivero of the University of Arizona. Many, but not all, of the texts referred to here can be found in *Infinite Divisions*, but no anthology can keep pace with Chicana writers today.

Certain passages of this book also appear in *Infinite Divisions*. These sections are integral to both volumes, and not all readers will have access to both. For that reason, this information has been repeated, with my apologies to those who find it redundant.

English translations of quoted material, unless otherwise noted, are my own.

Why a cultural analysis? Because Chicana literature has become a vast and enormously complex field. This book is an attempt to trace and contextualize certain themes or areas in Chicana literature, including the meaning and importance of identity, of gender, of sexual preference, and of being a Chicana. It examines the importance of growing up and being a witness to the historical, social, and cultural processes that formed the writers. It explores the meaning of living a border existence: existing in worlds that may contain you but are never completely yours. Most significantly, the book is an attempt to show how Chicana writers, with the self-realization of their emerging consciousness, have managed to make themselves the subjects of their own discourses.

For women growing up in a culture that taught them that to survive, you should not speak out, and that your loyalty was to your family and the collectivity, not to yourself as an individual, writing is a subversive act. Many Chicana writers, although not all, are from working-class families. They may be the first in their families to be educated. Yet the phenomena that seemed to silence women at the same time enabled them to speak out—for and with the collectivity, as well as for themselves. In the writers' memories, in their witnessing, are many references to the chain of women who came before them and who supported them, evidence of the bonding with other women through which Chicana writers find their sustenance and their strength.

A central concept in this book is the idea of seizing subjectivity or becoming the subject of your own discourse. For many years Chicanas have been unable to write or to publish their writing if they did write. They were also working within a system in which language denied them. Thus to be able to write meant they had to "seize the language" (Ostriker) and become the subjects of their own narrations, and not the objects. This implies an extraordinary measure of empowerment for those women who were supposed to stay at home, be good wives and mothers, and be caregivers: active within the domestic sphere but not the public one. To find language, then voice, then consciousness of self and to be able to insert themselves as subjects has been very difficult, particularly for minority women writers.

There is, of course, a strong oral tradition in our culture, an oral tradition in which women were active participants. Nevertheless, many of the Chicana writers writing today are first-generation writers who tell their mothers' and grandmothers' stories as well as their own. There have been few role models to allow these writers to break cultural stereotypes and restrictions and emerge with public voices into discourse. Thus becoming the agent of one's own subjectivity, having the courage and the freedom to speak out on public as well as private issues, has engendered a new generation of writers who explore their universe. Becoming the speaking subject for those who have been mute and "other" not only breaks all sorts of boundaries but also is the source for enormous creativity. Having multiple identities in various cultures also allows for shifting perspectives in all areas: since the subject need not be stable, then it can become multiply voiced — that is, it no longer has to be unified and static but is free to be complex and disparate. Having multiple identities also allows for contradictions and paradoxes within the problematizing discourse. This subject of consciousness is the central site of knowledge but "problematizes it by representing it as a weave" (Alarcón, "The Theoretical Subject," 366), that is, many threads coming together to form some sort of shape and structure. And it is this shifting, complex, and ever-changing subjectivity that is electrifying Chicana literature.

Implicit in this book is my belief (and my desire to demonstrate) that Chicana writers are influenced not only by the popular and oral heritage of Mexican culture (seen in such figures as La Llorona and La Malinche) but also by female Mexican writers such as Sor Juana Inés de la Cruz and Rosario Castellanos. These early writers have had an important impact on many Chicana writers, particularly those who are more conversant in Spanish. Chicana writers, then, are doubly enriched by popular and formal Mexican tradition as well as by Anglo-American traditions.

Acknowledgments

I owe more gratitude than I can express to Alice and Ted Washton and their daughters Ricki Washton Long, Harriet Washton, and Kate Washton, who took me in and supported me when I needed it most, and who continue to do so. They have been my family. And I want to thank my daughter Tey Marianna Nunn for being here (and there).

As in all works, many people helped put this project together. First and most important, I owe a great many thanks to the writers themselves, who took time to talk with me, share their ideas and concerns, and send me their work. I am indebted to the Center for Regional Studies and the Southwest Hispanic Research Institute at the University of New Mexico for their continuing support in many ways. For the patience of Joanne O'Hare, my editor at the University of Arizona Press, I am grateful. Thanks also to Alexis Noebels, who made this read better.

I want in particular to thank five dear friends who have listened to me in my joys, my rages, and at all other times: Margarita Cota-Cárdenas, Erlinda Gonzales-Berry, Pat Mora, Sandra Cisneros, and María Dolores Gonzales-Velásquez. Gracias, comadres, por su apoyo.

Y como siempre, a Mikko Passi, mi lector y compañero.

Women Singing in the Snow

Introduction

chicana critics in the wilderness—theories and praxis

In 1995, Chicana critics writing on Chicana writers are still in the wilderness, the margins of mainstream criticism. Although our authors are becoming better known (Sandra Cisneros is a prime example), not a single article on Chicana literature by a Chicana critic has been published in *Publications of the Modern Language Association (PMLA)*, *Critical Inquiry*, or other mainstream journals. It may be that Chicana critics don't bother to send work to such journals knowing a priori that our concerns and our formalization of them are so far afield from the center that it would be useless. We continue to publish in journals and books related to minority issues, with publishers like Third Woman Press, Bilingual Press, Arte Público Press, and in volumes concerned with Chicano issues. When such volumes are published by mainstream presses (e.g., *Criticism in the Borderlands*, Calderón and Saldívar, 1991), the women's work must be combined with that of the better-known male Chicano critics. Perhaps we prefer it this way, but our young untenured colleagues continue to be besieged in our universities and plagued by the persistent questions: Is this work valid? Is this work legitimate? Is this journal refereed? What kind of a journal is it anyway? Our retention at universities remains tentative at best, our recognition in the larger world small. For these and other reasons, Chicana literary critics in the United States remain a small group, probably numbering about twenty. Marta Sánchez's *Contemporary Chicana Poetry* (1985) stands as the lone book written by a Chicana critic on Chicana literature.

We probably have not produced the "definitive" theoretical books on Chicana writing because we remain cautious about majestic declarations and cognizant of the temptation to generalize, define, usurp, or speak for others. We do not want to essentialize nor be reductive, in either our literature or our criticism. It becomes a politics of representation in an age when some critics question if it is possible to represent at all. We are aware that the dangers and interpretive pitfalls are like those of Bernice Zamora's cobra master, whose duty "is fraught with fettered chores" (74; Rebolledo and Rivero, 279). We are our own shifting subjects. Nevertheless, many books on Chicana writers are in the gestation stage and should be coming forth soon.

A growing corpus of critical thought and praxis evinces an evolving infrastructure of a Chicana feminist theory. In particular, critical ruminations on postmodernity, postcolonialism, and their ramifications have appeared in the last several years. For example, how can the speaking subject (the authorial voice) be dead when it is just beginning to evolve? Are we readers? And how are we as readers resisting, intercultural, feminist? What are our critical stances? First World, nativist? What is/are our positionality(ies)?

By privileging purely theoretical discourses over praxis, we risk creating dialogic schisms about the validity of such praxis. Certainly, various ideological and philosophical perspectives on our literature serve to position us within a discursive framework and may even help elucidate the literature. My own bias, having undergone various theoretical illuminations over a period of time (from archetypal to structuralist, from radical feminist to revisionist contextualist), is to agree with the positionality of both Gloria Anzaldúa and Debra Castillo.

Anzaldúa, elaborating on her "mestiza consciousness," articulated what had been in the air for some time. When *Borderlands/La frontera* was published, many Chicanas recognized Anzaldúa's description of the multiply voiced, shifting subjectivities and ideologies as our own. She courageously enunciated an ideological stance of the utility of choice: survival. We did not need to heed solely First World or Third World perceptions, theories, definitions, or ideologies. The theoretical basis of our analysis could be of our own choosing. Indeed, so could the ingredients. We could, and did, pick from multiple possibilities to ensure our survival. We had already learned how to do that in our own daily lives fraught with "open wounds" (Anzaldúa, *Borderlands*, 3). So, too, in our writing, whether creative or critical, we need to use whatever is useful.

For example, Debra Castillo, in her illuminating book *Talking Back* (1992), elaborates a theory of feminist ideology/praxis concerning Latin American women writers. In so doing, she includes Chicana writers as part of the Third World continuum. Using women's everyday housework as a metaphor, Castillo frames a theoretical basis of support for the practice of eclectic criticism: Use that which is useful, that which is at hand. Noting that, in practical terms, critical theories have their apex and decline, suc- ceeding each other in ever-widening rings in the pond, Castillo believes that often-contradictory strategies for an evolving critique could be formed around a central metaphor of the recipe and cooking. The recipe, which stands for the theoretical basis underlying the textual analysis, is repre- sented as a loose format around which things may be added or taken away. "A recipe is not a blueprint and any experienced cook will concur that it is almost impossible to stick to the script, even the first time through. It is less a formula than a general model; less an axiom of unchanging law and more like a theory of possibilities" (xiii). Castillo envisions this theoretical basis to be a reciprocal exchange between the doer and the receiver, emphasizing that the Latin root of "recipe," *recipere,* indicates this exchange. Castillo sees Latin American feminist writing as well as Chicana writing as nonreductive and a challenge to "a monumentalizing or totalizing view of literature" (16). It, too, is multiply voiced and operates within shifting positionalities. Although not meant to be conclusive or comprehensive, current writing on critical issues in Chicana literature can be formulated in the following man- ner, and perhaps critical praxis can be articulated in the following ways.

Although many male Chicano critics continue to ignore Chicana writers in favor of the now-canonical male figures of the tradition, others have begun to broaden their theoretical framework. The women (usually Cisneros and Anzaldúa) may be included as chronologically recent phe- nomena and tacked on toward the end of the book. That is not to say the critical discussion of their work is not useful, because it is, but as an addi- tion, they are set apart from a contextual continuum. One such example would be Ramón Saldívar's *Chicano Narrative,* in which he discusses Cis- neros, Cherríe Moraga, and Isabella Ríos, stating that they are "building an instructive alternative to the exclusively phallocentric subject of contempo- rary Chicano narrative" (175). Saldívar, however, consciously acknowl- edges the limitations of his study regarding women. Hector Calderón's article "At the Crossroads of History, on the Borders of Change" (1988) mentions only three women critics, and of those, only their work on male writers. Yet a volume edited by Calderón and José David Saldívar, *Criticism in the Borderlands* (1991), shows a genuine effort to include articles by women: Norma Alarcón, Elizabeth Ordóñez, Rosaura Sánchez, Angie Chabrám, Barbara Harlow, Teresa McKenna, Alvina Quintana, and Sonia Saldívar-Hull. Furthermore, in the introduction, the editors welcome the interest in feminist scholarship and view their book "paired with the recent books by Moraga and Anzaldúa (1983) and Herrera-Sobek and Vira- montes (1988) in Latina feminist studies" (6).

Some Chicano critics have focused on the work of women — either on the work of a single author, such as Julián Olivares on space in the work of Cisneros, or Francisco Lomelí on Ríos's *Victuum*. However, the work of these women is often analyzed from a male theoretical framework (Bachelard; Olivares, 160) or molded to fit into male formulas such as generational stages. In 1985, Lomelí noted that although gains had been made in bringing Chicano literature into "some degree of world prominence," there was "an alarmingly low number of critical studies devoted to novels written by Chicanas" ("Chicana Novelists," 30). He attributed this to a lack of supportive environment, to psychological discouragement, and a lack of exposure. Worse still was "the underlying implication that issues women writers raise are not of great magnitude or importance" (32). Juan Bruce-Novoa, a critic who included the work of Chicana writers in his 1982 book *Chicano Poetry,* has introduced the uncanonized and largely ignored writers such as Cecile Piñeda. Perhaps some of the most useful criticism by men is the recuperative work by Genaro Padilla on the California Bancroft narratives and New Mexico writer Cleofas Jaramillo.

Chicana critics of Chicana literature seem to be operating from a totally different perspective. From the beginning, Third Woman Press and volumes published by Arte Público Press and edited by María Herrera-Sobek and Helena María Viramontes brought Chicana literature and literary criticism to the forefront. In many of these texts, it becomes evident that working on emergent colonial literature requires acknowledging what the writers were trying to do in their own social context. If current theory claims that the speaking subject is dead, that may well speak for the positionality of First World writers. But Chicana literature is a budding literature replete with its own characteristics, and one of these characteristics is the seizing of subjectivity — evolving into a speaking/writing subject. Thus postmodernism can only be approached in Chicana literature as an acknowledgment of multiple points of view on the part of the writers and of the critics themselves.

The arguments as to whether Derridian, Lacanian, French feminist, and Anglo feminist criticism and response is vital to the analysis of Chicana literature have critics in various camps. Although I don't think any critic, even myself (see "The Politics of Poetics"), would argue that we should disregard First World critical approaches, some sensible limitations are needed on the overlay of these critical theories on our literature as we try to evolve and articulate our own theories. I would argue, as does Debra Castillo, that some of these theories can help us to understand and contextualize the opus of Chicana literature.

I am not such a nativist that I believe we can produce a "pure," "un-contaminated" product or theory. Clearly, in today's world, with the inter-mingling of ideologies, languages, and commodities, this is impossible. I believe, however, in the *salpicón* analysis of literature: a bit of this, a bit of that. Moreover, I would argue, as I have before, that theory must be appro-priate and well integrated in its application to the literature, that the critic's biases need to be acknowledged, and that praxis is as important as theory.

Characteristic of contemporary literature — especially in Latin Ameri-can and Chicana literature, and perhaps part of the reason postmodernist critics think the speaking subject is dead — are the quantities of popular culture, oral traditions, and folklore that inform our literature and are inte-grated with it. Songs, *dichos* (sayings), traditions, oral narratives, and popu-lar history pepper our literature. These forms also place emphasis on the collectivity, as can be noted in the analysis of the importance of the *corrido* (the ballad) in the border narrative, and the appearance of such folk figures as La Llorona in literature. This is a field currently being analyzed by critics such as Herrera-Sobek in *The Mexican Corrido: A Feminist Analysis* and Saldívar-Hull in her discussion of Mexican romances and dime-store novels in the work of Cisneros and others. It is the rare Chicana author who does not have the refrain of a song (*bolero,* corrido, or *ranchera*), or a dicho, or a memory of the oral tradition slip across the text. This use of folk and popular culture acquires a life of its own and often places the poem or the narrative into a historical/cultural context as well as adding a mythic di-mension to the work.

Critical attention has also focused on how the colonized subject breaks the silence and seizes subjectivity. Among the critics who successfully analyze the multiply voiced subject in Chicana writing is Norma Alarcón, perhaps the most purely theoretically based Chicana critic. Alarcón has shown, through various critical articles, how the oppression of Chicana writers combined with their sense of communal and social ideology has produced a shifting, split, multiply voiced speaking subject that claims an authority only as it speaks for a collectivity. Basing her theoretical frame-work on French and Anglo-American feminist theory, Alarcón has articu-lated the importance of going beyond theory into an analysis of the social reality surrounding the writers, and the politics of struggle involved in that reality.

Part of this analysis involves the deconstruction of power relations, which Alvina Quintana addresses in "Politics, Representation and the Emergence of a Chicana Aesthetics." Quintana examines how Chicano op-positional movements challenged and resisted dominant cultural models but at the same time were subordinated and repressed by the ideologies of resistance. This, she sees, forced Chicanas to resist those ideologies, which in turn allowed "new aesthetic opportunities" that gave Chicanas a strategic position from which to enhance or refute them, contributing to what she sees as a "multiplicity of voices and experiences" (259). Similarly, Saldívar-Hull in "Feminism on the Border: From Gender Politics to Geopolitics" questions the hegemonic power of Eurocentric feminist critics who do not "recognize" Chicana theory. For Saldívar-Hull, the problem is that "Chicanas ask different questions which in turn ask for a reconstruction of the very premises of 'theory.' Because the history of the Chicana experience in the United States defines our particular *mestizaje* of feminism, our theory cannot be a replicate of white feminism nor can it be only an academic abstraction. The Chicana feminist looks to her history . . . to learn how to transform the present" (220).

Chicanas who define themselves primarily as creative writers also change genre by "doing" criticism (e.g., Anzaldúa). Often, as in Latin American writing, the perspective in these texts is political, ideological, and social as well as critical. Certainly, many of the principal ideas of feminist critical thinkers such as Luce Irigaray and Julia Kristeva are embedded in Anzaldúa's texts. A mixture of politics, poetry, oral tradition, personal essay, and autobiography, Anzaldúa's *Borderlands* is the epitome of a creative/critical praxis that tries to identify and imbue a purely Chicana-Mestiza-India (and all the aforementioned complications) theoretical discourse with practice. Here Anzaldúa, in seizing the subject, shifts from the personal to the collective, from the emotional to the political, from the details of her lived personal life to its connections with the mythic. It is a text that, as Saldívar-Hull has pointed out, "complicates things," which Chicana critics often do ("Feminism," 203). Rather than being reductive, as many European and Anglo theoretical frameworks are, Anzaldúa's theoretic praxis is more baroque, thereby allowing very useful shifting zones of representation and significations. Another example would be *Nepantla* by Pat Mora, a series of essays that transpose genre, mixing the personal with the political, and poetry with narrative. Mora is not afraid to interject critical thinking about what it is to be a writer and what responsibilities that entails.

Many Chicana critics have been working to contextualize Chicana literature based on broad themes such as growing up, oppression, violence against women, and what it means to be a writer. These themes, which can be found in the work of many Chicana writers, place the individual and her concerns against the backdrop of the greater social and cultural picture.

Although more purely theoretical critics may undervalue this thematic, contextual criticism, it is useful for understanding the sociopolitical representation of meaning in Chicana literature. In *Chicana Voices: Intersections of Class, Race and Gender* (Córdova et al., 1990), several articles elaborated contextual themes. Yolanda Broyles's "Women in El Teatro Campesino: '¿Apoco estaba molacha la Virgen de Guadalupe?'" examines the participation (and exclusion) of women in El Teatro Campesino and discusses the struggle and example of women who strove to "reclaim a fully human female identity on stage" (186); Clara Lomas discusses the issues of reproductive freedom in "Libertad de no procrear: La voz de la mujer en 'A una madre de nuestros tiempos' by Margarita Cota-Cárdenas"; and Alvina Quintana discusses voice and silence in Chicana writing in "Women: Prisoners of the Word." More recently, writers have begun to explore the urban experiences and struggles of Chicana writers; for example, Cota-Cárdenas's articles, "The Chicana in the City as Seen in Her Literature" and "The Faith of Activists: Barrios, Cities and the Chicana Feminist Response," and Herrera-Sobek's "The Street Scene: Metamorphic Strategies in Two Contemporary Chicana Poets." Other critics analyze symbolism and imagery in Chicana literature, as does Laura Gutiérrez Spencer in "Fairy Tales and Opera: The Fate of the Heroine in the Work of Sandra Cisneros" and "Cactus Flowers and Other Floral Images in Pat Mora."

Documentation of the continuum of Chicana social and cultural history has also been receiving a great deal of emphasis. This recuperative work has been added to by historians and critics alike. Clara Lomas, Rosaura Sánchez, Genaro Padilla, and I are among the literary critics examining the work of authors who were writing before the Chicano Renaissance. Among the first of such publications was *Pasó por aquí: Critical Essays on the New Mexican Literary Tradition, 1542–1988,* edited by Erlinda Gonzales-Berry (1989). The book spanned New Mexican Hispano authors from the early colonial period to the present. Several more books have recently appeared, including *Reconstructing a Chicano/a Literary Heritage: Hispanic Colonial Literature of the Southwest,* edited by Herrera-Sobek (1993), and *Recovering the U.S. Hispanic Literary Heritage,* edited by Gutiérrez and Padilla (1993). Both books contain important contributions to the history of Chicana literature and form part of several projects designed to uncover and publish works by Mexicano/Chicano authors of the United States. Many of these projects are sponsored by the Recovering the U.S. Hispanic Literary Heritage Project and Arte Público Press. In addition to the important collections already published, several presses, including the University of Arizona Press, University of New Mexico Press, and Arte Público Press, are sponsoring reissues of out-of-print texts such as *The Squatter and the Don* by María Amparo Ruiz de Burton, edited by Rosaura Sánchez and Beatrice Pita (1992); *Mexican Village* by Josephina Niggli, with an introduction by Herrera-Sobek (1994); *We Fed Them Cactus* by Fabiola Cabeza de Baca Gilbert, with an introduction by Tey Diana Rebolledo (1994); and *Romance of a Little Village Girl* by Cleofas Jaramillo, with an introduction by Padilla (forthcoming). The reissuing of these texts not only will make these works available to the general reading public but will open them up for further analysis and inclusion into the canon.

Chicana critics also seek to elaborate a "different" creative space for Chicana criticism, which Cordelia Candelaria refers to as "The Wild Zone," "a distinct female cultural space derived from biological and historical imperatives," thus capturing the idea of "a separate area of human consciousness defined outside a male-identified, male controlled civilization" (3). She also sees the wild zone as a metaphor for the ethnic and racial minority experience in the United States. For Candelaria, the wild zone's emphasis is on "the shared collective experience of women excluded from decision-making rights and privileges of the patriarchy" (9). This theory would account for the levels of mediation between literary and social domains. Candelaria calls for a feminist literary theory dependent upon a feminist social theory, relating texts to changing ideologies as they affect women as social subjects.

Yvonne Yarbro-Bejarano has also been working on defining a space for Chicana writers and critics, particularly Chicana lesbians. In challenging articles, Yarbro-Bejarano combines textual criticism with images and iconography by Chicana visual artists in order to expand and elucidate cultural self-representation (e.g., "Insider/Outsider"). She also acknowledges the "Mestiza" position as that of an insider/outsider for whom the positionality is shifting. Yarbro-Bejarano thus offers not only a multiple cultural critique of the mixture between visual and textual arts using the iconography of altars and *ofrendas* (sacred offerings) to illuminate Chicana literature, but she also contextualizes the mythography whereby someone like "La Llorona," the crying woman, can become a *gritona,* the hollering woman. She continues to incorporate these multiple cultural critiques as she makes a space for Chicana lesbian writers and critics. This can be seen clearly in "De-constructing the Lesbian Body: Cherríe Moraga's *Loving in the War Years.*" Here, Yarbro-Bejarano discusses "the cartography of lesbian desire, the unspeakable speaking and the unrepresentable desire" of the Chicana lesbian, which "maps" the oppression and the suppression of subjectivity in Moraga's writing (143). Yarbro-Bejarano is a critic whose work engages us all in further dialogue and understanding of lesbian issues.

It is clear from this limited discussion that the critical theories and practices that Chicana critics are just beginning to formulate will be as varied as they will be illuminating. Furthermore, as younger Chicana scholars trained in Chicana literature (as we were not) take their places in the academy, spaces for Chicana criticism will be opened, and the critics can emerge from the wilderness and come home.

1

Early Hispana/Mexicana Writers

the chicana literary tradition

The number of known texts written by Mexican American women in the United States between 1848 and 1960 is very small. In the early years (1848–1910), Mexican American women generally were unable to read or write unless they came from wealthy families. Formal education for women was not considered a prime necessity, although many were trained in the "gentler" arts: fine sewing, embroidery, and music.

The women who immigrated from Mexico were often pioneers: they needed to survive on isolated ranches or to earn a living in more urbanized areas. There was little leisure time for reading and writing. Still, there were those who wrote, and some of their writing continues to be preserved within the family, languishing in trunks and boxes—unpublished and undistributed. Although much is lost, more and more material written by Hispanic women between 1848 and 1960 is coming to light. Nevertheless, early Hispanic women writers are often mentioned only in passing, if at all, in the general accounts of Hispanic cultural production in the United States. They are part of the culture of silence that until the Chicano Renaissance of the late 1960s effectively obscured those women who did write and who, for the most part, remain unread and unpublished.

The material in this chapter and in chapter 2 comes from four main sources: 1) oral histories from the California Bancroft collection and the New Mexico and Arizona Works Progress Administration Federal Writers' Projects; 2) oral folktales and stories emerging from the *cuento*/"*estoria*" (story) tradition; 3) creative written material published in Spanish (mainly in Spanish-language newspapers); and 4) creative written material published in English, much of it between 1920 and 1950 (although at least two novels in English were published in 1872 and 1885). This material includes poetry, narratives about folklore and traditions, recipes and stories about recipes and the gathering of food, and writing about women-centered issues such as health care and health-care providers, relationships between women, and relationships between men and women. The material also describes women's roles within their families and communities. Although this chapter is not intended to be a definitive study of early Hispana/Mexicana writers, it is meant to suggest the possibilities for research and perhaps entice researchers into further work that needs to be done.

Oral Histories: The Bancroft Narratives

In the 1870s, historian Hubert H. Bancroft collected oral histories of California and the Southwest in an attempt to document the early history of the region. As Rosaura Sánchez notes, most of these early histories lay forgotten in the archives of the Bancroft historical project as part of the "silenced voice, the voice of the subaltern" ("Nineteenth-Century California Narratives," 279). Although these narratives functioned only as raw material for Anglo historians, Chicano scholars are beginning to research these narratives for details of Hispano/Mexicano California life, and the narratives themselves are beginning to be translated and published. As Sánchez notes, "we have to acknowledge that it is to one such entrepreneurial researcher and publisher that we owe even the existence and accessibility to us today of a number of manuscripts narrated by the Californios themselves" (280). Genaro Padilla concurs, saying that "women's narratives were considered merely supplemental to men's; indeed, even when they were considered 'reliable and fascinating'" (*My History, Not Yours,* 111). Of the materials collected by Bancroft and his assistants, at least twelve are narratives or testimonials by women. These testimonials are "doubly voiced" according to Sánchez, because the oral histories were filtered first through the recording by a second person and then again when translated into English (284). Nevertheless, in reading the narratives by these California Hispanas, one is able to discern a distinct, although muted, female voice.

At times an exasperation, a value judgment, a triumphal moment, or an outrage reaches through the translations, as in the memoirs of Doña María Inocencia Pico ("Reminiscences of California," 1878) when she discusses how young girls became married, "for there existed the evil custom of marrying off girls at a very tender age, whenever they were sought in matrimony" (5). Pico also emphasizes her role in ransoming her husband when he was captured by opposing forces. She did this by sending the opposing general a generous supply of delicious provisions, "chicken, mutton, cakes, cheese, enchiladas, good wine, excellent whiskey etc. All this, richly decorated, along with fine napkins" (6). Thus with her good judgment, not to say bribing of the general, did she secure the freedom of her husband, and he was returned unharmed. In the narrative of Doña Eulalia Pérez, "Una vieja y sus recuerdos" (1877; Rebolledo and Rivero, 39–42), we have an account of her "interview" and her "tryout" as cook for the mission, including a lively account of how she won the "cooking contest."

The voices that come to us from these California narratives not only cement the place of women and their activities in the population of the new frontier but also show us their ingenuity and survival skills. And although the voices are sometimes accommodating to the new order after the Treaty of Guadalupe Hidalgo of 1848, they are also the voices of resistance, anger, and loss. One example that Padilla points out is the resistant signature of Apolonia Lorenzana ("Memorias," 1878) who inscribed her initials on the final page "as a gesture of defiance against an impending threat of historical and cultural death" (*My History, Not Yours,* 147). This was a portent of the future, since it has only been in the last several years that these texts have been uncovered from the archives.

Oral Histories: The Federal Writers' Project

In the 1930s and 1940s, a great deal of interest in the Southwest was sparked by the Federal Writers' Project.[1] In New Mexico, Arizona, and Texas, program participants gathered oral histories, trying to preserve the history and culture of the "old-timers." Because many of the Hispanic informants were older women, valuable information about their lives, education, and traditions was preserved, as well as important folktales about women and their roles.[2]

The oral histories came from people who were in their sixties or older, some of whom came from families of the earliest Spanish settlers. Others had arrived in the nineteenth and twentieth centuries. In Arizona some of the more interesting interviews were conducted by Romelia Gómez of Cochise County,[3] who interviewed elderly Hispana women (many of whom spoke no English) and completed a series of three-page vignettes about their lives. Perhaps because she was Hispana herself and more interested in women's personal lives than most male interviewers, Gómez seems to have been able to better glimpse what these women's lives were like. These interviews also offer insight into the restrictions that prevented women from writing. In an interview with Doña Isabel Hernández, Gómez wrote that "Isabel Juárez (for that was the family name) never attended school in Bisbee and cannot understand or speak English at all." According to Gómez's interview with Martina Diaz, "the respectable families were very proud and they imprisoned forever a girl who committed an indiscretion." Gómez says Casimira Valenzuela (who was 82) was "vague about dates and complete details, as her memory fails her and she can neither read nor write." Señora Lola Romero knew "no English at all, never having attended school in the U.S. Her younger sister was the only one of the family to attend school on the arrival of the family in Bisbee. She went to Central School which was later torn down to make way for the larger brick building of today. There was no compulsion in the attendance of the children at school, so her sister, like most of the Mexican children going to school then only went when she felt like it." Doña Apolonia Mendoza and an older sister also attended school at Central for a short while, "during which time she says they learned nothing at all, so their mother took them out of school so they could help her in earning the family's living, which she did by taking in washing from families living on Chihuahua Hill" (Gómez, AZFWP interviews).

The husbands of these women came to Bisbee mainly as miners, and many of the women had to earn their living doing laundry or serving as domestics because they had few other opportunities. Bisbee was not without culture, however. A Mexican theater group performed regularly, and there were also musical events and many *bailes,* or dances.

The New Mexico Federal Writers' Project: Cuentos and "Estorias" (Historias)

Beyond life histories, the Federal Writers' Project is important because it yielded a valuable source for Chicano literature: a collection of oral folktales known as cuentos or, in New Mexico, "estorias." Many of the informants who shared these folk stories (and songs) were women. While some of the stories are variants of European tales, we are fortunate that others are of local origin and chronicle the lives of people in remote areas such as the small villages in northern New Mexico. These estorias and *memorate* (popular recollections of real-life events) not only portray dramatic situations in which women play an important part, but they also contribute to some understanding of the symbolic literary role of women during these times. Even if they could not read nor write, women could tell stories fired with imagination and symbols that were subsequently passed down from generation to generation. Many contemporary Chicana writers are "first-generation" writers who are telling the estorias of their mothers and grandmothers, thus preserving this oral tradition.[4]

The collection of creative estorias and other oral folk material from the New Mexico Federal Writers' Project is very rich indeed. In general, the stories were told in Spanish and then translated either by the interviewer or the project director, again a double voicing. Several women, including Guadalupe Gallegos and Rumaldita Gurulé and others, provided much information on a variety of topics. The New Mexico collection is particularly rich in women's materials because in 1940–1941 Annette Hersch Thorp gathered materials for a never-completed project that was to be called "Some New Mexico Grandmothers." In addition, much of the collection of folktales came about because several questions were asked of all respondents (Weigle,[5] xix–xx):

Are there any stories concerned with animals or animal life, or the relation between human beings and animals, which are native to your community?

Are there localized ghost stories, witch stories, etc.?

Are there any of the so-called "Tall Tales," where the story teller gets the effect either through exaggeration or understatement, stories that are not in print but that are passed around by "word of mouth"?

Are there any persons in your community who are believed to possess power to see into the future? Tell some of the current stories about such persons.

These standard questions clearly influenced the selection of informants by field writers as well as the type of material they collected, and Thorp indicates the stories were often told by women.

> Story telling was looked forward to on winter nights. All the family, big and little gathered around the fire-place, and by the light of a kerosene lamp, or ocote wood "pitch," would shell corn, or the women sewed, while some grandmother or neighbor viejita "old woman" told stories until time for bed. The beds were made down on the floor. The colchons [sic] "Mattress" were stuffed with wool, and folded on bancos against the wall in the day time. At night they were layed [sic] on the floor. The stories that were told by these grandmothers were religious ones. About Santos, and the miracles they used to perform. And about brujas, "witches," and those who had been embrujada "bewitched." Brujas were taken for granted by all. The men as well as the women believed in brujas, and were careful not to offend anyone they were not sure of. (NMFWP, 17 Dec. 1940)

Many of the stories about women are tales aimed at regulating female behavior — stories with a moral or describing some punishment if the female steps outside prescribed boundaries. One such story is "Las tres gangozas" (The three sisters), told by Guadalupe Gallegos. This story is about three beautiful sisters who had a speech defect causing them "to speak with a sniffle," and therefore none were married. Three young men went to the girls' mother, a widow, to ask for her daughters' hands in marriage. She accepted but was unable to be at home when the young men came to call, so she warned her daughters not to speak while the men were present. At first the girls heeded their mother, but suddenly the coffee began to boil.

> "The coffee is boiling," said the eldest sister forgetting her mother's warning.
> "I'm going to tell mother that you talked," said the second sister.
> "I'm the only one who didn't talk," said the third.
> Upon hearing the defective speech of the sisters, the young men were very shocked and forgot how beautiful the girls were. They jumped up and left immediately, leaving their hats behind.[6]

Although the drama of these stories is enhanced by humor, both the drama and humor are aimed at making sure the moral of the story is remembered. These folktales may not have been simply moralizing or regulatory, however; they may also have been used by women to question the roles assigned to them by their culture. These tales may have expressed dissent and also helped women to see themselves as exercising power over and within their world.[7]

In addition to the moralizing tales mentioned above, the Federal Writers' Project contains a series of stories about some singular female figures in New Mexico folklore, including the *curandera* (folk healer), the *bruja* (witch), and mythic female ghost figures such as La Larga and La Llorona.[8] The curandera in these folktales is referred to with respect for her healing powers and her knowledge of herbs and plants. This respect is clear in a story told by informant Rumaldita Gurulé called "An Old Native Custom: La Curandera" (Rebolledo and Rivero, 43–45):

> In the days of long ago when there were no médicos in the now land of New Mexico . . . healers called curanderos played important parts in the life of the native communities. Their curealls were of the lavish gifts of nature and free to all who collected them. . . .
> In the earliest days of Las Placitas, a little house nestled close to Cerro Negro. . . . A house which became a kind of sanctuary for weary souls and a little temple of health for the sick. It was La Casa de La Curandera, Jesusita.
> The name Jesusita and all of its forms have since been banned by the church. This Jesusita was a pious, honorable curandera devoted to the saints and her remedios. . . .

La Curandera was a very small person, with slender, graceful hands with which she did half of her talking and much of her healing. She wore many petticoats, made of cloth she wove herself, and always she kept them fresh and clean. To one of them she fastened a little sack filled with the hair of every different form of life she could find. This would save her from the power of the witches as would the piece of cachana she wore about her person. . . . Jesusita feared the witches even more than she feared the devil; but then she was born in 1830.[9]

Because of their transformative powers, sometimes these curanderas could also be brujas. Gurulé told a series of stories about Placitas, New Mexico, in which a battle occurs between Quiteria, a young nurse healer, and Doña Tomasa, the witch nurse. Doña Tomasa is jealous of Quiteria, who has been taking her patients away, but Doña Tomasa often manages to outwit Quiteria and win her old patients back. However, as in the following story, Quiteria learns quickly and, if necessary, will resort to her growing knowledge of witchcraft to try to gain control of the situation.

"Quiteria is the best nurse and she is young," the people said, and it made Doña Tomasa, the witch nurse, very jealous. So Quiteria was afraid of her and she tried to keep out of her way. The witch nurse might play an evil trick on her. Then one day somebody whispered to Quiteria that if she stood on Tomasa's shadow, Tomasa could not move, and then she would have power over Tomasa. At noon one day Doña Tomasa came to visit Quiteria. "Ah," thought Quiteria to herself, "I must keep her until her shadow grows a little." So she invited the witch nurse to eat dinner with her. The woman was hungry so she stayed and drank the good *atole* (a drink made of milk and the meal of the roasted and ground pueblo corn) and ate the tortillas. But she was in a hurry and soon she was leaving. Quiteria picked up her new *reboso* and followed Tomasa out the door. "See how fine my new reboso is? Touch it," and Quiteria came very close to the witch nurse and stood on her shadow. The witch nurse tried to move. She could not. So she acted very natural as if she did not wish to move. She talked of the people to Quiteria. She talked of the crops. She rolled many cigarettes and smoked them. Hour after hour passed. Then she knew Quiteria was keeping her there on purpose. She must get away. She cried out, "I am sick. Run quick. Get me some water!" Quiteria saw that she looked very pale, so she ran into the house for the water. When she returned, Doña Tomasa was gone.[10]

This story is not just about having or not having power over someone but is also about generational change, the young replacing the old. Its moral, however, is that in order to function, the new system must learn the ways of the old. Doña Tomasa continually outwits her young rival, but Quiteria is learning. The tale is also about *respeto,* or respect, so important a cultural trait for Hispanos. As much as the young woman wants to control the older woman, when the older woman asks her for something, Quiteria does so out of respect for her age.

Sometimes the witches were just people who lived in the community. For example, a story called "The Tale of the Sick Woman," narrated by Senaida Sebastian in 1939, describes the strange happenings around a sick woman who felt that every night she was being beaten and a pair of hands were trying to strangle her. Because no one else could see her visions, no one believed her, and she continued to be quite ill. She kept insisting that a neighbor of hers wished to kill her, but no one could see anything, so more and more people in the neighborhood came to keep her company.

> The crowd was so great that at one time some of the men stepped outside for a breath of fresh air and were greatly surprised to see the clothesline on which the woman hung her washing full of owls, a strange sight to see at night. The owls were making short flights and hooting all the while and the men felt that they were bad omens. One of the men went inside and returned with a rifle which he fired at the owls, wounding one of them. Several of the persons who had been sitting up with the sick woman upon returning home saw a ball of fire fall to earth, and this ball of fire hooted just like the owls had done. The following day, a neighbor woman, 23 years of age, was found to be suffering from a bullet wound. This young woman was the one whom the sick woman had seen beating and choking her.[11]

A dress had been the cause of the quarrel between the two women. A doll made from the material of the dress was burned while prayers were said, and from that moment the sick woman recovered.

The heroines in this sampling of folktales are women of power and ingenuity, and the tales are highly imaginative and descriptive. Details about clothing, personal characteristics, food, houses, and places were important, and humor was always welcome for comic relief. And although many of the cuentos and estorias may have had their antecedents in European folktales, nevertheless the local tradition, creative ingenuity, and the imagination of the storyteller changed the tale as it was told, becoming a bountiful source for the written tradition that was to follow. Also important is the fact that many of the powerful symbols, characters, and images found in the estorias and cuentos have also become part of the written tradition (e.g., Rudolfo Anaya's powerful curandera Ultima in *Bless Me, Ultima*).

Chicana writers are also drawing from contemporary oral histories and folk materials. In the past fifteen years there has been much interest on the part of Chicano historians and folklorists in continuing to collect such materials, and various books have resulted from this recollecting of life stories. These recent oral histories reveal many of the same perspectives on life in the new territories and the sense of loss of culture (as well as social and economic power) reflected in the writings in the English tradition between 1920 and 1950. Oral histories such as Patricia Preciado Martin's *Del rancho al barrio* (1983) (from the Mexican Heritage Project in Tucson, Arizona) and her *Images and Conversations: Mexican Americans Recall a Southwestern Past* (1983), as well as Nasario García's *Recuerdos de los viejitos* (1987) and his *Abuelitos: Stories of the Rio Puerco Valley* (1992), evoke the vanishing cultural landscape. Preciado Martin has also begun to document oral histories of Arizona women in *Songs My Mother Sang to Me* (1993). Contemporary writers have used the images from these oral histories to re-create the same sense of nostalgia. For example, in *Images and Conversations*, Preciado Martin uses the image of a fig tree to graphically symbolize a disappearing culture.

> In 1858 José M. Sosa built a small residence for his family on Main Street — Tucson's Old Camino Real. . . . In 1878 the property was sold to Leopold Carrillo . . . in time he dug a well, built corrals and chicken houses, planted herbs and flowers — and a fig tree. The fig tree, nourished by the sweet water drawn from the well, flourished in that desert garden. Through the years it grew, its spreading branches finally embracing the garden walls. On warm summer nights, the family would gather outdoors to enjoy the cool evening breeze. Undisturbed by the noise or concerns of modern urbanites, they would count the stars and fall asleep beneath the protective canopy of the sky and the fig tree.
>
> Through the years the fig tree continued to grow and give fruit to succeeding generations. In the twentieth century a bustling Mexican neighborhood grew up around the house of the fig tree. It was a community of vitality and culture and tradition, built with the love and labor of those who dwelled there. But the laughter and songs of the descendants of those early Mexican pioneers would in time be silenced by the bulldozers of progress and urban renewal. Only the Sosa-Carrillo house would be spared, standing alone in a wilderness of asphalt, brick, and glass — mute evidence of the past. And miraculously that same fig tree still branched and flowered in stubborn affirmation of those families who gave it root, greening forth in solitude — a symbol of history and nostalgia in a modern wasteland of concrete, an inheritance which still gives sustenance to those of us who pass this way. (9–10)

The Spanish-Language Literary Tradition

In the West and Southwest, in addition to the oral tradition, there is a long and respected literary tradition in Spanish. In New Mexico, poets and essayists were writing before 1880: Miguel de Quintana in the eighteenth century, and Chicoría, García, El Viejo Vilmas, El Pelón, and El Negrito Poeta in the nineteenth century. These were exceptions, however, as most early schools in the West were private and only the children (mainly sons) of the rich could afford to attend.

In the 1850s and 1860s, Archbishop Lamy brought the Sisters of Loretto and the Christian Brothers to New Mexico to set up schools. The Sisters of Loretto established their school in Las Vegas in 1869 (and another in Santa Fe), and the Jesuits set up a school for boys in 1877 and founded a Spanish newspaper, *La Revista Católica,* in 1875 (Cabeza de Baca Gilbert, *We Fed Them Cactus,* 80–124). The Sisters of Loretto maintained a long and respected tradition of educating the daughters of the well-to-do. Around this time, Protestant schools were also established, including the Menaul Presbyterian School in Albuquerque, founded in 1881. In 1860 New Mexico passed the first law to establish public schools, and by 1886, 40 percent of the youth of New Mexico were attending schools (although it is difficult to say how many of them were women). Instruction was in Spanish, and only 10 percent could speak and write both English and Spanish (E. Arellano, 5).

Between 1880 and 1890, some forty new Spanish-language newspapers were introduced in the territory of New Mexico, with similar growth in Texas, Arizona, and California. Most of these Spanish-language newspapers carried a literary page or cultural supplement that contained poetry, short stories, and "serial" novels. Often the authors were well-known writers from Mexico, Latin America, and Spain. The works of American, English, French, and other European writers were presented in translation.

All this literary activity encouraged many Hispanos to write, and original work was often solicited for the literary pages. In many communities, literary societies were formed, both as independent organizations and as part of mutual aid societies. Although these societies were composed mainly of men, occasionally the poetry and drama societies also included women, for example, the Hispanic American Dramatic Club of Las Vegas, New Mexico (E. Arellano, 6).

In his exploratory article on early Hispanic literature, "La poesía nuevo mexicana," Esteban Arellano does not mention any women published in Spanish-language newspapers during the nineteenth century. However, Juanita Lawhn, who has studied a San Antonio, Texas, Spanish-language newspaper, *La Prensa,* between 1913 and 1920, has shown that many women published poetry and narrative as well as essays in *La Prensa,* engaging furthermore in a lively polemic on women's rights. Lawhn cites 380 Spanish-language newspapers printed between 1855 and 1959, yet she argues that since the editorial boards as well as the publishers of these papers were men, the editorial opinions expressed were generally "one-sided, the reading made available through the newspaper to women was thus controlled, and the indoctrination of male norms and male expectations prevailed through the issues of *La Prensa*" ("Women Publishing," 2).

A perusal of other Spanish-language newspapers supports similar conclusions. A few well-known women writers such as María Enriqueta and Rosario Sansores (Mexican exiles) were published consistently over a period of time, but local women writers tended to have a few pieces published and then not be heard of again. For example, María Guadalupe Valero published fifteen poems between 1924 and 1925, and May Stadden de Rojas published seven poems in that same period (Miguélez). Neither became well known. Columns of advice about love and beauty as well as essays about the ideal behavior for young women were written by both women and men. Nevertheless, Lawhn demonstrates that many of the women writers who were published in *La Prensa* "rebelliously confronted, challenged, and destroyed the stereotypical images that were created and disseminated both in the male-dominated literary section and in the editorial essays" ("Women Publishing," 4).

A new area being researched by Clara Lomas is that of women writers who were exiled during the Mexican Revolution of 1910. Lomas has shown that these women not only were politically astute and active but also clearly aware of women's issues, and they published articles attempting to involve women in the revolutionary cause ("The Articulation of Gender"). What impact these writings had on women in the Southwest is still under analysis.

Among the local writers, poetry was the most popular genre, and much of the poetry conformed to romantic ideals of what women's writing should be: there were elegies, occasional or circumstantial poems for Mother's Day or patriotic holidays, and tributes to husbands, mothers, and cultural symbols. At least one critic argues that publishing the "great writers" in effect stifled the creation of local poetry because local writers tended to carefully imitate widely accepted literary styles rather than rely on their own creative talents. Some native talents arose, nonetheless, and among them a woman, Carmen Celia Beltrán, who was actively publishing in Spanish-language newspapers between 1920 and 1940 (Miguélez, 33).

One early example of women writing in Spanish is a poem published in *La Bandera Americana* on February 4, 1921, by Margarita V. Sánchez, titled "Acróstico: Al dulcísimo nombre de Jesús" (Acrostic to the sweet name of Jesus). This poem cleverly uses the first letter of each stanza to spell out the name of Jesus and affirms the writer's devotion to him as well as her poetic agility. Another example is "Día de campo" (A day in the country), published by Margarita Arellano in *El Nuevo Mexicano* in June 1932. The poem adroitly mentions all the young women who went together on a picnic, explaining that they were wearing pants (*vestidas de hombre*) borrowed from their brothers, none of which fit properly. The poem includes some phrases in English, illustrating the increasingly common code switching among Spanish speakers. As clothing changes, so do the times, and in the poem we have the image of the emergence of independent young women.

As mentioned, Beltrán of Tucson, Arizona, was one of the foremost local contributors to Spanish-language newspapers, in which she had many poems published, and she wrote radio dramas as well. She continues her creative writing to this day. Some of her previously published work has been collected in *Remanso lírico: Cantos y poemas,* which includes forty-six poems, four songs, and six translations of popular songs. Many of these are occasion poems (e.g., to the twelfth of October [Columbus Day] and to the fifteenth of September [Mexican Independence Day]), but she also wrote religious poems to Santa Teresa and prayers to God, as well as romantic texts in the style of Mexican poet Amado Nervo. The volume also contains some women-centered texts, including several tender poems about motherhood. In two poems to her daughters, she writes that their birth brightened her sad days forever (15, 16). In another poem, a mother singing a child to sleep remembers with nostalgia her own childhood in all its innocence and illusion, ending in a tragic present where, the father gone, the mother is alone with her child (48). A radio program written by Beltrán for Mother's Day has a similar theme: "La cuna vacía" (The empty cradle) focuses on a mother's feeling of emptiness on the death of her sons during the Mexican Revolution. Also of special interest is the poem "A la Virgen morena," to the Virgin of Guadalupe, in which the Indian Virgin is credited with the independence of Mexico since she cheered on the insurgent army.

Beltrán's poetry conformed to literary standards of the day (Romanticism and Modernism), and she was respected in local poetic circles. Her creativity can be seen in her attention to local events, such as those specific patriotic events important to Mexicans, and to Mexican symbols such as the Virgin of Guadalupe. She also features people central to her personal life, her mother and daughters, as well as events important in the lives of women such as the traditional quinceañera (coming-out party) on a girl's fifteenth birthday ("Quinceañera," Rebolledo and Rivero, 65).

Another early writer—and the only woman included in Anselmo Arellanos's *Los pobladores nuevo mexicanos y su poesía, 1889–1950*—is María Esperanza López de Padilla. In her autobiographical sketch, López de Padilla (b. 1918) explains that when she was a child, her father and his friends recited poems they never wrote down (A. Arellano, 45). Her mother also knew many verses, prayers, and sayings by heart. López de Padilla was not as influenced by established writers as was Beltrán. Her poetry is characterized by her relationship to the landscape and to the people she knew. One text, "Simplicidades" (Simple things), sings of common ordinary objects and images that bring the lyric speaker happiness—romantic images such as poppies in the breeze and the wind blowing through her hair, but also clothes drying on the line, the bathing of her children, and white curtains in the window (Rebolledo and Rivero, 69–70).

In another poem, "María Esperanza," López de Padilla tells the story of her baptism and how her name was chosen. Her father chose Esperanza (Hope), but her mother and godmother wanted María (in honor of the Virgin). Her parents were from northern New Mexico and her godparents from the north of Mexico, and both families had recently arrived in Pueblo, Colorado, to work in the steel mills. With her baptism, the two families sealed their friendship forever. The poem offers cultural information as well as information about the patterns of migration in the Southwest. Although code switching is minimal (the only words in English are in a single line, "Y allí en los steel works se encontraron" [And there in the steel works they met]), it symbolizes her family's economic dependence on non-Hispanic institutions (Anselmo Arellano, 148; Rebolledo and Rivero, 68–69).

Finally I would like to mention the serialized epistolary autobiography written by a young girl, Olga Beatrice Torres, in 1913, *Memorias de mi viaje. Memorias* recounts the life of a young Mexican girl whose family flees the revolution and goes to live in El Paso, and the book documents Olga's impressions of the United States and its people. In the introduction to her translation of *Memorias,* Lawhn analyzes the process by which Olga becomes a Chicana, through her changing perspective and through language, demonstrating how the young woman consciously incorporates anglicisms into Spanish, thus acquiring a "new" language.

The English-Language Literary Tradition

When considering the early Chicanas writing in English, critics have been prompt to identify Estela Portillo Trambley as one of the first. Portillo Trambley was beginning to publish her short stories and plays in the early 1960s. Nevertheless, there is a long tradition of literary antecedents in English before Portillo Trambley, including two novels written by María Amparo Ruiz de Burton, *Who Would Have Thought It?* (1872) and *The Squatter and the Don* (1885).[12] The English-language literary tradition, primarily the material written between 1920 and 1950, is the third source in Chicana literary tradition. This material is rich in variety and ranges from texts published by writers such as María Cristina Mena (in *Century* and the *American Magazine*) and Josephina Niggli (in magazines as diverse as *Mexican Life* and the *Ladies Home Journal*) to self-published texts by writers who were known only locally, such as Cleofas Jaramillo.

In her research on early Chicana narratives, Gloria Treviño argues that not only were Chicanas active in creating a literary tradition in English, but they were also consciously pursuing the creation of a "female space," one that "articulated the concerns particular to the minority woman" (2). Treviño focuses on three women: Mena, Niggli, and Jovita González, the best known (at least until recently) of the early Chicana writers who wrote in English.

María Cristina Mena was born in Mexico in 1893 and came to the United States at the age of fourteen. She lived in New York, where she began writing, and her marriage to a well-known dramatist, Henry Kellet Chambers, allowed her to further involve herself with New York's literary life. Treviño sees Mena's value within the Chicana literary tradition as important because "all of her short stories take place in Mexico and deal with aspects of Mexican society" (2). Although Treviño agrees that many of Mena's female characters are presented as stereotypes within traditional love-story plots, she nevertheless succinctly demonstrates that Mena had a "feminist" consciousness about the subordination, limitation, and oppression of women. When female characters are foregrounded, particularly in many of her short stories, Treviño believes Mena "incorporates an element of resistance which expresses the desire to change the Mexican woman's inferior social position" (3). Mena also successfully incorporates humor and irony in her work to undermine stereotypic images of women as objects of beauty.

Josephina Niggli (b. 1910) also was born in Mexico (although of Scandinavian American parents).[13] Niggli's family fled the Mexican Revolution when she was three, but they returned to live in Mexico from 1920 until 1925, when they moved to San Antonio, Texas. As Treviño points out, Niggli is one of the few writers to have published three major collections of her fiction and plays before 1960. Known primarily as a playwright, she published one-act plays and many essays on drama, such as *Pointers on Playwriting* (1945) and *Pointers on Radio Writing* (1946). Her plays, which are folk-oriented about life in Mexican villages, led one biographer to comment that "Niggli's work combines a deep understanding of the Mexican personality with a sure knowledge of custom and folkways" (Shirley, 270). Among her plays with Mexican folk culture themes are *Tooth or Share* (1935), *Red Velvet Goat,* and *Sunday Costs Five Pesos* (both published in 1936). Niggli's plays continue to be performed by local theater companies, including a summer 1986 production of *Sunday Costs Five Pesos* by the Las Vegas (New Mexico) High School Players. Niggli also wrote a series of historical plays about Mexico, for example, *Azteca, Soldadera,* and *This Is Villa.* Many of these plays were compiled in the collection *Mexican Folk Plays* (1938). She later wrote a narrative piece called *Mexican Village* (1945).

Questions of national identity, of crossing frontiers, and of being an outsider in Mexican as well as American culture are important themes in all of Niggli's work. Many of her characters are of mixed heritage, and they struggle with issues that arise from this heritage—being a Mestizo in racially conscious societies. Often her themes are of alienation.

Some male critics classify Niggli as a member of a generation of women writers (which included Nina Otero-Warren, Jaramillo, and Cabeza de Baca) who greatly romanticized the Mexican past and presented "quaint" images of Hispanic culture. Niggli did in fact struggle with issues of race and class, and with the conflict and alienation that national as well as cultural identity can bring, but like Beltrán, she wanted to portray the national events of Mexico that would bring pride of culture to those of Mexican descent living in the United States. She therefore wrote of the Mexican Revolution, of the Aztec Empire, and of the Virgin of Guadalupe (the first Mestiza Virgin).

According to Treviño, Niggli was particularly good at depicting female reality, as evidenced in her portrayal of María de la Garza in *Mexican Village,* a strong character who "defies and challenges the codes of conduct for village women" (13). Beautiful and mysterious, she makes her own rules and lives an independent life outside the village. Another character in *Mexican Village,* Tía Magdalena, exhibits similar strength and independence. She is a curandera/bruja figure who is admired for her knowledge and likewise feared because of her "powers."

In Niggli's play *Soldadera,* seven of the eight characters are women who participated in the Mexican Revolution, and the play shows the effects of death and violence on their lives. But the struggle for justice encompasses both women and men. In *Soldadera,* the violence and destruction that have entered their lives have almost entirely taken away their humanity. One of the characters, Adelita, symbolizes the idealist, the innocent woman, the one who believes killing and violence are not necessary to change the social order. When the women determine that in order to protect the hiding place of the revolutionary soldiers, it is necessary to kill a political prisoner who has fallen into their hands, Adelita says to them, "What do you know about the Revolution? It's beautiful, it's glorious, it's heroic. It's giving all you've got to freedom. It's dying with the sun in your face, not being eaten to death by little red ants in a bottle. If this is your Revolution, I don't want to see it" (*Mexican Folk Plays,* 109). She is answered by Concha, the leader of the group, "Yes, this is the Revolution. We had to forget how to weep and how to be kind and merciful. We are cruel, because the Revolution is cruel. It must crush out the evil before we can make things good again" (109). Adelita, known in folklore as the famous revolutionary soldadera (and perhaps prostitute) of the Mexican Revolution, in this play acquires realistic dimensions as she loses her innocence (and her life) in the fulfillment of her commitment to the revolution.

In her thematic use of Mexican folkways, history, and symbols, Niggli went beyond a mere quaint portrayal of Mexican life. She was eager to portray Mexico and its people in a complex manner so they would be better understood by Americans. Her exploration of the alienation that people felt because of mixed heritage and confused identity, and her portrayal of women as complex, independent characters place her in a literary category that goes beyond quaint and puts her in the company of writers who were beginning to explore Chicana reality. However, as María Herrera-Sobek points out in her introduction to *Mexican Village,* even though Niggli's "concern with history and tradition coming to grips with an increasingly modern world" is laudable, her ethnic identification is problematic because Niggli does not necessarily see herself as Mexican or Chicana (xx). It is more probable that we should classify her work as Chicanesque.

Unlike Mena and Niggli, who were writing from distant nostalgic perspectives, Jovita González, born in Roma, Texas, and raised in ranching communities, exhibits "an awareness and concern about the socio-economic problems affecting Chicanos during that period" and was "among the first Chicanas to record the history of her people in the southwest" (Treviño, 7–8) (e.g., "America Invades the Border Towns," a brief history of the social effects of Anglo domination on Texas Mexicans). González was collecting folktales and stories in the late 1920s and 1930s — well before the Federal Writers' Project — and she also wrote original cameos of Texas Mexicans that described the life and times of the border. As Treviño points out, although women protagonists are assigned subordinate roles in González's stories, she nevertheless was consciously choosing to explore and describe those roles (8). González is certainly one of our foremothers who should be further researched.

As we have seen, numerous women have told or written of their lives and experiences when they could. As more and more previously unrecognized texts are recovered, we will be able to better understand the impact of women on the social and cultural structure of their times and our own.

2

The Nuevomexicana Writers

From the 1930s through the 1950s, three women writers in New Mexico were deeply and energetically involved in preserving Hispanic/ New Mexican culture. Fabiola Cabeza de Baca Gilbert, Nina Otero-Warren (formerly Otero), and Cleofas Jaramillo not only were active in their communities and in public life, but each of them also produced several books that recorded the folklore and ways of Hispanic New Mexico and at the same time revealed details of their lives and their families. The books are also highly original works that were meant to preserve, in writing, the Hispano oral tradition.[1] They were written by a first generation of New Mexican Hispana women writers who were conscious of their heritage and cultural identity, and who were writing, in part, because they wanted to communicate their sense that this culture and identity was somehow slipping away, that it was being assimilated through history and cultural domination. Their writing represents an act of resistance to this domination.

Genaro Padilla, in his illuminating article on folkloric autobiography in New Mexico, "Imprisoned Narrative? Or Lies, Secrets, and Silence in New Mexico Women's Autobiography," points out that the dominating culture, in order to subvert the conquered group's ideological consciousness as much as possible, must make "the subject culture forget the details of its domination" (44). Padilla states that many Hispano writers were influenced by Anglo-American intellectuals who came to New Mexico at the beginning of the twentieth century. These writers invented for New Mexico an aesthetic discourse of myth and romance that inscribed itself upon the popular consciousness and "provided one of the few forms through which Hispanos could compose their lives for public view" (45). However, when written by Hispanas, this same discourse, applauded by Anglos in such books as *The Land of Poco Tiempo* by Charles F. Lummis and *Death Comes for the Archbishop* by Willa Cather, has been severely criticized by recent Chicano critics. For example, Raymond Paredes, in a generally perceptive study, condemns these early accounts, saying that the writers had a "hacienda" mentality, that they ignored social concerns, and that in general it is difficult to take their writing seriously because they were too sappy and genteel (49). Furthermore, Paredes says, "The Mexican American literature in English that emerged from New Mexico during the 1930s evokes a past that, while largely imaginary, is presented with rigid conviction . . . the writers described a culture seemingly locked in time and barricaded against outside forces. Here the New Mexico Hispanos pass their lives in dignity and civility, confronting the harsh environment with a religiosity and resolve reminiscent of the conquistadores themselves" (51–52).

Despite his desire to dismiss these writers, Paredes does note that there is "something profoundly disturbing about this body of work. It seems a literature created out of fear and intimidation, a defensive response to racial prejudice, particularly the Anglo distaste for miscegenation and ethnocentrism" (52). Although one of the few male Chicano critics to even consider the early women writers in a serious way, Paredes overlooks those parts of their writings that contrast with the "romantic" view and criticizes these writers for internalizing prevalent class, gender, and racial attitudes. Nonetheless, Paredes's commentary raises some interesting questions as to what should be included in the literary canon. To ignore the writings of the middle and upper-middle class is to ignore literary history as well as the origins of much women's literature.[2] Also, although many male critics have no problems with the "masculine" concerns of long, boring descriptions of skirmishes between natives and soldiers, or with the "sappiness" of the long-winded, sugar-coated love quatrains published by romanticizing male authors of the 1890s and early 1900s, they tend to dismiss early efforts by women to write and break into print because of their nontraditional forms and their "feminine" concerns.

Padilla, on the other hand, perceives the writings of the three Nuevo-mexicanas mentioned above to contain "sparks" of dissent: "What we must look for are momentary struggles in the narrative, revealed perhaps only in whispers of resistance, quelled immediately but signaling like a flash through the dense texture of language and reified memory. In such whispers we discover those gaps in the narrative where the native cultural 'I' voices itself against the imperial 'Other' to speak through the bars of the ideological prison in which it is confined ("Imprisoned Narrative," 44).

While I agree with Padilla's assessment of this resistant discourse, I believe it is much more prevalent in the writings of these women than previously thought. The strategies of resistance used are not totally self-conscious, but there are too many "strange" happenings in the texts for them to be naive or innocent strategies. Given the statements these writers made about preserving the culture, wanting to contribute to a better understanding of Hispanos, or just writing to "get it right" (Jaramillo, *Romance,* 173), these writers had to be conscious that in both form and content they were constantly subverting the "official" text. First of all, the books were written for the dominant culture in English, as if to prove that the authors could write in and control the dominant language. Second, the texts contain a great deal of contestation. The "strange" occurrences, which elsewhere I have called their "narrative strategies of resistance" (Rebolledo and Rivero, 17–18), include:

A consciousness of being colonized and the struggle to retain their ethnic heritage by naming that heritage in every way possible. Often this is manifested by detailing the cultural signs embedding that cultural identity. Cabeza de Baca, for example, endlessly lists landmarks (hills, roads, valleys) and explains what their Spanish names had been and the history behind them. She also recounts long tales that specify family names and friends' family names, as if to show what Anne Goldman calls a "cultural pedigree" that claims a traditional space. Cabeza de Baca also details long accounts of other forms of cultural resistance, such as social banditry, which betrays her admiration for these Hispano bandits.

All the New Mexico writers display a sentimental attachment for the past, generally a nostalgic edenic one. This longing questions the viability of the present authority. This past is seen in terms of a unified Hispano community, and not necessarily as the past of any one individual. Recollections of this Hispano past reflect a nostalgia for a centered and not conflicted cultural space, while the Hispano present is seen as decentered and marginalized.

Along with many other Chicana writers, the early Nuevomexicana writers experimented with the blending or blurring of various genres of writing, mixing the oral and the written, history and creative autobiography, recipes and narrative, family history and romance. The mixing of genres was acceptable because it was a *recuerdo,* a memory, and because this narration was underscored by the *"estoria,"* or storytelling, tradition. In this Hispano storytelling, mixing genres, with strong attention to personal detail as well as deviation from that detail when appropriate, was acceptable and even expected. In general, everyone had already heard the story in some form, unless it was news, and knew how the narration ended, so the vivid retelling with as many clever and astonishing interpolations was highly regarded. This attitude toward storytelling contrasted with a perception in the Anglo written tradition that narratives must keep moving along and should tell the story without lingering over the very details that the estoria audience would be expecting. Padilla also argues that recuerdos do not have the direct authorial authority of an autobiography because they are collective, not individual memories, even though seen through the "I" ("The Recovery of Chicano Nineteenth-Century Autobiography," 287). Thus the discourses of creative literature, history, sociology, ethnography, psychology, and geography are woven together by an intensely reflexive personal subjectivity. All are incorporated into the personal autobiographical "I"; that is, it is the personal storytelling binding them all together.

Also, because it was acceptable for women to tell the stories, although not to write them, and because the passing on of recipes and traditions was thought to be women's work, this mixing of genres allowed expressions of a highly feminine voice. Thus, fortunately, detailed narrative accounts of women's activities and perspectives were preserved. As Goldman points out, by "constructing an empowering image of cultural tradition via her own cooking labor" and by her views on other types of labor as well, "the autobiographer writes herself into a prominent place in the narrative" (174). The self-reflection seen in the Nuevomexicana writers is intimately connected by their literary and social history as well as their personal interactions in it.

Moreover, continually interwoven into the ethno / auto / social biographies as well as the cookbooks are "translations" from not only the Spanish language into English, but from Spanish perspectives to English perspectives. At times these "translations" are humorous, subtly criticizing Anglo culture and Anglos' understanding of Hispanic culture. Hispanos usually come across as superior beings, morally and spiritually, while Anglos are often ridiculed for their lack of understanding.

Beyond their thoughts about the strategies of resistance these women have used in their writings, Goldman and Padilla have continued to explore ever-deepening perceptions of these strategies as more consciously planned than originally thought. As Goldman points out, many of the books carry with them a glossary of Spanish terms, which for her signifies that "reproducing the recipes . . . does not necessarily lead to cultural ownership"

(184). Cabeza de Baca in *The Good Life* was careful to point out that words may have more than one meaning and that she was explaining the particular meaning as used in that particular circumstance. Goldman asserts that "By calling attention to what is left over, the remainder that escapes translation, the author problematizes cultural access, depicting a web of associations and meanings ultimately ungraspable by the nonnative speaker" (184). As more texts become accessible to us, and as we read these texts more closely, we become amazed at how subtlely, yet consistently, the resistance manifests itself, and moreover, how clearly it was embedded as an icon for these authors.

These Hispana New Mexican writers were documenting their lives during the time when the land and society in New Mexico was shifting from Hispano to Anglo control. They came from old, landed, upper-class New Mexican families, and their stories generally reflect these class origins. They generally extol the Spanish (and not the Mestizo or Indian) heritage and see the pastoral tradition of the past as a utopia where humans were integrated with nature and tied to the land. Because many of their books, like other stories in the cuento tradition, are first-person accounts that draw on stories of older family members or people employed by the family (e.g., "El Cuate," the ranch cook in Cabeza de Baca's *We Fed Them Cactus*), these writers' narratives often extend back into the nineteenth century.

Because these early Hispanic New Mexican women were writing during a period of significant cultural transition, their work deserves serious study, particularly in light of their confinement within fairly rigid gender roles and the fact that writing was not considered a suitable pursuit for women (except for the occasional poem). In fact, it is a wonder they wrote at all. The assumption implicit in many critics' writings is that "true" Mexican American literature cannot ignore social concerns and that the Chicano/Mexican American culture is a monolithic concept best described as a "culture of resistance." However, as we define what is resistance, we see that these writers not only were describing the loss of their lands and culture, but they also were actively resisting culturally defined roles for themselves and for all Hispana women. Close readings will show that the paradise depicted in the beginnings of their books becomes a land of transition and struggle (almost a purgatory) in the early twentieth century.

In *We Fed Them Cactus,* Cabeza de Baca tells about the arrival of Hispano pioneers in the Llano Estacado, the establishment of ranches and communities, the arrival of Anglo settlers and homesteaders, and the Hispanos' gradual loss of the land due to drought, fencing, homesteaders' plowing practices, taxes, and other political realities. There is rich documentation of ranch life, cowboy images, politics, education, and recreation. By the end of the book, with her father's death marking the end of an era, the life of abundance is over, and the tone is one of sadness and loss.

> The Hispano has almost vanished from the land . . . but the names of hills, rivers, arroyos, canyons and defunct plazas linger as monuments to a people who pioneered into the land of the buffalo and the Comanche. These names have undergone many changes but are still known and repeated. Very likely many of those who pronounce them daily are unaware that they are of Spanish origin. . . . Corazon Peak took its name because its shape resembles a heart. Cuervo is the Spanish word from crow, and the creek received the name from the abundance of crows in that area. La Liendre was originally settled by a family who were small in stature, whose nickname was liendre, meaning nit. Las Salivas were the mines. Los Alamitos signifies little cottonwoods. (66)

Otero-Warren's *Old Spain in Our Southwest* (1936) and Jaramillo's *Romance of a Little Village Girl* (1955) have similar time frames and record many of the same changes.

Nina Otero-Warren

In Otero-Warren's book, most things of value are presented as an end product of Spain, evidenced by the title *Old Spain in Our Southwest,* yet one must also look at her work as an early attempt to preserve in literary images a vanishing way of life. Otero-Warren's awareness of instability is clear. "This southwestern country, explored and settled nearly four hundred years ago by a people who loved nature, worshiped God and feared no evil, is still a region of struggles" (3). And while she concentrates on quaint folkloric vignettes praising the lost Spanish heritage, she nevertheless communicates to us her growing sense of disjunction from the landscape, illustrating her feeling of alienation and isolation in a time of transition.

Otero-Warren envisioned the Indian as well as the traditional Hispano shepherd as integrated with nature both in religious belief and in understanding of the land. She, however, remains on the edge, longing for the sense of integration denied her, in part because she is a woman, but also because she represents a culture and class undergoing profound change.

> In the only room of my house, a melancholy candle was flickering as if gasping for breath. . . . I had a feeling of vastness, of solitude, but never of loneliness. . . . The night was alive with sounds of creatures less fearful than

humans, speaking a language I couldn't understand, but could feel with every sense.

In the night the storm broke, wild and dismal. The wind hissed like a rattler, and as it struck the branches of the trees, it made a weird sound like a musical instrument out of tune.

At dawn, the clouds parted as if a curtain were raised, revealing the outline of the mountains. The hush following the storm was tremendous. . . . As the shepherd was extinguishing the camp fire, there appeared on the top of the hill a form with arms stretched to heaven as though offering himself to the sun. The shepherd from his camp and I from my window watched this half-clad figure that seemed to have come from the earth to greet the light. A chant, a hymn — the Indian was offering his prayer to the rising sun. The shepherd, accustomed to his Indian neighbors, went his way slowly, guiding his sheep out of the canyon. The Indian finished his offering of prayer. I, alone, seemed not in complete tune with the instruments of God. I felt a sense of loss that they were closer to nature than I, more understanding of the storm. (4–5)

The language throughout this description emphasizes Otero-Warren's feelings of exclusion, nostalgia, and loss.

The romanticized class differences noted by Paredes are also clear in this text. Although the Hispano may be poor, Otero-Warren says, "he takes his place in life with a noble bearing, for he can never forget that he is a descendent of the Conquerors" (9). Yet, "Near the house of the patrón were the houses of the peones who were not slaves, but working people who preferred submission to the patrón rather than an independent chance alone" (10). Nonetheless, Otero-Warren was aware that the old system was unjust. "The men of the village liked to hunt, and hunting was more of a necessity than a sport, as a means of obtaining food; game was plentiful. . . . There was very little money in the country and whatever there was was usually in the chests of the patrones" (50).

Otero-Warren was also aware of the growing tensions between Anglos and Hispanos as Anglos entered the territory and populated the state in ever-growing numbers.

"Strangers do not understand our hospitality," said Don Antonio's brother-in-law. "A young attorney from the States came to the hacienda a short time ago on business. He brought his wife. My señora received her guest in her usual courteous manner. The shutters of the guest room had been opened, the room well aired, the sun allowed to look through the deep windows. The high bed, with its feather mattress, was made ready. A silver basket, filled with fruit, was placed beside the candle on the bedside table. On retiring for the night, my wife told the American lady: 'My house, all that it contains, is yours.' She did not know that this phrase, perfectly sincere, is our way of making a guest feel at ease. One hardly accepts a house and its belongings! My señora had left a set of jewelry, a brooch, bracelet and earrings on the dresser of the guest room. The American lady took these away with her, thinking it was a gift to her. It was her understanding of our hospitality, 'My house is yours.'" (33)

This description of cultural misunderstanding is amusing to Hispanos and is certainly part of a cultural "translation" marking Anglos as inferior.

Also significant are the details Otero-Warren provided about daily life. For example, among her descriptions of the work that women did, we discover that it was the women who plastered walls in houses and churches. "They worked all day save for the afternoon siesta time. They protected their skin from the hot sun by a face powder which they made for this purpose. This face powder called cáscara was made of dried bones finely ground, mixed with herbs and made into a paste" (11).

We also see the incorporation of the oral tradition in the "stories" told in the text. In "The Field Crosses of the Farmers," Otero-Warren tells of seeing small crosses on the stumps of trees left after the clearing of her land during planting time (Rebolledo and Rivero, 50–52). When she asks the foreman Anastacio why he is "planting" crosses in her fields, he answers that it is to protect her crops, and he tells her the tale of a woman who lived in the community, who because of her strange words and actions was considered a witch. Nevertheless, because she lived alone, the community felt an obligation to care for her, as they cared for all those who were infirm and unable to look after themselves. One spring day, the woman warned that a great storm was coming, but the people laughed at her because the skies were clear. Days passed, and the villagers forgot the warnings of the woman, who now insisted that all would be lost unless "they planted little crosses in their fields." One night a cold wind blew, the rain turned to hail, and many of the crops were destroyed. The only crop that was saved belonged to an old couple who had believed the witch. They had nailed wooden crosses to their fence posts and to the tree stumps. And Anastacio concluded, "Since that time, Patrona, when we plant seed, and before the day's work is ended, we erect small crosses" (Otero-Warren, 123–28).

Otero-Warren was herself a woman active in and concerned about her community. She was strongly influential in bringing about the vote for women in New Mexico in 1920. Two years later, she ran for Congress on the

Republican ticket, and although she lost by 10,000 votes, it was a remarkable achievement since she was the first woman to challenge an all-male political establishment. (It would not be until 1946 that a woman would be elected to Congress from New Mexico.) For many years, Otero-Warren served as the superintendent for Santa Fe County and Indian schools, striving to better the educational system for New Mexican children.

Cleofas Jaramillo

Cleofas Jaramillo was also concerned with the disappearance of cultural traditions, many of which are described in *The Genuine New Mexico Tasty Recipes* (1939), *Shadows of the Past* (1942; Rebolledo and Rivero, 57–63), and *Romance of a Little Village Girl* (1955). Her mother was a storyteller, and *Spanish Fairy Tales* contains Jaramillo's English translations of twenty-five of her mother's stories. Jaramillo was active in trying to preserve Hispano culture, not only through her writing but also by founding the Sociedad Folklórica.

It was in June 1935, by her own account, that Jaramillo saw an article in *Holland Magazine* about Spanish and Mexican food, an article that, in her opinion, was not accurate. She thought, "Now, why don't we who know our customs and dishes do something about preserving the knowledge . . . we who know the customs and styles of our region are letting them die out" (*The New Mexican*, Feb. 26, 1954). In her cookbook, Jaramillo preserves that aspect of culture embodied in native food, encouraged no doubt by her brother Reyes Martínez, who was involved with the Federal Writers' Project.

Also preserved in her writing is a series of unforgettable portraits of the women in her family. One of them was her grandfather's spinster sister who was "quite amusing."

> She was very stately, tall and fair, with a delicate skin, for the sun or wind never touched it. She wore her long silver braids like a crown around her shapely head, which was always covered with a silk skullcap to protect it from the air. She ground roots and herbs, rubbing them on her temples and back of her head, to cure her continuous headaches, which she said were caused by *aire en la cabeza*, air in the head.
>
> At night she pushed her bed into the farthest corner, away from doors and windows, placed two chairs on the side, and spread the bed cover over them, to screen off the air, which she said made whirls in the corners. (*Shadows of the Past*, 29; Rebolledo and Rivero, 62)

Jaramillo's work is important, moreover, because although she was influenced by "los cinco pintores" (a group of painters in Santa Fe including Fremont Ellis, Willard Nash, Jozef Bakos, Will Shuster, and Walter Mruk) and writer Mary Austin, and she wrote in English, it is clear that the language issue concerned her. The loss of the Spanish language emphasized what she saw as a disappearing culture, and she felt "alien" writing in English. In *Romance,* she laments her "appalling shortage of words, not being a writer, and writing in a language almost foreign to me," and she offers an apology for her "want of continued expression in some parts of [her] story" (vii). Such an apology, however, is a convention in the Spanish oral tradition. Before beginning a song or a blessing, the speaker/singer often asks pardon for not being able to do it well.

Jaramillo also had the feeling that she was being co-opted and that people outside the culture were trying to steal her writing. Although such fears might at first seem paranoic, they were not groundless. In a sense, Mary Austin, Mabel Dodge Luhan, and others who helped create the mystique of New Mexican culture were in effect appropriating the culture they found so fascinating. As Padilla asserts, the artists "were more sympathetic than usual, not marking native people negatively . . . but nevertheless essentializing them, setting them into the sediment of the earth instead of relating to them as social beings, mystifying and mythifying their cultural practices. . ." ("Imprisoned Narrative," 47).

This nonnative discourse also functioned as a silencer for the authentic voices that existed within that culture, as evidenced by Jaramillo's recollections of seeking a publisher for her work. "I tried sending my manuscript to some of our Western universities. After holding it for several months, they would return it, saying that they did not have the funds with which to publish it. One professor said he was writing a book. Would I permit him to use two or three of my stories in his book? I then understood. All they wanted was to read my manuscript and get ideas from it, so I decided to have it published by a small private press here in my city" (*Romance,* 168).

Romance of a Little Village Girl, in which Jaramillo reflects on almost seventy years of her life, is more strictly autobiographical than her other texts discussed here. Each chapter is framed in a romance, or ballad, form, blurring the lines between poetry and narrative. By so framing her narrative, Jaramillo hints at traditional heroic Spanish epic poetry. Also reminiscent of epic poetry is Jaramillo's narration of her descent, like that of Otero-Warren and Cabeza de Baca, from an edenic girlhood in northern New Mexico to a more ambivalent present where she feels the loss of traditional New Mexican Hispano culture. Like Cabeza de Baca, Jaramillo traces the history of the "New Spanish Province" from its colonization to the present day (including the role that her family, the Martins [later Martínez] and the Luceros, played in its settlement).

For example, Jaramillo details the Hispano perspective as the area became an American territory in 1848, noting that "After existing surrounded by the struggle of life and death . . . for almost three centuries under Spanish rule, with one stroke the new colony was brought under the rule of a foreign government under a new, unknown constitution, which helplessly the Spanish population must accept" (*Romance*, 6–7). Only slowly, according to Jaramillo, did the Hispano *ricos* become aware that they needed to control the rapidly deteriorating situation.

> The Spanish Dons could not prevent their leisurely sons from patronizing these gambling places and squandering fortunes. Eventually it dawned on the parents that times had changed and the new generation was changing with them. The only remedy they could see was to send their sons to Eastern schools, where they could learn the English language and deal with this energetic race. Some of these boys came back from Georgetown and other schools speaking good English but still playing the part of the fine gentlemen they had been brought up to be. They would not take to work. The fortunes of the Dons soon passed out into the hands of strangers, for minimum sums. Adobe mansions began to crumble into ruins, their owners having lost their means to keep them up . . . servants were discharged and Doñas now became their own maids. (*Romance*, 8–9)

Although this passage is simplistic in its analysis of the complex reasons why the Hispanos lost their fortunes and their lands, nevertheless we see the frustrations and bewilderment felt during this time of loss and change. Jaramillo's own father prospered over these years, however, because of his energy and his various business interests: sheep raising, farming, and retailing. He was, moreover, a man who "kept up with the times" (10). Her mother, too, was energetic. "If my father was out busy . . . and someone came who wanted something at the store, mother dropped her work and went and waited on the customer. Our store supplied the simple needs of the people, from dry goods and groceries to patent medicines, which mother would tell the people how to use" (11–12).

Another interesting chapter in *Romance* is an account of English-teaching schools. According to Jaramillo, Spanish-teaching schools had been established in Taos in 1721, and Padre José Antonio Martínez had his own college there in 1826, but by the time Jaramillo herself attended the convent school in Taos when she was nine, Spanish — and Hispanos — were scorned. "We were not allowed to speak any Spanish and the first English words were, 'Put some wood in the stove'" (29). The Taos school had only six boarders and fifty day students, though, and the nuns had a hard time keeping the school open. After five years, Jaramillo transferred to Loretto Academy in Santa Fe, where in her class there was just one other "Spanish" girl. Here, after she asked, she was allowed to formally study Spanish (52).

Romance records Jaramillo's life in precise detail, particularly the Spanish customs and rituals that governed it: religious ceremonies, holidays, courtships, weddings, and funerals. In 1898 she was married to wealthy, good-looking Venceslao Jaramillo. *Romance* documents the subsequent birth and death of two children, her travels, her husband's life in politics, and the birth of a third child, Angelina. After her husband became ill and died, Jaramillo found that their extravagant life had been lived at great cost. With all their fortune lost, Jaramillo became a businesswoman in order to survive. Her strength throughout her life is clearly evident, particularly when her young daughter Angelina is brutally murdered.

Like the writing of Otero-Warren and Cabeza de Baca, *Romance* is a text in which the landscape underlies the narrative content. At the beginning of the narration, Jaramillo's home is a paradise with crystal-clear springs and bountiful meadows. This pure and clean landscape, with no social disorders to jar the sensibilities, was a welcome contrast to boarding school.

> I climbed up on the seat by my father and rode along inhaling the fresh fragrance of the newly-awakened sage and wild flowers. The desert plain seemed turned into a fairy-land. Icy winter had given place to warm summer, melting snow and filling rivers and causing ditches to overflow. Here and there we dropped into a verdant little valley, the sparkling river fringed with new green plants and drooping willows. From the edge of the highest ridge we looked down into the Arroyo Hondo . . . which in its rich verdure seemed to lie asleep, the deep silence enveloping the valley broken only by the rattling of our carriage wheels or the distant barking of the dog. (41–42)

By the end of the narrative, this scene has completely changed. Returning to her old village, Jaramillo feels not joy, but sadness and loss.

> After dinner, my nephew took me in his car for a visit to my old home at Arroyo Hondo. In fifteen minutes I found myself gliding down the once-steep hill now almost level, and I was surprised to see before me the little sunken green valley. What a different aspect it now presented! High pitched roofs, a new, modern-looking schoolhouse — with nothing left but memories of our once lively, happy home, now in melting ruins. . . . With a sigh I turned away from this sad sight. (187)

Even the Virgin that once stood in the chapel "seemed to have a sadder and a lonelier expression that day" (188).

The displacement perspective that underlies the narrative is also clear in Jaramillo's recollection of taking a *gringa* writer, Ruth Laughlin Barker, to the house of a friend because Barker wanted to see an old Nuevomexicano house to describe in her new book. Jaramillo tries to find house after house, but they have all disappeared.

> . . . we rode on to Arroyo Seco to see the fine Gonzales home. We were standing right before it but I did not recognize it. "Where is Juanita Gonzales's home?" I asked a man in the yard. "This is the house," he answered. The whitewashed porch with the blue railing post was gone and the whole house was in ruins. Juanita, whom her mother always had kept so well-dressed at school, came to the door with torn hose and shabby shoes. She asked us to come in. I asked her if she had some of her mother's fine jewelry or table silver. She brought out a silver set with an exquisite design and silver grape bunches on the lids. My friend became interested right away to buy it. Juanita asked $35.00. I am sure it was worth more, but my friend continued to bargain until finally she said, "I will give you a $15.00 check." I shook my hand at the side "no," but Juanita only smiled at me, showing her pretty dimples, and answered, "Alright." This is how our rich Spanish families have been stripped of their most precious belongings. "Why did you do it?" I asked as I was going out the door. "I need the money to fix the house," she said. (*Romance*, 119)

At times, the discourse in *Romance* achieves a critical perspective of realism and an underlying cultural critique; for example, when Jaramillo describes the disjuncture between cultures, exemplified by the death of her first child after she had gone to a hospital in Denver in order to have good medical care.

> On the second day, when the nurse brought in the baby from his bath, I felt his little hands and they were ice cold. "The baby is so cold," I said to her. "Just on the outside," she answered, putting the baby back in his basket up on the table by the window. I almost cried. I wanted to keep him by me to keep him warm. By next day his kidneys had stopped functioning. The baby specialist circumcised the baby as a cure. He cut a blood vessel and the baby bled to death. (108)

This telling scene is contrasted in the next chapter with a discussion of what the *médica,* or curandera, tells her. "Hearing what had happened to our baby, the médica said: 'That trouble comes from catching cold. We roast an onion, split it open, and while it is still warm, place it over the baby's bladder. Muy pronto (very soon) the functioning is released" (109). The narrative perspective is clear; if Jaramillo had given birth to her baby within her cultural preserve and context, the baby would have lived.

Fabiola Cabeza de Baca

Cabeza de Baca's *We Fed Them Cactus* is especially valuable for its historical perspective. The title itself is symbolic since the cactus is a central symbol not only for her but also for many contemporary women writers. The cactus holds water in reserve over times of drought and protects itself with thorns. The book refers, on one level, to the drought of 1918 when Hispano farmers fed the cactus to their cattle for survival. On another level, it refers to the Hispanos themselves as survivors able to weather misfortunes.

At the beginning of *We Fed Them Cactus,* Cabeza de Baca describes, as did Jaramillo, an earlier New Mexico landscape that was a rich, nourishing, and fruitful (yet domesticated) Garden of Eden. "There are wild flowers in abundance, and when the spring comes rainy, the earth abounds in all colors imaginable. The fields of oregano and cactus, when in full bloom, can compete with the loveliest of gardens" (1). It is clear that her family depended upon the land, and that the relationship of land, weather, and landscape was dominant. "Money in our lives was not important; rain was important . . . rain for us made history. It brought to our minds days of plenty, of happiness and security, and in recalling past events, if they fell on rainy years, we never failed to stress that fact. The droughts were as impressed on our souls as the rains. When we spoke of the Armistice of World War I, we always said, 'the drought of 1918 when the Armistice was signed'" (11–12).

We Fed Them Cactus is an extraordinary account of the evolution and change suffered by a people expressed through landscape.[3] By the end, as in Jaramillo's account, the land is described as a purgatory. Bitterness over lost land and nostalgia over lost culture are implicit in the description of a barren wasteland that before had been a paradise.

> The land between the years 1932–1935 became a dust bowl. The droughts, erosion of the land, the unprotected soil and overgrazing of pastures had no power over the winds. The winds blew and the land became desolated and abandoned. Gradually the grass and other vegetation disappeared and the stock began to perish. There was not a day of respite from the wind. . . . In the mornings upon rising from bed, one's body was imprinted on the sheets which were covered with sand. . . . The whole world around us was a thick

cloud of dust. . . . The winds blew all day and they blew all night, until every plant which had survived was covered by hills of sand. (177)

The tragedy of the Hispanos of New Mexico is reflected in the interrelatedness between the land and her father's life. In addition, the loss of her father's land parallels the loss of land of all Hispanos. The land is gone forever, having passed into the hands of Anglos.

> The land which he loved had sucked the last bit of strength which so long kept him enduring failures and sometime successes but never of one tenor. Life so cruel and at times so sweet is a continuous struggle for existence — yet one so uncertain of what is beyond fights and fights for survival.
>
> He is gone, but the land which he loved is there. It has come back. The grass is growing again and those living on his land are wiser. They are following practices of soil and water conservation which were not available to Papa. But each generation must profit by the trials and errors of those before them; otherwise everything would perish. (178)

One narrative strategy of resistive discourse in *We Fed Them Cactus* is the use of collective voices to tell the stories. Not only do we have Cabeza de Baca's grandmother's, father's, and El Cuate's voices as recourse to historical authority, we also hear the voices of Señor Mariano Urioste (the tollkeeper of the road over Vega Hill into Las Vegas), Doña Jesusita García de Chávez, and Lola Otero de García, who remembered tales about the lives of women; Don Miguel Benavides and Señor Antonio Trujillo, taken captive by Indians as children; and Don Luciano López, who told about the Caballeros de Labor and the bandit Vicente Silva. Over and over, Cabeza de Baca emphasizes that the stories she recounts are part of the oral tradition and history of the community. She names the storytellers as those who lived the experiences and had intimate knowledge of the facts. Thus she emphasizes a communal authority and voice, not an individual one. Her own voice is simply one that shared in the collective experience. No voice has more discursive authority than any other; together they enrich (and preserve) the extensive oral tradition.

We Fed Them Cactus is also an account of how women functioned in this community. Throughout the narrative are glimmers of a life contrary to stereotypical images of Hispanas. Cabeza de Baca apparently had a somewhat free childhood, growing up under the supervision of her grandmother. "As a child, I was a problem to my grandmother and was forever running away from her. She called me from morning to night trying to locate me" (84). This is in contrast to the childhood of Cleofas Jaramillo, who depicts the women and children as usually enclosed behind the tall walls of the houses and only rarely free to go on an excursion out in the country. "I can still see myself, like a wild bird set free of a cage, running from one berry bush to another, filling my little play basket, my heart beating with delight at the sights of beautiful mariposa lilies, blue bells, yellow daisies, feathery ferns" (*Romance,* 10).

Even though she may have enjoyed more freedom than most young Hispanas, Cabeza de Baca nevertheless had to accept certain restrictions and learn to behave like a lady of her class.

> Each boy on papa's ranch had from ten to twelve horses as remuda. I had my own horses, too, but they were gentle ponies. True to aristocratic rearing, I had to lead a ladylike life and should not resemble that of our uncouth neighbors whose women were able to do men's work. I always envied any woman who could ride a bronco, but in my society it was not done. How skillfully they saddled a horse! I often watched them but it was never my privilege to have to do it. When I arose each morning, my horse was already saddled and tied to a hitching post waiting for me if I cared to ride. (*We Fed Them Cactus,* 129)

Cabeza de Baca admired the pioneer Hispanas and the women who lived on the ranches, who "had to be a hardy lot in order to survive the long trips by wagon or carriage and the separation from their families. . . . [and] had to be versed in the curative powers of plants and in midwifery, for there were no doctors within a radius of two hundred miles or more" (59). Her own grandmother was called every day "by some family in the village, or by their empleados, to treat a child or some other person in the family. In the fall of the year she went out to the hills and valleys to gather her supply of healing herbs" (59). This same grandmother was later able to convince the villagers to vaccinate for smallpox after terrible outbreaks of the disease, thus representing both the traditional medicine associated with curanderas, and the progress being made by modern medicine.

In *The Good Life* (1949), Cabeza de Baca incorporated the oral tradition (as well as her training as a home economist) into a text that combines creative tales about the mythic Turrieta family, living in an isolated village in New Mexico, with recipes for the preparation of traditional foods. Because this book was meant to be used as a guide to food, the most important characters are women. Among these women is a singular character, Señá Martina, the curandera of the village with a mysterious past (Rebolledo and Rivero, 52–56). "The medicine woman seemed so old and wrinkled to Doña Paula and she wondered how old she was. No one remembered when she was born. She had been a slave in the García family for two generations and that was all any one knew. She had not wanted her freedom, yet she had always been free. She had never married, but she had several sons and daughters" (10; Rebolledo and Rivero, 52).

Doña Paula, the mother of the family, and Señá Martina exemplify a mythos of cultures in harmony as they are mutually dependent. In fact, much of the book is a dialogue between the two women.

> "Señá Martina, you will have to tell me the names of the plants and what their uses are. I can never remember from one year to another," said Doña Paula.
>
> "You young people believe too much in doctors and you have no faith in plants," answered Señá Martina. . . . "Doña Paula, why don't you put down all the prescriptions that I give you each year? You who can write need not rely on your memory only, as I have for years. I cannot live forever and when I am gone you will have no one to ask."
>
> "You are right," said Doña Paula. "I shall write them down." She had said the same thing for twenty years. (14; Rebolledo and Rivero, 53)

Señá Martina grumbles and limps her way through the narration, becoming by the end a thoroughly likeable character. She arrives at the house on Christmas Eve, limping and complaining that if she had not promised, she would not be there to help because her rheumatism is getting worse every day. Yet in the same breath she asks, "What do you want me to do?" When she dies, the entire community is saddened.

> The men carried the body on a litter as there was no coffin for Señá Martina; she had asked to be given an Indian burial. She had often said to Doña Paula, "I do not want a coffin. There is no need for pomp and expense because once we are dead nothing matters anymore. The coffin rots and we return to the earth as was intended." . . . Doña Paula was the chief mourner for Señá Martina, who had been closer to her than even her own mother. She had depended on her since she came to El Alamo as a bride and theirs had been a silent friendship, deeper than words could express and only the heart could feel. (43)

For Cabeza de Baca, the curandera symbolizes the old ways of healing as well as knowledge that is passing on. As these women who have stored the tradition in their memories die, the only way to preserve it is to incorporate as much as possible into the literary, written tradition. Cabeza de Baca does so in her books, consciously attempting to capture as much of the orality of that tradition as possible, using narration as well as inner monologues, prayers, songs, sayings, and recipes. Thus the feminine discourse of this tradition is intimately tied into the portrayal of a female way of life, the work they do, and the traditions and rituals they hold dear.

Cabeza de Baca, who worked for thirty years as an extension agent, started her long, distinguished career of public service as a country school-teacher. In *The Good Life,* she has left us an account of the time when she taught reading, spelling, history, grammar, arithmetic, physiology, penmanship, and geography. She had definite ideas about teaching English to Spanish-speaking children, without denying the children the value of speaking their native languages. "We had bi-lingual readers for the primary grades. These were the adopted texts of that day. In this way, the English-speaking children learned Spanish and the Spanish-speaking learned English" (161). Looking back on her teaching career, Cabeza de Baca says, "I know I have never been happier and I have never been among people who were more hospitable, genuine and wholesome than those who lived on the Ceja" (170).

All three writers discussed here are remarkable for their concerns and their production in a time when most Hispanas/Mexicanas had little education, or if they were educated, little leisure or encouragement to write. They did so against the overwhelming dominance of Anglo culture and language, and against the patriarchal norms of their own culture. Their narratives are valuable not only because they preserve accounts of folk life but also because, in particular, they record the details women considered important, details rarely included in male narratives. Thus we are able to glimpse something of the female experience usually left out of history.

These early writers and the storytellers have many things in common. There is a desire to preserve the "old ways": the traditions, the stories, the cultural history and rituals, and the foods, and to do it more or less "truthfully" (Vásquez, xi). The strong, resourceful female is an integral part of both estorias and written tales. The figure of the curandera/bruja or healer is a cultural symbol, even an archetype, who stands out as a continuous link from the estoria/cuentos to the early written tradition, and who continues to be an important literary symbol for contemporary writers such as Pat Mora, Carmen Tafolla, and Sandra Cisneros. The careful description, both realistic and imaginary, of people, houses, villages, and traditions is essential because it is through these detailed images that we remember. And the perspective on landscape—from the edenic past to a disintegrated present —is not only evidence of a vanishing cultural scene but also a symbolic representation of the loss of Hispano control of the land to Anglo domination. Preservation of language, however, is as important as land, and although some of the writers chose to write in English, there is considerable emphasis on Spanish, Spanish names, and Spanish perspective. Finally, many of the writers rely on, revere, and empower a community discourse, a collective storytelling.

At this early stage, however, the writers were still "explaining" things —describing and detailing. Romantic, nostalgic, yes—but at the same time complex and revealing. And quite clearly we can discern a "feminine" voice, for we have women working, laughing, sharing, talking, caring for each other. The women brought to life in these pages are strong women. They are survivors—women who used their intelligence and ingenuity to survive in a harsh land, and who did it with laughter, tenderness, and a strong sense of self. Contemporary Chicanas could not ask for better ancestors.

3

From Coatlicue to La Llorona:
Literary Myths and Archetypes

Mythology often functions as a collective symbolic code that identifies how we should live. Cultures use myths and the stories of heroines and heroes to create role models. These stories enable us to differentiate correct behavior from incorrect, transmit moral values, and identify those traits considered desirable by a group or society.

Women's lives are particularly circumscribed by cultural values and norms that try to dictate how women should behave and who their role models should be. If, however, the existing mythology (as defined by patriarchy) is unable to fulfill the increasing demand for women as active, energetic, and positive figures, then women writers may choose myths and archetypes, historical and cultural heroines, that are different from the traditional ones. They may create new role models for themselves or choose existing models but imbue them with different (sometimes radically different) traits and characteristics. Thus the female figures chosen by female writers may coincide with traditional figures; they may show different aspects or attributes from those figures; or they may be totally different figures. How Chicana writers choose, define, and image their myths and heroines is the subject of exploration in this chapter.

Christian and Pre-Columbian Archetypes: The Generation of Myths

Roman Catholicism has long emphasized the importance of the Virgin Mary, and followers of the cult of *Marianismo,* or Mariology, strive to emulate the Virgin's faith, self-abnegation, purity, care of her physical as well as spiritual child(ren), and passivity. This tradition, emphasized by the church, has heavily influenced many Hispanas who look to the Virgin to intervene for them in their daily lives (Warner). In Mexico, the Virgin of Guadalupe, the first dark Mestiza Virgin, who miraculously appeared to the Indio Juan Diego in the early colonial period, is an important symbol of syncretism. The Virgin appeared in an area known to be the sacred worshiping place of an important pre-Columbian Nahuatl goddess, Tonantzín. This appropriation of an already-sacred space facilitated the native Mexicans' acceptance of the "Indian/Mestiza" Madonna. Moreover, the Virgin of Guadalupe represents the merging of European and Indian culture since she is, in some senses, a transformation or "rebirth" of the native goddesses.

Tonantzín is, interestingly enough, an aspect of the great Nahuatl goddess Coatlicue, "the strangest goddess of pre-Spanish America. . . . The metaphysical conceptions of death and resurrection which came together in her as the 'filtheater' belong to the oldest ideas of mankind. . . . a temple was erected for her as Tonanzin [sic] (our mother), on the site of which there stands today the church of the 'Virgen de Guadalupe,' the patron-saint of the Mexican Indians" (Anton, 58). Because there is a significant connection between the European, albeit Indianized, madonna and the female Nahuatl deities, it is interesting to compare the main characteristics of these various deities to those of the Christian deities, and to see which aspects of these important cultural images contemporary Chicana writers define for themselves as significant.

Coatlicue is an extremely complex goddess of many aspects, transformations, and features, and she is considered to be probably the most ancient of the Nahuatl deities (Anton, 58). She is both goddess and monster, beneficent and threatening. Coatlicue is sometimes seen as a decapitated earth goddess. "When her adversaries had mutilated Coatlicue — says the myth — her hair turned to grass, to trees, to flowers. Her skin was transformed into fertile soil, her eyes to holes filled with water, wells and springs. Her mouth changed into great caves, which offered shelter to men. Out of her nose were formed hills and valleys. She it was who secured life with her sacrifices" (58–59).

Another Nahuatl goddess, Tlazolteotl, is also seen as a goddess of filth and as such is linked to that aspect of Coatlicue. Filth, in the Aztec world as in the Christian world, was symbolic of sin, but Tlazolteotl has four phases, related to the four phases of the moon, and in the third phase, she has the power to cleanse or "forgive" all sin. According to the noted Nahuatl scholar Miguel León-Portilla, a text in the *Florentine Codex* shows that Tlazolteotl, like Coatlicue, is not a static goddess but one whose aspect can change from a voluptuous seducer to a cleanser of sins ("Afrodite y Tlazolteotl," 5). Tlazolteotl was commonly associated with sexual excesses, and "her priests heard the confession of those found guilty of adultery" (Anton, 59). She was also connected with witchcraft.

The origin of Tlazolteotl's name, which León-Portilla defines as both *tlazolli* (garbage, waste) and *tlazotli* (precious thing), also points out the duality of her nature. León-Portilla compares her to Aphrodite in her erotic aspect and says that just as Aphrodite converges into Theameter (the mother goddess), Tlazolteotl converges into Tonantzín (our little mother) ("Afrodite," 4). Another Nahuatl scholar, C. A. Burland, describes Tlazolteotl as remover of corruption.

> It was said that evil, perverseness and debauched living were the gifts which Tlazolteotl offered. She inflamed and inspired them and likewise could forgive them. At her wish she removed the corruption. She cleansed and washed away all these evils with the cleansing green and yellow waters in her hands. And thus she pardoned, and removed the corruption when confession was made in her presence. The heart was opened before Tlazolteotl, and the guardian of her image, the one who saw for her, was a seer wise in reading the sacred almanac. In his hands he kept the picture writing made with ink, and the colours for painting. The knowledge and wisdom of the book was well known to him. (135)

This ritual ceremony of cleansing was not only a magical sanction, but generally occurred only once in a lifetime, often marking the transition to old age (136).

Coatlicue (incorporating aspects of Tonantzín and Tlazolteotl) was seen as a goddess of love and of sin, with the power to create and devour life; thus she was "the symbol of ambivalence . . . personification of awesome natural forces, monster who devoured the sun at night [and] brought it to life in the morning. . . . Coatlicue, therefore, represents all aspects of a dual nature and is a cyclical figure" (Anton, 59).

The importance of the Coatlicue figure in Chicana literature is just beginning to be realized. We will see in chapter 4 how this shadowy figure resolves a representational problematic for writers. This powerful symbol is also subject to transformative representations in Chicana writers' desire to make these traditional symbols their own. Pat Mora, for example, explores the cultural and mythic aspects of Coatlicue, humanizing and modernizing her as she envisions her as a talk-show hostess dispensing advice in "Coatlicue Rules: Advice From an Aztec Goddess." In this poem, Mora not only makes use of the mythology surrounding the goddess but transforms it, with a great deal of humor, into the things that make up the lives of ordinary women as well.

As Mora weaves in the mythic with the ordinary, Coatlicue is seen as an extraordinarily wise, and also wry, woman, who as she contemplates her history learns also to tolerate it and benefit from her experience. Her advice is certainly worth taking: beware of offers to make you famous; retain control of your own publicity; protect your uterus; avoid housework (she repeats this twice); listen to inside voices and verify they are yours; insist on personal interviews. The final piece of advice is to be careful about what you swallow: a double-edged reference to the fact that Coatlicue became pregnant by swallowing a feather (the sort of miraculous impregnation common in myths). The advice could also be interpreted as a warning to women to not get taken in by the patriarchy. Thus Coatlicue is a goddess to be heeded not only for her life-giving and life-taking capacity but also for her sage and practical advice.

La Virgen de Guadalupe

In contrast to the dual nature of Coatlicue, the Catholic Virgin is often represented as a one-dimensional figure. She is pure and free from sin. Her central role was as a mother: the mother of Christ and the mother of all Christians. She is regal and dignified. She is also a helper to those who are ill or in need. She intercedes on behalf of humans before God and Christ her son — so she is a transmitter (or translator, if you will) through which and not to which Catholics pray, "since love and honor paid to Mary is always an expression of thanksgiving and adoration to her son" (Johnson, 247). The Virgin of Guadalupe, the Mestiza Virgin, is a unilateral figure: she personified nurturing, beneficent aspects and not the supposedly negative life forces of the powerful Tonantzín/Coatlicue who judged, created, and destroyed. She was competent, wrathful, independent. Her powers were autonomous, as were those of most Nahuatl deities. Therefore, as the images of Tonantzín/Coatlicue and the Virgin of Guadalupe were merged, the powerful aspects of Tonantzín were dropped. The Catholic Church considered such qualities inappropriate for the Virgin, Mother of God, and instead heavily promoted the all-knowing, all-powerful "male" traits of God the Father, a symbol interpreted through "traits associated with ruling men in a male-oriented society: aggressiveness, competitiveness, desire for absolute power and control, and demand for obedience" (Johnson, 247).[1]

The Virgin of Guadalupe was not the only Virgin venerated by Mexican Americans in the United States; for example, La Conquistadora, a figure that accompanied the Spaniards to the New World, was also important (she is venerated in California and New Mexico today). But Guadalupe was the most central one. Young Catholic women were admonished to behave like the Virgin of Guadalupe, and role models were created to emulate her. Thus Chicano literature abounds with dutiful mothers, wives, daughters, teachers, nurses, and other helpful, nurturing, compassionate figures of all kinds. "The message was that Mary could be used as a secret go-between, a kind of heavenly powerbroker who could 'fix' things and, in a literal sense, 'get her way.' This was an image the church not only cultivated but institutionalized" (Ohanneson, 41–42).

Thus for Chicano culture, the Virgin of Guadalupe represents characteristics considered positive for women: unselfish giving, intercession between earth and spirit, and the ideal qualities of motherhood. She is the higher being who can be appealed to on a very personal level. In the intimate relationship the culture has with its saints, there are stories of individuals putting the image of the Virgin in a corner or "punishing" her in some way if she does not perform properly.

Many women feel the Virgin has much more power than the "official" ascendancy given to her by the church. For one thing, she is seen as having a mother's hold over her son — that it is not just through him that she derives her power, but that from the respect he has for her, she only has to look at him for him to obey her commands.[2] In her images in Chicano culture, she stands alone — without her son — and in her dress she wears the ancient symbols of Tonantzín.

The Virgin is the patron saint of the Chicanos and the visual image of contemporary popular culture (as evidenced, for example, in lowrider manifestations). Her image was central to the 1960s strike marches from the grape fields of California to Sacramento when the United Farm Workers walked with two banners: one displaying the red and black thunderbird symbol of the UFWA, and the other, the Virgin of Guadalupe.[3] Notwithstanding the Virgin's strong image in popular culture, she is represented in a problematic manner by many Chicana writers, and at times even — ironically — as a symbol of failure. On the negative side, the Virgin is often seen as not active enough, a somewhat passive figure created by the patriarchy, an image giving them mixed messages: How can one be a mother and a virgin too? How could Mary " 'get around' Jesus to do anything and still be the sweet, gentle handmaid of the Lord?" (Ohanneson, 42).

The Virgin is also often seen as the image of the unattainable. She has failed to intercede politically for her people in the United States; she is powerless — like a traditionally submissive "madrecita mexicana" — and she advocates acceptance and endurance, not action. For example, in her poem "444 Years After," Carmen Tafolla plays on the image of Juan Diego (who took the roses the Virgin had given him to the bishop to prove her existence) and the migrant workers in the fields, and questions whether or not the Virgin could be incorporated into modern life.

> If I gathered roses for you . . .
>
> .   .   .   .
>
> —would my jeans jacket sprout
>   an embroidered vision
>   of the same old Lupe
>   with stars in her cloak
>   but standing on a pick-up
>   truck with melons?

(Get Your Tortillas Together, 44; Rebolledo and Rivero, 256)

In Tafolla's version, she would have to "steal" the flowers (playing on the stereotype of thieving Mexicans) rather than be given them by the Virgin. Furthermore, she would give the Virgin only half of the dozen; the other six she would give to her lover, thus dividing her offerings between her sexual, earthy life and her spiritual one. The poem is built around the repetition of the conditional "if I gathered roses for you" (repeated three times), and followed by the problematic question, "Would you understand?" Tafolla's answer is a tentative "I think so," followed by "so, I'll still gather roses for you. (And for him)." This poem is one of many that illustrate the often-ambiguous attitude of Chicana writers toward the Virgin.

In another interesting juxtaposition, the Virgin is connected with the Statue of Liberty, which is also seen sometimes as a symbol of failure because it promises justice and equality for all. But although some consider those promises broken, others still see hope. For example, in the posters for Denise Chávez's play "Hecho en Mexico," the Virgin and the Statue of Liberty are superimposed on each other and are together transformed into a Chicana revolutionary.

Even nonbelievers find symbolic figures such as the Virgin hard to ignore. In Pat Mora's powerful poem "To Big Mary From an Ex-Catholic," the speaker fears the repercussions of not believing—if the claims of the Catholic Church turn out to be true—and she wonders if Mary is really a vengeful goddess. She also addresses her as "Big Mary," ironically referring to the traditional interceding-yet-powerful image she carries in Chicano culture. But again this image contains mixed messages: Is she the great mother? Big mama? Or a manipulative woman?

Will you kick me in the teeth?
Will your foot spike so fast
from under your blue robe
no one will see
but I will bleed?

My fault. I stopped the bribes
hoarded soft petals
didn't lay them at your feet
didn't speak to you at all.

(*Borders,* 77)

Mora here underscores the tradition of young girls (and women) who
during the month of May lay flower petals at the Virgin's feet during pro-
cessions that end with the coronation of the Virgin on May 31 as *Regina y
Emperatriz de Cielos y Tierra* (Queen and Empress of Heaven and Earth).
Mora also refers to the "gifts" (she calls them bribes) believers offer Mary;
"if you do such and such for me, I will donate money to the church, offer
flowers, etc." Mora continues with the skepticism of uncertain belief that
perhaps all ex-Catholics maintain.

If some day in a dark church
I wait for a nod, smile, wink
will you just smash your foot
into my mouth?

(77)

This, of course, ties in with the prevailing "punishment and purgatory"
images taught to young Catholic girls.[4]

In an attempt to repossess the Virgin and imbue her with active and
contemporary qualities, writers such as Demetria Martínez and Sandra Cisneros break through the stereotypes to create a complex image of a Virgin
who is more powerful because of her contemporary representation. For
example, in "Hail Mary," Martínez represents the Virgin as a figure who was
burned at the stake, kicked out of her home as an unwed mother, and raped
by the soldiers of El Salvador in 1982, soldiers "who shined their rifles at
cathedral doors" (*Turning,* 111). But beyond her various stages of martyr-
dom, she represents the Virgin as "witch" and bitch, who

made love with
life instead of a man,
birthed a troublemaker

(111)

Martínez thus presents the Virgin as taking an active part in life and making her own choices. This activization of the Virgin can also be seen in the visual arts, such as Yolanda López's painting of the Virgin as herself in tennis shoes, or as her mother and grandmother actively working. The Virgin is also portrayed as a karate expert by artist Ester Hernández, and she appears as a tattoo on the back of a young lesbian in "La ofrenda."

Cisneros offers a promising revision of Chicanas' attitude towards "la Virgencita" in "Little Miracles, Kept Promises" (*Woman Hollering Creek*, 116–29; Rebolledo and Rivero, 257–66). While the Virgin figures as one among many saintly interceders for all the prayers offered to the saints by Chayo, the principal protagonist in the story, it is the Virgin who solves her problem. (Chayo thought she was pregnant but it turns out to have been her thyroid.) In repayment of the favor, Chayo cuts off her beautiful long hair and hangs it on the altar next to all the other favors asked and miracles granted. Yet in Chayo's narrative, she too had been ambivalent toward the Virgin.

> I'm a snake swallowing its tail. I'm my history and my future. All my ancestors' ancestors inside my own belly. All my futures and all my pasts.
> I've had to steel and hoard and hone myself. I've had to push the furniture against the door and not let you in. (126; Rebolledo and Rivero, 264)

For Chayo, the Virgin of Guadalupe represented the passivity of her mother and her grandmother, helpless before the violence of their husbands and sons. She wanted a different image for herself. "I wanted you bare-breasted, snakes in your hands. I wanted you leaping and somersaulting the backs of bulls. I wanted you swallowing raw hearts and rattling volcanic ash. I wasn't going to be my mother or my grandma. All that self-sacrifice, all that silent suffering. Hell no. Not here. Not me" (127; Rebolledo and Rivero, 265). For Chayo then, her reconciliation with the Virgin comes about because she recognizes that beneath the patriarchalization of the Virgin, just softly below the surface, lie Tonantzín and all the powerful Aztec/Nahuatl goddesses that gave her life.

If the existing images of the Virgin of Guadalupe, because of their negative connotations, cannot be considered entirely progressive, how can this strong image, so important to the culture in general, be redeemed as a mythology for contemporary women to live by? Part of the solution has been a circuitous route working around the positive but passive figure of Mary, back to the strengths and power seen in the Nahuatl deities, as in Cisneros's story. Other writers attempt to incorporate the power and control of these goddesses with the goodness of the Virgin, thereby creating a third, more acceptable cultural heroine: the curandera. The literary route that leads to the mythic image of the curandera evolves moreover through a number of heroines, each of whom contributes particular characteristics seen as valuable to their creators, amplifying the wide spectrum of cultural heroines available as literary images.

Guerrilleras, Soldaderas, La Adelita: Women Warriors and the Active Life

In the early days of the Chicano Renaissance (1968–1974), the heroines of the Mexican Revolution were prominent figures in the literature.[5] These soldaderas, known also as *guerrilleras* (women resistance fighters), followed their men into war and at times fought beside them — as in the particular case of one heroine popular in legend and corridos, La Adelita. It is clear that an identification exists between the revolutionary fighter for justice, land, and food, and contemporary writers who believe that the pen and the sword are related. Inés Hernandez identifies with the revolutionary heroines, in one poem saying, "Guerrillera soy" (I am a warrior woman) (Rebolledo and Rivero, 232) and in another poem linking the guerrillera figure with the life-giving force of birth and creation.

The guerrilla fighter
there in the mountain of her mind
profound heart
mother-woman
strong and tender
is awaiting
the prophesy of her people
the birth of her daughter
Revolution.
("Untitled")

Another poet, Ana Montes, also identifies La Adelita with the struggle of the Chicanas. As La Adelita struggles for justice, she does what is necessary, even if it means dying, to participate fully in the vision as well as the tragedy of revolution. Montes says,

> Adelita,
> today you are called
> > > Chicana.

(23; Rebolledo and Rivero, 231)

The formal spacing of the poem visually reinforces the equation past/present, Adelita/Chicana. As previously discussed, these revolutionary heroines were also important for early writers such as Josephina Niggli; such common links underscore the strength of these cultural heroines.

Sor Juana Inés de la Cruz: The Life of the Mind

Sor Juana Inés de la Cruz is an important cultural heroine who symbolizes the intellectual woman. In her "Respuesta," an autobiographical essay about her early education and her desire for learning, Sor Juana emphasized the importance of formal training (in her defense of education for women) as well as empirical observation and intuitive knowledge. She saw clearly that if she accepted traditional norms, married and had a family, she would have no time for reflection and intellectual pursuits. Even as a recluse in a convent she often complained about her lack of privacy and time to study because her sister nuns would come to visit. Because she was well known and esteemed in the artistic and intellectual community of Mexico in the late seventeenth century, Sor Juana was treading dangerously on entering the discourse of the public domain. She was considered a troublemaker by church authorities, whom she sometimes (and very subtly indeed) defied, as when told it was unseemly for a woman and a nun to pursue intellectual study. In her *Respuesta a sor Filotea de la Cruz,* Sor Juana argued that for her to stop studying would be to defy God, who gave her intelligence for some reason. Ordered to put away her books, she technically complied but continued her empirical studies by observing physics and other sciences in the laws evident in cooking and household duties. Thus not only did she continue her scientific observations, but in so doing, she elevated the everyday work of women into the realm of science.

The tragedy of Sor Juana's final years of silence is sobering to many Chicana writers. Ordered to end her studies as an act of obedience, she gave away her magnificent collection of books. She nursed her sister nuns during an epidemic and died at the young age of 44. In her silence, Sor Juana seems to embody all the negative and repressed characteristics of the Virgin of Guadalupe. Nevertheless, Sor Juana's other qualities — her fierce love of knowledge, the brilliance of her writing, the power of her language, and her independent spirit — intrigue and inspire contemporary writers. She was not a quiet, long-suffering woman, but an intellectual who, for most of her life, made and lived her own choices.[6] Sor Juana appears as a constant figure in both Chicana poetry and prose.

Estela Portillo Trambley, in her historical play *Sor Juana* (Rebolledo and Rivero, 233–55), presents her as a woman who, through the example of her confessor Father Antonio, finally resolved her internal conflict between the life of the mind and life itself. Portillo Trambley sees Sor Juana at the resolution stage of her lifelong struggle against her passion. In the play, Sor Juana has always believed that knowledge was the path to salvation, to God, and she has felt guilty because of her lack of humility, because of her faith in herself as an intellect. In a sense, Portillo Trambley turns the traditional perspective of Sor Juana around by presenting her at the end of her life (after she had forsaken her quest for knowledge) and imbuing her with a contemporary "social" conscience, revealed in Sor Juana's explanation of her final penance.

> What I have written to be truth is not the truth I see before my eyes each day . . . except for love and dignity. I see that in the barrios every day. It embarrasses me to sound full of self-importance. They will say that all good things evaporated in Mexico with the coming of rebellion, that I was forced to give up my possessions, my writing. They will make of me a martyr. I am not. I simply faced myself and found myself wanting. My knowledge could not dissolve the terror of death and violence. My books could not suspend the suffering of so many! Words became only words; for that reason I saw them as a form of deceit. It would be a prideful thing to say such things with words. (191)

Sor Juana's struggle is of course the same faced by many Chicana intellectuals and writers, who are often torn between community social activism and a more detached intellectual or creative life.

As disturbing as it seems to be for Portillo Trambley that Sor Juana made many of her life choices because of the impact of the men in her life (Bernardo, the nobleman she was supposedly in love with who married another, and Father Antonio), nevertheless the play does emphasize Sor Juana's feminist independence, and the sexism and lack of opportunity for women in colonial Mexico.

For many writers, Sor Juana remains an important image of female intellect and striving for knowledge. In "Mi reflejo," Lydia Camarillo sees Sor Juana as one of many foremother heroines who come together to form the literary and artistic reflection of the contemporary Chicana.

> Don't you remember me?
> > Your chauvinism impedes my inner growth,
> > quemaste mis libros,
> > you smashed all women's hopes,
> > you destroyed my life.
> ¿Ya no te ACUERDAS de mí?
> > I am the scientist:
> > the gifted;
> > the one with all wisdom,
> > Yo soy la mujer hermosa.
>
> (73; Rebolledo and Rivero, 268–69)

Mora, in "Maybe a Nun After All," identifies with the image of the nun working in seclusion in her cell — but the cell has become a modern motel room.

> Motels are my convents.
> I come alone
> give workshops, readings.
>
> I lock my door twice,
> smell solitude, taste quiet
> away from fast music, telephones,
> children tugging, "Mom, Mom."
>
> I remove my dust-
> y clothes, slip on
> a loose white gown.
> Before I sleep, I say
> my poems, old, new
> say lines over and over
> wrestling with demon words.
>
> I wake early
> mumbling phrases,
> litanies

holding a pencil
rather than beads.

I shower, wrap my hair
in a white towel.
My face is pale, my body
hollow.

(*Borders,* 76; Rebolledo and Rivero, 283)

Playing on the idea of a "room of one's own," Mora sees (as did Sor Juana) a convent-like seclusion as desirable. With poems replacing prayers, and a pencil substituting for rosary beads, she fashions her own litanies and images herself as a nun, all in white.

Mora, too, rewrites Sor Juana's autobiography in poetic fashion in "The Young Sor Juana," focusing on the significantly revealing moments of Sor Juana's life. Juana recounts how at three, she ran away to school with her sister, and at seven, when she wants to dress like a boy to study, she says that instead,

. . . I hide
in my grandfather's books, sink into the yellowed
pages, richer than cheese. . . .

(*Communion,* 78)

At sixteen, she cuts her hair off when she doesn't learn fast enough.

I'll set the pace and if I fail, I'll hack and slash
again until I learn. I'll pull and cut, this foolish lushness.
Again I'll feel my hair rain softly on my clothes, gather
in a gleaming puddle at my feet.
My hands are strong, and from within I rule.

(78)

Alicia Gaspar de Alba has made the figure of Sor Juana even more revisionary in her "Juana Inés," a short story about the life of Sor Juana. Gaspar de Alba sees Sor Juana as a lesbian, and her most terrifying and terrible secret is the one she cannot speak. From the beginning, Juana is seen as "unnatural" because of her brilliance. She should "learn how to embroider, how to crochet, like your cousins; those are safe things for girls to know" (3). Yet Juana demonstrates her brilliance in European knowledge as well as Nahuatl and Mayan knowledge. Her "unsafe" knowledge also incorporates her own awareness of her love of and for women. She is yet another example of the ever-evolving complexities of cultural archetypes by Chicana writers. Sor Juana and her legend as a woman of passion — passion for knowledge and the intellectual life — have left a deep admiration in many Chicana writers for this singular figure.

La Malinche, La Llorona: Revisions of Negative Mythology

A female figure opposite to that of the Virgin Mary is Eve/Lilith. As the Virgin represents the spiritual, nourishing, and positive aspects of women, Eve/Lilith is the seductress, temptress of man's flesh and sexuality, and incorporates all the power that lies behind passion, energy, and desire (and certainly even the more threatening power of knowledge) (Stevens, 90–101). Eve has been syncretized into the Malinche/La Llorona figure in Mexican as well as Chicano culture. La Malinche/Malintzín/Doña Marina (depending on your perspective) is the Nahuatl woman of noble birth who was sold into slavery by her family. When she was fourteen, she was given away again, among twenty other women, to Hernán Cortés when he arrived in Mexico. Malinche was able to speak both Maya and Nahuatl, and she communicated in Maya with Geronimo de Aguilar, a Spaniard who had been shipwrecked on the Yucatan coast and who spoke Spanish and Maya. Because of her language abilities, Malinche had a central role as translator.

She later became Cortés's mistress. Her name became so closely identified with that of the conqueror (and his with hers) that in Mexico, by the twentieth century, the word "Malinche" or "Malinchista" became synonymous with a person who betrays her or his country. (At present it specifically refers to those Mexicans who relate excessively to American-produced commercial goods.) The historical figure Malinche had a child by Cortés, but when Cortés was ordered to bring his Spanish wife to the New World, Malinche was married off to one of his soldiers, Don Juan de Jaramillo. Her child by Cortés was sent to Spain to be educated, and Malinche died young, in relative obscurity (Díaz del Castillo, 85–87).[7]

The image of La Llorona, the weeping woman, brought together Indian and Spanish folklore and legends. In both cultures there were prevalent images of women whose children had been murdered, or who themselves murdered or abandoned their children and could not rest thereafter. The restless spirits of these women roamed from then on and appeared to those who rode or walked deserted roads, particularly crossroads. In some tales, if La Llorona murdered her own children, her anguished cries could be heard during the night. La Llorona was a syncretic image connected both to Spanish medieval notions of *ánimas en pena,* spirits in purgatory expiating their sins, and to the Medea myth. She was also closely identified with pre-Columbian Aztec cultural heroes such as *Mocihuaquetzque,* valiant women who died in childbirth (and who were the only Aztec women to achieve afterlife in the place of the warriors). These women were held sacred by Aztec warriors, who believed that carrying the third finger of a Mocihuaquetzque's left hand into battle would protect them. The women were believed to have supernatural powers; thus *brujos,* or witch doctors, would try to obtain a piece of their hair or their left arms to be used in rites of magic. Because of these reputed powers, the families of the Mocihuaquetzque had to guard their graves so their bodies would not be mutilated. However, when they had achieved their afterlife, they were known as *Cihuapipiltin,* or night ghosts, who lay in wait at crossroads, wished epilepsy on children, and incited men to lewdness. They were also vaguely connected to attributes of Coatlicue, who also at times roamed the crossroads.

The anguished forces of ánimas en pena and the Cihuapipiltin were the same creative and destructive powers attributed to Tonantzín/Coatlicue. La Llorona was associated with rivers and bodies of water — and when children drowned, Hispanos often blamed the influence of La Llorona. Today in New Mexico, for example, there are signs with the symbol of La Llorona warning children to stay away from ditches.

In folklore, the images and mythology about La Llorona and La Malinche merge until in many areas they are transformed into a unitary figure. The image is a negative one, tied up in some vague way with sexuality and the death or loss of children: the negative mother image. As La Malinche, she is connected to Cortés and is believed to have somehow favored him and betrayed her people. As La Llorona, she is known to appear to young men who roam about at night. They believe she is a young girl or beautiful young woman, but when they approach her (with sexual intent in mind), she shows herself to be a hag or a terrible image of death personified. The union of the two figures is clearly seen, for example, in Rudolfo Anaya's *The Legend of La Llorona,* in which the historical figure of La Malinche evolves into that of La Llorona.

La Malinche and La Llorona are also important cultural symbols for Chicana writers. But in general, the two figures are never confused nor united: their identities remain clear and defined. At the same time, the representation of La Malinche has undergone constant reevaluation and transformation since the 1970s. Many stories and poems have been written that use La Malinche as a central symbol, often from varying perspectives.

Because she is complex, La Malinche is represented by Chicana writers both as a figure to be redeemed and as one to be transformed.

As the personification of the native Indian woman "conquered" by the Spanish/European male, La Malinche is seen as the victim of family and historical circumstances, traded twice against her will. Many Chicana writers find it difficult to place the symbolic blame of history on a woman who was a victim and not an instigator.

La Malinche also represents the subordination of the Indian race to the European white race. For a long time, in both Mexico and the United States, the Indian roots of Mexicano Chicano culture were denied, and Mexican Americans attempted to assimilate into the dominant culture. The resuscitation of La Malinche as part of the process of mestizaje brings her into the forefront as the symbolic mother of a new race. Recognition of La Malinche as a complex figure with both positive and negative aspects would imply, therefore, integration of these Indian roots, as seen, for example, in Tafolla's poem "La Malinche" (Rebolledo and Rivero, 198–99) and the dream sequence in Erlinda Gonzales-Berry's *Paletitas de guayaba* (Rebolledo and Rivero, 207–12).

One element of Malinche's historical importance has been her ability to translate for Cortés, giving him knowledge and power over the native tribes. History tells us that La Malinche chose to aid Cortés, saving his life on more than one occasion. Because Chicana writers identify with the act of interpretation as they consciously shift from one language and culture to another, and because in the power structure they always have to consider their relation to the dominant culture, it is not surprising that many feel closely aligned with the figure of La Malinche. This ability to translate is seen also as the ability to move easily between multiple cultures as well as languages.

Malinche was also used as an object of sexual desire; thus she is often portrayed as a whore, standing for the stereotyping of a "lower" culture's sexuality. Lesbian Chicana writers have also been portrayed in this sense as "Malinches." Cherríe Moraga, for example, sees the limitation of Chicana autonomy as part of the "sexual legacy" of the myth of Malintzín, defined as any Chicana who defies tradition (particularly sexual) tradition, and is therefore labeled a traitor or lesbian (Alarcón, "Traddutora, Traditora," 79).[8]

Chicana writers do not view La Malinche as the passive victim of rape and conquest but instead believe her to be a woman who had and made choices. Because she possessed the power of language and political knowledge, for them La Malinche is a woman who deliberately chose to be a survivor—a woman with a clairvoyant sense who cast her lot with the Spaniards in order to ensure survival of the race, a woman who lives on in every Chicana today. It was often because of her diplomacy and intelligence that a more total annihilation of the Indian tribes of Mexico did not occur. It is in this capacity as intercessor (translator) and helper that La Malinche takes on the attributes of the Virgin of Guadalupe.

To illustrate the incorporation of La Malinche into contemporary Chicana literature, let us examine first the "Marina Poems" by Lucha Corpi, and then two short narrative pieces on La Malinche, which are incorporated into recent novels. The first narrative is "Malinche's Discourse" in *Puppet,* by Margarita Cota-Cárdenas (Rebolledo and Rivero, 203–7). The second is a dream sequence found in *Paletitas de guayaba,* by Erlinda Gonzales-Berry (Rebolledo and Rivero, 207–12).

The personal identification of many Chicana writers with La Malinche is seen over and over again. It is clear, for example, for Corpi, who when interviewed about her Marina poems was asked whether the empathy she shows for Marina reflects Corpi's identification with her through her own experience. Corpi answered,

> "Yes. They say that Marina was even from the town where I'm from. There is a hill called 'el Cerro de la Malinche' where they say she was born. The town is a few kilometers from Tabasco and they say Marina was from the tribe of the Tabasqueños. It is possible that the Tabasqueño empire extended to my town, because it is so close. Marina could be from there. Another identification with Marina was the matter of her son. With my divorce there was the question of whether my son would live with my ex-husband or with me. For the first time I was confronted with the possibility of my son growing up away from me . . . Martín Cortés, Marina's son by Hernán Cortés, was taken from her as a baby and raised in Spain. When he came back she wasn't his mother, she was the Indian woman his father had raped." (quoted in Brinson-Piñeda, 6)

In *Fireflight*, in which the poems appear, Corpi says that

> Doña Marina was a young Indian woman given in slavery to Hernán Cortés after his arrival in Mexico. She served him as guide, interpreter, comrade-at-arms and nurse throughout the conquest and bore him a son. When Cortés was preparing his marriage to a Spanish lady of noble rank, he made a handsome gift of land to Marina and married her to one of his lieutenants. Contemporary accounts of the conquest speak of the extraordinary beauty, intelligence, courage and loyalty of this woman, but the attitude of subsequent generations of Mexicans has been ambivalent. She has been idolatrized as a mother-goddess or reviled as a traitor—her Indian name, Malinche, has become a synonym in Mexico for treachery. These poems were written by way of vindication. (77)

The poem has four sections: I. Marina Mother, II. Marina Virgin, III. The Devil's Daughter, and IV. She (Marina Distant) (translation by Catherine Rodríguez-Nieto).

I. Marina Mother

They made her of the softest clay
and dried her under the rays of the tropical sun.
With the blood of a tender lamb
her name was written by the elders
on the bark of that tree
as old as they.

Steeped in tradition, mystic
and mute she was sold —
from hand to hand, night to night,
denied and desecrated, waiting for the dawn
and for the owl's song
that would never come;
her womb sacked of its fruit,
her soul thinned to a handful of dust.

You no longer loved her, the elders denied her,
and the child who cried out to her "mamá!"
grew up and called her "whore."

(77; Rebolledo and Rivero, 196)

As other critics have noted, Corpi chooses the Spanish name Marina[9] and in the first section employs Christian imagery to denote Marina's sacrifice ("with the blood of a tender lamb"), sexual victimization ("she was sold from hand to hand, night to night / denied and desecrated"), and negation as a legitimate mother ("her womb sacked of its fruit"), denied finally even the love and respect of her lover Cortés, her people, and her child, who "grew up and called her whore." Yet the title of the poem, "Marina Mother" undermines the negative images that others (not the author) have of Marina.

Although Christian images, stereotypes, and expectations prevail on one level, on another, the pre-Columbian symbols balance the image. Marina is "made of softest clay" and sun — reflecting a belief of the Nahuatls and other Mexican pre-Columbian people that humans were created from the earth and infused by the vitality and life-giving force of the sun. Also, at her birth, her name is placed into history by the elders, who write it "on the bark of that tree / as old as they." The bark here refers to a specific tree as well as to the sacred parchments, to the codices of the tribe. For her name to be entered at all tells us that as mute as she may be imaged, Malintzín was no ordinary woman, since ordinary women did not have their names entered on anything.

In addition, Corpi portrays Marina as a mystic, steeped in tradition; that is, she was the holder of ancient ritual and knowledge, a knowledge that does not disappear because you are silent. Indeed Marina is also acknowledged as being a "nurse." The owl, a symbol connected with the curandera and the bruja as well as with Minerva, the goddess of knowledge, never comes, nor does the dawn. Although this may represent denial and negation (as in Marta Sánchez's interpretation of the owl's song as a presage of a death that never comes [*Contemporary Chicana Poetry,* 189]), it could also represent that which awaits, suggesting that Marina lives even today.[10]

II. Marina Virgin

Of her own accord, before the altar
of the crucified god she knelt.
Because she loved you, she only saw
the bleeding man, and loved in him
her secret and mourning memory of you.

She washed away her sins
with holy water, covered her body
with a long, thick cloth
so no one would know
her brown skin had been damned.

Once, you stopped to wonder
where her soul was hidden,
not knowing she had planted it
in the entrails of that earth
her hands had cultivated —
the moist, black earth of your life.

(*Fireflight,* 79; Rebolledo and Rivero, 197)

In this section, Corpi uses Christian imagery to describe Malinche's conversion to Christianity because of her love for "you." This addressee, who in section 1 was clearly Cortés, here on first reading might be her son or Cortés, but on a closer examination, it is an ambiguous "you" transported to a future time, which could refer to the present generation. The intent of such an undifferentiated addressee is a transitional one, shifting from a specific referent in her own historical reality to a more encompassing present. The "virgin" in the title not only refers to the Virgin of Guadalupe, but also to the idea of cleansing and renewal. Thus, like the woman sinner at the feet of Christ who washed his feet with tears, Marina "washed away her sins / with holy water." While the primary image is Christian, as Sánchez points out, we must not forget that the Nahuatl goddess Tlazolteotl also had the ability to forgive sins and did so with the waters of yellow and green. And when the future "you" once "stopped to wonder / where her soul was hidden" — that soul which in Marina Mother was "thinned to a handful of dust" — we are told that ". . . she had planted it / in the entrails of that earth."

While it may be simple to think of the dust-to-dust imagery, this metaphor is more complex. Not only does it refer in general to a female image of the womb, but also to the pre-Columbian custom of burying a newborn child's birth cord in a place that would signify its destiny. Often the umbilical cords of males were planted in battlefields or other places signifying activity, whereas those of females were often planted in the hearth, so they would stay at home. Mora plays on this image of limitation and freedom in her poem "Aztec Princess."

> Her mother would say, "Look in
> the home for happiness. Why do you stare out
> often with such longing?" One day
> almost in desperation, her mother said,
> "Here. See here. We buried your umbilical
> cord here, in the house, a sign that you,
> our girl-child, would nest inside."
>
> That night the young woman quietly dug
> for some trace of the shriveled woman-to-woman
> skin, but all she found was earth, rich earth,
> which she carefully scooped into an earthen jar
> and carried outside to the moonlight
> whispering, "Breathe."
>
> (*Chants*, 28; Rebolledo and Rivero, 195–96)

A Nahuatl child was also, at the time of birth, given a ritual blessing by the female or male elders that would prescribe the ideal circumstances of its life. To a female, the elders would say,

> You must be in the house like the heart in the body. You must not leave the house. . . . You must be like the ashes and the hearth. . . . Now you have come into the world where your parents live amidst cares of toil, where glowing heat, cold and winds prevail, where there is neither real joy nor satisfaction for it is a place of work, cares and wants. . . . You must not sigh, nor weep to have come. Your arrival has been longed for. Yet there will be work and toil for you, because this is the wish of our master and his decision that we shall obtain all that is needed for life only through sweat, only through work. (Anton, 18–19)

Like Mora, Corpi emphasizes the recurring image in Chicana literature of planting the center of oneself (the umbilical cord, the female to female connection, the soul) into the earth (one that is moist, rich, and fertile) that the woman herself cultivates. In the "Marina" poems, it is a "soul" that will grow again precisely because it is connected to "that" earth which is the same earth of "your life," or that of the narrator/receiver in the present.

III. The Devil's Daughter
When she died, lightning struck in the north,
and on the new stone altar the incense burned
all night long. Her mystic pulsing
silenced, the ancient idol
shattered, her name
devoured by the wind in one deep growl
(her name so like the salt depths of the sea) —
little remained. Only a half-germinated seed.

(*Fireflight*, 81; Rebolledo and Rivero, 197)

In section 3, Corpi shows Marina connected to a power not sanctioned by the Christian church (the new stone altar has simply replaced the old stone altar).

As stated earlier, all those powers seen as not proper for Catholicism were branded as heretical, *brujería* (having to do with witchcraft), and devilish. All those powers Marina had known, psychic and mystical, disappear in an atmosphere laden with mystery and possibilities — as if somehow a prophecy would come to pass. What Marina is and stands for, her "puls-ing," becomes, in effect, a latent transition, a "half-germinated seed"—a seed that can only continue to germinate under the proper conditions, as it does in the poem's fourth section.

IV. She (Marina Distant)

She. A flower perhaps, a pool of fresh water . . .
a tropical night,
or a sorrowful child, enclosed
in a prison of the softest clay;
mourning shadow of an ancestral memory,
crossing the bridge at daybreak,
her hands full of earth and sun.

(83)

She, Marina Distant, appears in the form of another girl child, a symbol of the fruit of that seed and moist soil, "a flower perhaps, a pool of fresh water." The soul that has been planted takes shape in a child "enclosed in a prison of softest clay." The connection between Marina and the child, "She," is shown not only in the parenthetical connection in the title but also as the child crosses the bridge at dawn, her hands full of earth and sun. The Indi-ans believed in the cyclical powers of life forces, in regeneration through sacrifice. While Marina waited for a dawn that was denied her, her inheritor crosses the bridge and achieves the dawn. The connection between the two, between myth and history, between denial and acceptance, comes not only through the mystic pulsing, through the shadows "of an ancestral memory," but also through the recognition of self—inheritance and history—and through the unstated connective powers of the bruja and the curandera. For if the dawn and the sun are achieved, is not the owl achieved also? The connection to the earlier progenitor, seen here as the creator of a new race, is made through writing—the ritual of the sacred parchments.

Many critics have failed to see the subtle yet extremely strong pre-Columbian subtext which in effect parallels the Christian text. Marta Sán-chez, for example, comments that Marina never speaks for herself (*Chicana Poetry*, 187). Yet the text makes it clear that this modern daughter of Marina becomes the recipient of Christian and pre-Columbian legacies equally. Alarcón recognized the Demeter/Persephone themes of the "forced disap-pearance of the Mother/Goddess which leads to the daughter's own abjec-tion. The daughter is doomed to repeat the cycle until the ancient powers of

70

the Goddess are restored" ("Traddutora, Traditora," 80). However, a close reading of Corpi's text reveals that in the creation of the modern "She," the powers have been restored. Marina is no longer mute because her muteness has been transformed by the modern writer.

In "Malinche's Discourse," Margarita Cota-Cárdenas also stretches the "dialogue" across history, weaving the speech of La Malinche into the speech of a teacher at a university, Miss Lencha. La Malinche and Miss Lencha are closely identified by the linguistic wordplay of their names, as well as by symbolism. The narration follows a stream-of-consciousness style, jumping back and forth between historical myth, dialogue, and thought patterns, as well as the class discussion about Chicano ideology. The structure of the dialogue captures the confusion, ambiguity, and conflict that Chicanos feel about the nature of La Malinche.

Closely identified with La Malinche in her traditionally defined aspect of traitor is Chicana feminism. During the early days of the Chicano Renaissance, it was decided at some level that in order to make headway, the group — by means of collective activity — needed to appear unified on all fronts. The women participated, and wanted to participate equally, with the men in the Chicano movement. Often, however, they found themselves staying home and taking care of the children, or in the kitchen in the traditional role of nurturer preparing food and coffee while the men plotted revolution. This is noted in the creative literature in such poems as "Para un revolucionario" and "You Cramp My Style, Baby," by Lorna Dee Cervantes.

The women who were concerned with women's issues or who voiced dissent were considered traitors, nonsupportive of La Raza — Malinchistas. It has taken some time for women's concerns and women's writing to be accepted as legitimate concerns for all Chicanos. Thus part of the ideological praxis of "Malinche's Discourse" — and what Miss Lencha is trying to teach the young generation of Chicanos in her class — is that the old stereotypes, the maligning of women by old myths, values, and attitudes, need to be rethought. In particular, to use the symbol/myth of La Malinche to malign contemporary women who are fighting for their own values and identity is especially vindictive. In "Malinche's Discourse," Cota-Cárdenas therefore not only attempts to bring the myth of La Malinche into some realm of personal perspective, as does Corpi, but she also provides La Malinche with a personal dialogue by way of explanation of her role in history. Furthermore, she examines the role of the conquistadores in their military as well as religious function, linking them to anyone who imposes an ideology on others. Thus she creates a nexus also for those Mexican Americans who try to limit other Chicanos (and Chicanas) by forcing a single vision of what being Chicano should be through cultural stigma. Cota-Cárdenas brings the question of the merchandising of ideology to the forefront from the beginning, as La Malinche seeks to distinguish how labels begin.

> Are you Malinche a malinche? Who are you (who am I malinche)? seller or buyer? sold or bought and at what price? What is it to be what so many shout say sold-out malinchi who is who are/are we what? at what price without having been there naming putting labels tags what who have bought sold malinchismo what other -ismos invented shouted with hate reacting striking like vipers like snakes THEIR EYES like snakes what who what (203)

For Cota-Cárdenas, La Malinche is trapped between two cultures, a woman caught in the crisis of identity, of her beliefs. Initially the crisis is that of the Indians caught, as they were during the Conquest, between the prophecies that said the god Quetzalcoatl would return, and their belief that Cortés was that god. Later they were caught between their native religions and Christianity. The Chicano is also caught between two cultural systems, and the Chicana is then caught between those two and, additionally, between gender differences in Chicano culture. Thus La Malinche becomes the formative symbol for all Chicanas caught "between two systems in a conflictive state" (206).

La Malinche has been "labeled" by others from an early age, a labeling that has continued in her historical legacy to the present. Cota-Cárdenas uses humor to underscore this reality.

> "Using the latest terminology and it's so useful nowadays, I'm going to tell you about my formative years: at the age of five, more or less, I left off being the favorite eldest daughter of my tribe, when some very immediate relatives sold me, to some more distant buddies, who bought me. . . at what price? I don't know, I only remember that I went kicking that I wanted my mama that why had my papa abandoned me yes yes I went yelling loud too why why and they said tie her up she's too forward too flighty she thinks she's a princess thinks she's her father's daughter thinks she's hot stuff that's it doesn't know her place a real threat to the tribe take her away haul her off she's a menace to our cause that's it only learned to say crazy things to say accuse with HER EYES and they didn't want then troublemakers in their country." (203–4)

These labels, specific here to La Malinche, are of course the very labels that cultures use to restrict and limit women's activity — socially and intellectually. Women are so silenced that they are left to speak only with "their eyes." Again La Malinche clearly defines the country as "their" country, signifying that it belonged to others, not to her, and she makes the connection between Mexico and the United States.

> "The country, well I suppose Mexico, Aztlán . . .? Well, it could have been a little more to the north or a little more to the south, it makes no difference now, what I was telling you was my version that's it, my version as . . . as a woman, that's right, and they can establish the famous dialectic with the other versions that you already know very well." (204)

This personal vindication of Malinche's version sets up the dialogue with the patriarchal version of history and myth.[11] The "message" La Malinche brings us is that one must take great care in accepting passively all that is told by the culture.

> "You know what, you know a lot about -isms and -acies but I advise you, my children, to look for the answer inside and to look further than the labels implanted and thrown out in reaction hate violence . . . What's wrong is that we're very smart, very bright, and we learn certain things very well that frankly keep on being the same pyramidal funereal hierarchal structure. . . ." (204)

It is important to the dialogue that the receiver / transmitter of this message be a teacher, one who can in turn continue the dialogue with the future generation. Miss Lencha explores the damages done by the stereotyping and labeling imposed by traditional cultural norms and argues that in order to be oneself, one must reject those labels. The dialogue with history seems to have a particular listener, "One who understands." Specifically the dialogue is directed first to the women, "my daughters" (207). No matter how she brings the subject up to her class, the males turn a deaf ear, and the females seem afraid to assert their opinions in front of the males for fear, again, of being labeled traitors.

> "Let's talk turkey, class . . . Well, that means that we ought to discuss today's topic openly and in-good-faith-ly, that's how I prefer it. Well then, Ester, what do you think of Miguelito's comment . . . Yes, what he said about the bad effect of feminism on the movement . . . What do you think, Ester . . . ? Is feminism bad or good . . . etc. . . ? Oh, you don't want to say . . . ? You're . . . afraid . . . ? What are you saying, Miguelito . . . ? . . . "that the chicano / mexican / latin family has to maintain itself intact, that traditions are more important for the good, for the future, Profesora. I think, that's just what my dad and my grandparents were saying last night, that all this stuff about women's liberation is just bourgeois women's junk, those women that have idle time to write and to draw and to . . . discombobulate

73

themselves . . . like my dad said last night . . . I'm sorry, but the movement needs its women . . . well to struggle for the causa . . . Ester, why are you crying . . . What's wrong with you . . . ?" (205)

Through the dialogue, Cota-Cárdenas shows that Miss Lencha suffers from a paranoia born of centuries of oppression—from a long-silenced sense of oneself, from lack of freedom to express openly what it is to be a woman—in a culture that has held up that "goodness" and nurturing acceptance of the Virgin as a role model. The paranoia is expressed in these terms:

"You keep being afraid of you don't know what of SOMEONE who wants you to shut up for you not to ask questions not to challenge not to NOOOOOOOOOOOOO and the insomnia with Puppet and other signs of the barrio about which you had never thought before or much and that now that there's no time left . . . (and this rage started to enter you suppurating and you begin to write poetry at all hours and you strike out at everything now)" (206)

Previously accepted cultural norms, now critically viewed and questioned, outrage the writer, who resents allowing herself and other women to be silenced.

In the final part of the dialogue, Miss Lencha is clearly transformed into Malinche as the students ask Malinche questions directly, the bridge between past and present having been crossed. They also directly call her "Profe Malinchi." The question is, can people really change? Malinche's answer is yes, unless you are dead. The students, humorously, do not hesitate to point out to Malinche that she is in reality dead. But Malinche, transformed into the teacher/writer Miss Lencha, refuses to accept this. She is not dead because she can still see.

" . . . Well how can you know if you're dead . . .? (hahahahaha keep it up little donkey) Isn't it too late by the time you realize that you've . . . Answer me that one, Profe Malinchi . . ."
. . . .
" . . . hee, hee, it's easy, it's easy to know, my daughters my sons it's easy: If you can still open your eyes, then, well you haven't blin blin blinked them for the last time, if you still can open your eyes, then . . . Well then I tell you that you can still kick . . . some . . . (207)

Those who are still seers, in all the symbolic meanings of that term, those who are still visionaries, believe that the world may still change. Once again La Malinche reaches out from the past to instruct the young and to revitalize her image. Miss Lencha has reached her own state of self-knowledge and self-awareness. Her goal is to communicate that to others. At the end of the narration, Cota-Cárdenas links La Malinche to the figure of La Llorona as a "comadre" (co-mother), playing on the conjoining but not identical nature of the two figures. "WELL MY COMADRE LA LLORONA IS CALLING ME I STILL HAVE TO TEACH HER TO NOT PUT UP WITH SHIT TO OPEN HER EYES BECAUSE THERE'S SOMETHING REALLY GOOD" (207).

Gonzales-Berry, in her novel *Paletitas de guayaba,* also uses the Malinche prototype to develop cultural ideas about assimilation/translation. For Gonzales-Berry, La Malinche, who appears to the young heroine Mari (a symbol for Marina) in a dream, is once again a "teacher," a woman who transmits her knowledge, her understanding of her situation, to the younger generation. Mari is a young Chicana traveling by train to Mexico City to study. In an atmosphere rich with sensual descriptions, Mari dreams she is propelled into a capital where the canals of ancient times still reach into the heart of the city. There she meets "La Señora" (a term of respect for La Malinche), who tells her, "How beautiful you are. . . . I've been very conscious that my behavior would produce a beautiful and strong race of people" (209).

Marina takes Mari through a historical discourse prior to the destruction of the great city of Tenochtitlán. She predicts the end of their race as they know it, pointing out the Spaniards' lust for power and the Aztec leaders' weakness as contributing factors. She also acknowledges that the Spaniards' own empire is disintegrating, and the New World will be their salvation. In the midst of this destruction, Gonzales-Berry interjects a hopeful note as the character of Marina tells Mari, "We women, we are strong. . . . our strength comes from the silence imposed upon us by social and legal hands that have gagged our mouths" (211). Marina continues by noting she is "at the crossroads of a treacherous road." She decided to join Cortés in order to alter the destiny of her people, who otherwise would be on the road to annihilation. "I will use the force of my voice and offer it to Cortés, converting myself into his tongue and his procuress. Yes, the necessary link between his world and ours. My object is to help him achieve his imperious plans through the word and through compromise. I see this as the only way to save our race because this is what most obsesses me in this critical moment" (211). In her feminist revision of history, Marina, as the voice, expresses her understanding of how women, as oppressed in her time as in the present, finally overcome their silence to speak.

> Look, the women in this society, as in yours, are mere objects; they are
> chattel; they are the property of their fathers first and then of their husbands.

The only honor that is given to them in this culture is to be sacrificed, if they are virgins. Great honor! . . . We are relegated to the world of shadows and silence, but this silence engenders the word that flounders about in its own bile and finally becomes resentment, outrage, and also song. And to this word is added another and another, and in the end they form a long and strong chain that surrounds us and strangles us. We can succumb, die asphyxiated by words that never found their voice, or we can conjure, with all the portents of heaven and hell, that voice and hurl it out onto the world of men. Before it, they will show their real tendencies — solitude, reticence hidden behind masks and sexual organs that discharge like bows and arrows, harquebuses, and guns. Can you imagine Mari if we unite every single chain of words of every single woman in the world what power that would generate? (210–11)

From Lucha Corpi's silent Marina to Gonzales-Berry's heroine who exhorts Chicanas to use the word, we have come full circle in the revision of La Malinche. She has been vilified, vindicated, made the figure of victimization and the mother of a new race. Perhaps most important is the transformation of La Malinche from a silent figure to one who presents her own dialogue with myth and history. The rich and complex figure of Marina / Malintzín / La Malinche gives Chicana writers much to explore.

Although equally complex for Chicana writers, the figure of La Llorona is quite different. She approximates in popular folklore all those ancient Nahuatl deities who had life-giving and -destroying abilities. Not only is one of these the goddess Tonantzín, near whose shrine the Virgin of Guadalupe appeared, but many other Nahuatl female deities also were recognized for that ability. Among these, as previously mentioned, is the terrible goddess Coatlicue. As Elena Guadalupe Rodríguez explains in "Tu canto" (Your song), La Llorona is often the "boogie man" of Chicano culture, appearing at windows scratching the glass and trying to find some way in.

> Your long nails, uncared for
> scratch boards and windows
> of disobedient children
> trying to find
> some small space
> to extend your hands and pull at their feet
> in the bed where they embrace their dreams
> from foot to head
> they are trembling with skin shivering

all curled up
terrified on hearing your shrill cries
they ask the Virgin
to let them sleep in peace.

(*Morena,* 66, translation mine)

This haunting of young children encompasses bad memories of childhood, and is at times connected to family violence, as Cordelia Candelaria notes in "Go 'Way from My Window, La Llorona."

You've hounded me beyond belief, scaring
My childhood away from me, spooking
My sleep to reels and reels of horror shows

. . . .

Married forever in sickness and in sickness
Till death parts them in sickness
And in loudness
at midnight, in beatings and blood
And weeping children and everyone big
Drunk and endings of kisses happily forever
Sickness, befitting the passionate prelude.
Go!
Follow your babies llorando
Into the rolling water del río
Let them stare you clear-eyed into Hell.

(*Ojo de la cueva,* 164; Rebolledo and Rivero, 216)

For Candelaria, the mythical childhood threat becomes connected more specifically to evil, sickness, and violence.

La Llorona is also symbolic of Chicano culture, whose children are lost because of their assimilation into the dominant culture or because of violence and prejudice. Thus Carrie Castro portrays La Llorona more compassionately as a victim of poverty and circumstances in "The Night Filled With Faint Cries."

At dusk
a woman wrapped
in rags of poverty

kneels at the mouth
of a river
in silence she bows
her head and peers
downtrodden
into a mirror of fate
in front of her flashes
a funeral procession
a reoccurring nightmare
of suffering and death

(*Morena,* 22)

La Llorona's vision of a funeral procession implies that she constantly lives
with guilt, and the memories of the deaths of her children. They, too, are
victims of the social system, and because of this, their history mirrors the
history of Chicanos everywhere.

. . . black horses pull
the empty coffins
denied to innocent hijos
whose mutilated bodies
lie scattered
for centuries
living on
as victims of lust
and lack of food
characters in a story
that won't die
for losing them
she's committed
to cry

(22)

Thus the tragedy for La Llorona is the tragedy of all children lost because of
violence, neglect, abuse. La Llorona has lost her children perhaps through
no fault of her own, but she is condemned to wander endlessly, reminding
us constantly of our mortality and obligations.

At midnight
the moon's reflection
turns her rags to white
with nowhere to sleep
she's left to wander
endless streets
and shed maternal tears
all the way from
Spain to Aztlán
her shrill cry
stirs the wind
and shakes the spines
of those who wait
to hear her faint echo
in the restless night air.

(23)

Although La Llorona represents ambiguity, guilt, and loss, and in-spires fear of the unknown, she is nevertheless part of us — a dark part we need to come to terms with. In "My Black Angelos," Gloria Anzaldúa connects La Llorona with "la bruja con las uñas largas" (the witch with long fingernails), linking her with fearful creatures like Medusa (with her wild masses of hair) and evil witches as fear of this unknown creature "drenches" the lyric speaker.

Taloned hand on my shoulder

. . . .

she picks the meat stuck between my teeth
with her snake tongue
sucks the smoked lint from my lungs
with her long black nails
plucks lice from my hair.

aiiiii aiiiii aiiiii
She crawls into my spine
her eyes opening and closing,
shining under my skin in the dark

whirling my bones twirling
till they're hollow reeds.

(*Borderlands*, 184)

In this poem, La Llorona stalks the speaker and infuses herself into her as finally La Llorona and speaker become one. "We sweep through the streets . . . we roam with the souls of the dead" (185). In spite of the fear, or the terror or disgust we feel, in spite of the desire we have to be "safe" from this horrifying creature and all that she represents, she is part of us and of our culture. She will continue to stalk us and to haunt us until we come to terms with her.

More recently, Sandra Cisneros in "Woman Hollering Creek" has used the underlying symbolism of La Llorona to turn the image into a source of strength for the Chicana. In this short story, Cisneros underpins the structure of the narrative with the myth of a woman heard crying at night. A young battered Mexicana wife, aided by several Chicanas who sympathize with her, manages to escape from the restrictive, violent atmosphere of her home and return to her family in Mexico. At the moment of her flight, the Chicana driving the getaway truck opened her mouth "and let out a yell as loud as any mariachi," afterward explaining, "Every time I cross that bridge I do that. Because of the name, you know. Woman Hollering. Pues, I holler" (*Woman Hollering Creek,* 55). This hollering is no longer the rage or anguish of women suffering. It is the pure shout of triumph, of the celebration of life. And the women begin to laugh, "a long ribbon of laughter, like water" (56).

However serious a figure La Llorona is in our culture, there is a humorous side to her also. Monica Palacios revitalizes the archetype, turning the Llorona myth into a funny but fatal lesbian romance. In "La Llorona Loca: The Other Side," Palacios presents the romance between Caliente, a really beautiful woman, and "La Stranger" (whose name was Petronilia de la Chihuahua y qué). La Stranger, however, takes up with Trixie, and Caliente becomes so angry with jealousy that she drowns La Stranger in the river, and then she also drowns. However, in La Llorona stories, La Llorona never really dies. She is always resurrected by her own actions and by her grief over those actions.

A week after the burial, a villager was getting water from the river and was startled by the eerie cry of a woman. At first the man thought it was really loud Carly Simon music, but as he listened closely, he could hear something about a "stranger." . . . a woman appeared from the bushes . . . [and] sobbed to him, "Have you seen La Stranger?"

The man ran back to the village to tell the others who had also heard the crying. From this time on, the people heard and saw this woman almost every night—searching, crying desperately for La Stranger. Her crying was so hysterical, everyone began to call her La Llorona Loca—the crazy crier. (51)

This Llorona does not search for her lost children, but rather for her lost female compañera/self. The ever-evolving aspects of La Llorona make her one more in a series of Chicana archetypes that have become contemporary and remain relevant in their retelling. Whether a menacing or humorous figure, La Llorona is alive and well in Chicana literature.

4

The Curandera/Bruja:
Resolving the Archetypes

Perhaps the most prominent contemporary archetypal heroine in Chicana literature is the curandera/partera (healer/midwife) who is also the bruja (witch). As do most complex symbols, the curandera/bruja encodes both positive and negative attributes—attributes judged as such by the individual writer. In general, the curandera/partera is the positive side—a woman whose life is devoted to healing, curing, helping—again, attributes commonly associated with the Virgin Mary. The other side, the bruja, is more problematical for the writers because the curandera is always also the witch; that is, she has the power to become one, but she may never choose to do so. Although the healer represents the virginal attributes approved of by the Spanish Catholic culture, the bruja has characteristics that are seen by traditional culture as negative. Yet these same "negative" attributes are incorporated by Indian and folk cultures as part of the vital life cycle. Like La Llorona, the curandera emerges from the history and traditions of multiple cultures: the complex and intricate healing knowledge that the Arab culture had brought to Spain, the medieval Euro-Spanish healing traditions, and the Native American (both Mexican and southwestern) traditions of herb women, folk doctors who taught the Spanish arrivals their knowledge.

The curandera possesses intuitive and cognitive skills, and her connection to and interrelation with the natural world is particularly relevant. She emerges as a powerful figure seen throughout Chicano writing. The tales of Fabiola Cabeza de Baca and Nina Otero-Warren, who were writing in the early 1900s, attest to the emergence of the curandera early in the literature. The cuentos of the oral tradition also echo the importance of this empowered figure.[1] The fact that the curandera has emerged as a powerful figure in the writing of women and men demonstrates not only her enduring representational qualities as myth and symbol but also the close identification of the culture with her mystic and spiritual qualities. Chicana writers feel a particularly intimate connection to her, seeing in themselves some of her intuitive and cognitive transformations as well as her healing abilities.

The image of the curandera as a "seer" is central to Chicano literature. Often a small child receives hints about her or his destiny from the curandera/bruja. However, in *Bless Me, Ultima* by Rudolfo Anaya, although the young boy is mentored and protected by La Grande, Ultima, the old curandera refuses to tell his parents where his umbilical cord is buried because she fears it will predetermine his future—a future which is for him alone to decide. Sandra Cisneros in *The House on Mango Street* has the child narrator, Esperanza, come in contact twice with brujas/curanderas. The first encounter is with a "witch," Elenita, who has all the trappings of her trade but who in reality is only an ordinary healer: she cannot "read" the heroine's future. However, all the ritual is there. "We stay in the kitchen because this is where she works. The top of the refrigerator busy with holy candles, some lit, some not, red and green and blue, a plaster saint and a dusty Palm Sunday cross, and a picture of the voodoo hand taped to the wall" (59). For five dollars, Elenita reads the cards, but when Esperanza asks about a house of her own (which is what she desires), Elenita sees "a home in the heart." This is not what Esperanza came to hear. "She comes back and can tell I'm disappointed. She's a witch woman and knows many things. If you got a headache, rub a cold egg across your face. Need to forget an old romance? Take a chicken's foot, tie it with red string, spin it over your head three times, then burn it. Bad spirits keeping you awake? Sleep next to a holy candle for seven days, then on the eight day, spit. And lots of other stuff. Only now she can tell I'm sad" (61).

The second encounter, with "The Three Sisters," yields better results. This time, however, the child is unable to define and decipher the "sisters" or what they tell her. "They came with the wind that blows in August, thin as a spider web and barely noticed. Three who did not seem to be related to anything but the moon: one with laughter like tin and one with eyes of a cat and one with hands like porcelain. The aunts, the three sisters, *las comadres,* they said" (96; Rebolledo and Rivero, 220). The occasion of the visit is the death of Lucy and Rachael's baby sister, and Esperanza feels strange in the presence of death. The old ladies call her over, give her a stick of gum to make her feel better, and ask her name.

> Esperanza, I said.
> Esperanza, the old blue-veined one repeated in a high thin voice.
> Esperanza . . . a good good name.

> My knees hurt, the one with the funny laugh complained.
> Tomorrow it will rain.
> Yes, tomorrow, they said.
> How do you know? I asked.
> We know.
> Look at her hands, cat-eyed said.
> And they turned them over and over as if they were looking for
> something special.
> She's special.
> Yes, she'll go very far.
> Yes, yes, hmmm.
> Make a wish.
> A wish?
> Yes, make a wish. What do you want?
> Anything? I said.
> Well, why not?
> I closed my eyes.
> Did you wish already?
> Yes, I said.
> Well, that's all there is to it. It'll come true.
> How do you know? I asked.
> We know, we know. (97; Rebolledo and Rivero, 221)

Esperanza has wished for her house and she is given the solution to her destiny by one of the "sisters," even though it will not be until the writing of the book that she understands it.

> Esperanza. The one with marble hands called aside. Esperanza. She held my face with her blue-veined hands and looked and looked at me. A long silence. When you leave you must remember always to come back, she said.
> What?
> When you leave you must remember to come back for the others. A circle, understand? You will always be Esperanza. You will always be Mango Street. You can't erase what you know: You can't forget who you are.
> Then I didn't know what to say. It was as if she could read my mind, as if she knew what I had wished for, and I felt ashamed for having made such a selfish wish. (97–98; Rebolledo and Rivero, 221–22)

Cisneros ends the narrative on a mysterious note, ringed by childhood rhymes of ritual and magic. "Then I didn't see them. Not once or twice or ever again" (98; Rebolledo and Rivero, 222). Of course the "sisters" have given Esperanza exactly what she needs to learn about her life: she can't erase what she knows, she can't forget who she is.

That the image of the curandera is one of comfort and security to

Chicana writers can be seen in "curandera" by Carmen Tafolla. For Tafolla, the image of the curandera conjures images, smells, and colors as the lyric speaker seeks herbs (and cure) from the curandera. She configures her as wise, dignified, and intuitive.

> Afuera de tu casa,
> > entre la hierba buena y el aníz
> > estoy planteada.
>
> Vine aquí a verte,
> > a preguntar tus ojos tierra-grises
> > > a escuchar a tu voz mesquite seco
> > > > a observar tus manos sabi-siglos
> > > > > a llevarme alguna hierba de una de tus botellas.
>
> [Outside your house,
> > between the mint and the anise
> > I am planted.
>
> I came here to see you
> > to ask your earth-grey eyes
> > > to listen to your mesquite-dry voice
> > > > to observe your ages-knowing hands
> > > > > to take away some herbs from one of your bottles.]
>
> . . . .
>
> The gnarled and earthing fingers of her mind
> > feel the current in my veins
> > > and see the twilit shapes within my bodycaverns
>
> (52)

Tafolla, the writer, clearly identifies personally with this image; the back leaf of her book, also titled *Curandera,* says, "She received her Ph.D. in Bilingual Education from the University of Texas in 1981 and is presently working on her Ph.C. (Curandera of Philosophy). She lives in Austin, Texas, with her husband, Dr. Ernest M. Bernal, daughter Ann, daughter Cielos (deceased), 2 cats (Canela y Carbón), 1 dog, 1 typewriter, a house full of books, a yard full of hierbitas, many dreams, some *remedios,* and a *molcajete*" (60). The images cited here are those of books, memories, herbs, and a *molcajete* (or stone mixing bowl) in which to mix all the elements together.

Not all curanderas depicted in Chicana literature are as mystical or mysterious as those already mentioned. Gina Valdés, in "Josefina's Chickens," introduces a curandera who is amusingly robust and full of humor. Josefina raises chickens, and her chickens have been keeping the entire barrio awake at night.

> Josefina was a bosomy woman in her late fifties and she wore her long white hair in two braids pinned on top of her head. She had a high laugh and when she laughed her bosom moved up and down. When she was not attending to her patients, she was working on an herb garden that filled her back yard. The rest of the time she spent caring for her 20 chickens. In the last few weeks, not only Josefina's cures, but also her chickens had become the main topic of conversation in the barrio. (16; Rebolledo and Rivero, 228)

Because she has helped cure them, no one in the barrio except Consuelo, Josefina's sister, is willing to speak to Josefina about the noisy chickens. Josefina, however, is aware of the problems her chickens are causing and wonders what could be happening.

> The truth was that Josefina herself had been worrying about the chickens. She went into her bedroom, locked the door, took out a small notebook and pencil from a locked drawer, sat on a wicker chair with the notebook and pencil on her lap and closed her eyes. A few minutes later she opened her eyes and began to write in the notebook. The first word she wrote was "bewitched." She thought of this for a moment. "Who could have done it?" "Consuelo," she wrote in her notebook. Consuelo hated her chickens more than anybody else. She hated them since the first day that Josefina had brought them home, even before they had begun to cackle at night. She crossed out Consuelo's name. "She has the motives, but she doesn't have the power," thought Josefina. "No. Consuelo couldn't bewitch a flea." A list of relatives and neighbors ran through her mind, but she dismissed them all. No one had the power. (16; Rebolledo and Rivero, 229)

Her brother Severino is running a still next door. Josefina sells the liquor as an expensive healing remedy. And Josefina's fame as a curandera grows along with her selling of the brew. The mystery is finally resolved when we discover that "What neither Carlota nor Josefina knew was that the liquor bottles weren't the only thing passing over the fence. When brewing was completed, Severino took the powerful sediments and threw them over the fence and into the chicken coop. The chickens went straight to it becoming hopelessly drunk" (17; Rebolledo and Rivero, 230).

Apart from the story of Josefina's chickens, the curandera emerges as a compelling figure in Chicano literature because she is a woman who has control over her own life and destiny as well as that of others. As mentioned before, she has a special relationship to and understanding of earth and nature — she understands the cycles of creation, development, and destruction, thus unifying the past, present, and future. She incorporates intuition and rationality; she studies power and bends with it or harnesses it; she takes an active role in her environment. When she harvests her medicinal plants, she is careful not to take so many that they cannot propagate in the future. She listens carefully, thus understanding human as well as animal behavior. She uses her knowledge of group as well as individual psychology, a psychology embedded in ethnic beliefs and practices. She can be seen as a cultural psychologist or psychiatrist because individual human behavior is always weighed against behavior for the good of the community. And she understands the community.

But the curandera is not always beneficent (and perhaps this is the reason Chicana writers are so attracted to her representation). She has the capacity to fight social evils, with destruction if necessary. She can and does sometimes seek vengeance and revenge, careful to retaliate only against a particular evil doer and not in general. She fulfills our desires to seek justice against those perceived as more powerful. She can be a witch — yet she is also a curandera. She can control the other, nebulous world, but generally she chooses the positive side, the healing world. However, when evil is being enacted against us, the curandera can provide public protection against that evil by exposing it in a ritualistic fashion. She is both at the center and at the edge. These qualities are embodied in Mora's "Curandera."

They think she lives alone
on the edge of town in a two-room house
where she moved when her husband died
at thirty-five of a gunshot wound
in the bed of another woman. The curandera
and house have aged together to the rhythm
of the desert.

She wakes early, lights candles before
her sacred statues, brews tea of yerbabuena
She moves down her porch steps, rubs
cool morning sand into her hands, into her arms.
Like a large black bird, she feeds on
the desert, gathering herbs for her basket.

Her days are slow, days of grinding
dried snake into powder, of crushing
wild bees to mix with white wine.
And the townspeople come, hoping
to be touched by her ointments,
her hands, her prayers, her eyes.
She listens to their stories, and she listens
to the desert, always, to the desert.

By sunset she is tired. The wind
strokes the strands of long gray hair,
the smell of drying plants drifts
into her blood, the sun seeps
into her bones. She dozes
on her back porch. Rocking, rocking.

(*Chants,* 26)

Thus, like the Virgin, the curandera has the capacity for intervention between earth and spirit, but as a symbol, she represents more than the helping, nurturing side. She has the capacity to heal—but like the Nahuatl
deities, she also has the capacity for death and destruction. And because she
also has those capabilities, she becomes an incredibly powerful figure. This
is illustrated in another poem by Mora, "1910."

In Mexico they bowed
    their heads when she passed.
        Timid villagers stepped aside
            for the Judge's mother, Doña Luz,
who wore her black shawl, black
    gloves whenever she left her home—
        at the church, the *mercado,* and the *plaza*
            in the cool evenings when she strolled
                barely touching her son's wrist
                    with her fingertips,
who wore her black shawl, black
    gloves in the carriage that took her
        and her family to Juarez, border town, away
            from Villa laughing at their terror when

he rode through the village shouting,
spitting dust,
who wore her black shawl, black
gloves when she crossed the Rio Grande to
El Paso, her back straight, chin high,
never watching her feet,
who wore her black shawl, black
gloves into Upton's Five and Dime,
who walked out, back straight, lips quivering,
and slowly removed her shawl and gloves,
placed them on the sidewalk with the other
shawls and shopping bags.
"You Mexicans can't hide
things from me," Upton would say.
"Thieves. All thieves.
Let me see those hands."
who wore her black shawl, black
gloves the day she walked, chin high,
never watching her feet, on the black
beams and boards; still smoking,
that had been Upton's Five and Dime.

(*Chants,* 31; Rebolledo and Rivero, 227)

In this text, we have the image of the curandera dressed in black and elevated above the store — walking (or perhaps dancing, flying) on the beams. Doña Luz (light) is important because she has the ability to react against evil, seen here in the form of racial prejudice. Mora skillfully juxtaposes the mythic repetitive image of this woman and the historical placement of her leaving Mexico (the revolution and the date of the poem) with Upton's dialogue (still a contemporary one): the shameful attitude of "you Mexicans" as opposed to "us Anglos," and his disgraceful treatment of a respected lady. Doña Luz is able to avenge herself as well as all Mexicanos who are treated in this manner. This is the power of the curandera/bruja who circumvents all the passive, helpless figures of "la sufrida madrecita mexicana" (the long-suffering Mexican mother) and shows what a strong woman is capable of. And the reader is left cheering Doña Luz's actions.

In "Hands," a short story by Mora, we see exactly what the curandera means to a woman who has gone to ask her for help (Rebolledo and Rivero, 222–26). In this narrative, a woman, Cuca, who typifies the traditional virtues of the church-going good wife, decides to seek the help of another woman, a bruja, to bring her philandering husband home. Previously it was Cuca who had given advice to other women; "she dispensed wisdom like Solomon" (33; Rebolledo and Rivero, 222). She had prayed often then for humility, had knelt before the heart of flickering candles at church, always feeling superior because she had no troubles and she was in love with her husband. But now her husband was in love with another woman, and Cuca had no women to turn to. She says, "I am thirty-eight. . . . And I want to run to my mother. But my mother is dead, and the Virgin ignores my prayers" (34; Rebolledo and Rivero, 224). She is fearful of going to the bruja because the priests have said the bruja is the very devil. Cuca had seen the woman at market once, "dressed in black — black blouse, long black skirt, black shawl wrapped around her head. The gossips said Bruja's gray hair reached to her waist and that when she danced alone in the desert, the moonlight did not dare touch the gray strands that spun round and round" (34; Rebolledo and Rivero, 223). When the bruja asks Cuca what she wants, she explains that she wants the witch to shrink the large breasts of the other woman. "I want you to make her flat like a boy. I want him to feel bones beneath her skin and to long for my warm softness" (35; Rebolledo and Rivero, 224). The witch asks for ten American dollars — an amount Cuca has carefully saved. "She had known she must either pay to have masses said or see Bruja. And one didn't ask the Lord to remove a woman's breasts" (35; Rebolledo and Rivero, 225).

Over the next month, Cuca carefully, patiently works the magic Bruja has given her — snipping the material from a doll's breasts, flushing it down the toilet, sprinkling a powder in front of the woman's house. When at last Cuca goes to spy on the girl, she finds her standing in front of the mirror, "running her hands over her hard, flat chest, moving her hands up and down, pressing into the bones" (36; Rebolledo and Rivero, 226). The contrast in this story between what you can ask the Virgin (and through her the Lord) to do for you versus what you can ask a bruja to do is very strong. And again the image of the bruja is very much like that of Doña Luz in "1910" (Mora, *Chants*).

In "Bruja: Witch," Mora plays on the same theme, giving us the bruja's own perspective as she tells us of the joys of feeling free — free of her earthly body. The bruja who "waits for the owl" becomes one with the owl in order to do her "work." (As previously noted, owls are closely associated with healers and witches — with out-of-body experiences and with knowledge.) She had been paid three American dollars to frighten a woman's husband home.

> I spy my victims. Through a dirty
> window I see two nude bodies trying
> to escape into each other.

> I laugh and call from a nearby tree.
> "Amigo, who is that woman?
> Not your wife, eh? You don't taste
> your wife like that. Let us see.
> Our whole village wants to watch."
> I laugh again.

> (*Chants*, 16)

The bruja remains then for a short while in her other form — integrated with the moon, nature, and the landscape.

> Then I fly into the night.
>
> . . . .
>
> I am free
> until the rooster's song plunges me
> down into my tired bones.
> I tilt and dip and soar.
> I smell mesquite. Beneath white
> stars, I dance.

> (17)

One of the most important powers the curandera/bruja has is her ability to transform. She can transform the ill into the cured, the straying husband into a faithful one. Using psychology, she can transform people's perception of a situation as well as the situation itself. Like the alchemist, from raw material she makes precious jewels. It is not surprising, then, that the Chicana writer would feel a close identification with this symbol.

Tafolla's clear connection with the image of the curandera has already been noted. Mora, too, has written an article explaining that for her, writing is a ritual that transforms reality as well as one that attempts to organize and heal. Writing identifies social ills, and self-awareness often leads to a healing process. Many Chicanas, including those who write, feel alienated and fragmented in today's society; writing, self-awareness, and a close connection with one's culture provide a sense of rootedness, unity, and power not unlike that of the curandera/bruja. Thus Mora can connect writing with chanting and ritual.

An understanding of the need to accept all aspects—negative and positive—of our mythology is clearly enunciated by Gloria Anzaldúa, who calls it the "Coatlicue state" (*Borderlands,* 46). Coatlicue, in her great and strange stone representation in the Museum of Anthropology in Mexico City, is shown as a goddess with a skirt of serpents. Anzaldúa links these serpents with her own growing-up experiences with snakes—recognizing that for her, the serpents (and Coatlicue) have special meaning.[2] "She, the symbol of the dark sexual drive, the chthonic (underworld), the feminine, the serpentine movement of sexuality, or creativity, the basis of all energy and life" (35). The Coatlicue state therefore represents deep psychic images of the "contradictory." Anzaldúa states that the wound caused by the serpent should "be cured by the serpent" (50). And so the Coatlicue state is one in which the contradictions, the dualities (or multiplicities) are accepted.

In an earlier book, *This Bridge Called My Back,* Anzaldúa explains the healing process more explicitly.

> It makes perfect sense to me now how I resisted the act of writing, the commitment to writing. To write is to confront one's demons, look them in the face and live to write about them. Fear acts like a magnet; it draws the demons out of the closet and into the ink in our pens. . . . Writing is dangerous because we are afraid of what the writing reveals: the fears, the angers, the strengths of a woman under triple or quadruple oppression. Yet in that very act lies our survival because a woman who writes has power. And a woman with power is feared. (171)

The curandera/bruja figure incorporates the figure of the Virgin with those of the pre-Columbian deities in all their attributes. As Cisneros's Chayo comments in "Little Miracles, Kept Promises,"

> When I learned your real name is Coatlaxopeuh, She Who Has Dominion over Serpents, when I recognized you as Tonantzín, and learned your names are Teteoinnan, Toci, Xochiquetzal, Tlazolteotl, Coatlicue, Chalchiuhtlicue, Coyolxauhqui, Huixtocihuatl, Chicomecoatl, Cihuacoatl, when I could see you as Nuestra Señora de la Soledad, Nuestra Señora de Remedios, Nuestra Señora del Perpetuo Socorro, Nuestra Señora de San Juan de los Lagos, Our Lady of Lourdes, Our Lady of Mount Carmel, Our Lady of the Rosary, Our Lady of Sorrows, I wasn't ashamed, then, to be my mother's daughter, my

grandmother's granddaughter, my ancestors' child. (*Woman Hollering Creek,* 128; Rebolledo and Rivero, 266)

The bruja/curandera is also connected to the figures of Malinche and La Llorona, thereby in a most powerful way redeeming the Nahuatl dualities and negative and positive aspects of the folk legends — fully incorporating all of the myths. In poem after poem, the message is repeated over and over: to become ourselves, in the fullest way possible, one must integrate the serpents, the "negative," and accept the power of self-knowledge and self-expression that comes with it. We are all Guadalupe, Malintzín, Coatlicue, La Llorona, Sor Juana, Adelita, and Doña Luz. It is the power that comes from this integration of myth, legend, and history that infuses Chicana writing and the Chicana writer.

5

Infinite Divisions

constructing identities and dis-identities

In the early years of the Chicano Renaissance, male writers and a few female writers burst onto the literary scene establishing a creative representation of the Chicano/a experience. This representation was expressed in terms of a political and social identity that emphasized Chicanos' rural and working-class roots; the seizing of the Indian and Mexicano heritage that differentiated them from Anglos; the imposition of linguistic reservoirs in terms of English, Spanish, and bilingualism; and a sense of exploitation, marginalization, and of being "Other" because of this heritage. It was necessary to establish an identity that defined the Chicano in these social, political, and cultural ideological terms. Group solidarity was emphasized as necessary for survival, and pressure was exerted on group members to represent this solidarity.

When Chicana writers expressed their own sense of lack of representation, as well as lack of inclusion, they were labeled "Malinches," or *vendidas* (sellouts). As Angie Chabrám points out, the gender objectification of Chicanas in such works as Armando Rendón's *The Chicano Manifesto* (1972) effectively removed or distanced the women from full-scale participation in the Chicano movement. Left out, "without the possibility of inscribing viable Mexicana/Chicana female subjects with which to identify at the center of Chicana/o practices of resistance, Chicanas were denied cultural authenticity and independent self-affirmation" (Chabrám-Dernersesian, 83). This perspective is borne out by myriad texts that document Chicanas' sense of exclusion. Margarita Cota-Cárdenas writes,

> he's very much aware now
>   and makes fervent Revolution
>   so his children

and the masses
    will be free

but his woman
    in every language
    has only begun to ask
    — y yo querido viejo
    and ME?

        (*Marchitas*, 42)

With "ME" in capital letters thus doubly emphasized, Cota-Cárdenas points out the necessity of female questioning of an oppressive patriarchal system. However, she questions it in a way that continues to value the male/female relationship, calling the male "querido viejo" (beloved old man), an affectionate term. Lorna Dee Cervantes reaffirmed this questioning of patriarchal cultural practices in "Para un revolucionario."

you speak of the new way,
a new life . . .
Pero your voice is lost to me carnal,
in the wail of tus hijos,
in the clatter of dishes,
and the pucker of beans upon the stove.
Your conversation comes to me
de la sala where you sit,
spreading your dreams to brothers.

    (381–82)

Cervantes, too, notes the connectedness to Chicano males, calling them "carnal," indicating close body and cultural/familial relationships. Thus while women needed to have their voices heard, it was not to be at the expense of the males in the culture; rather it was to be considered as equals to them.

Constructing Chicana Subjectivity

The problem for Chicanas was how to represent a discourse that had effectively been silenced for generations. As Norma Alarcón has pointed out, Anglo feminists had already seized the speaking subject and created a solidified and unified identity. This meant that they had already become a subject of consciousness, of power and of domination. However, when early Chicana writers began to try to define their identities from their own perspectives on the social and political situation, it was a struggle to define themselves both as women and as members of the ethnic group. Because theirs was a subjugated or subordinated discourse, excluded from both mainstream and minority discourse, they were trying to "inscribe" themselves in a collective and historical process that had discounted and silenced them. The very notion of identity requires individual demarcation or, as Elizabeth Meese says, "the setting apart of an individual" (160). Yet Chicanas were focused on community and relationships. Thus emphasis was placed on the communal, not the individual. While these interconnections were not antithetical, they made the search for identity within the sociopolitical context very complex.

The problems and multiple answers to "Who am I? How do I see myself? How am I seen by others?" are thus constantly being refigured and repositioned, so the issue of "identity" in feminist work is one that will not go away. On a wider scale, and particularly within the work of minority women and other colonized groups, it is not only a question of the individual process of "subject positioning" but also one of ideological processes that are fully implicated in social formations of the individual and the group (see Weed, *Coming to Terms,* xx).

During the 1970s and early 1980s, there were many declarations of "Yo soy" (I am) — representations often unified with the main cultural symbols recognized within Chicano culture. However, these representations were intermingled with a sense of departure from tradition, and styled along the lines of change and transgression, symbolically linked with the Mexican Revolution of 1910, a revolution in which women actively participated. As Lydia Camarillo wrote in 1980,

> Si somos espejos de Cada una,
>   Soy Malinche
>   Soy la Virgen de Guadalupe,
>   Soy Sor Juana Inés de la Cruz.
>   Soy Frida Kahlo,
>   Soy Mujer.
>
> I am the reflection of the oppressed.
>   I am half the struggle . . .
>   Y mi compañero la otra.

I have come to knock at your door,
  A Decirte,
  "NO MAS!"

WE ARE THE REVOLUTION!

  ("Mi reflejo," 2; Rebolledo and Rivero, 271)

[If we are the mirrors of each other
  I am Malinche
    I am the Virgin of Guadalupe
      I am Sor Juana Inés de la Cruz.
      I am Frida Kahlo
      I am Woman.

I am the reflection of the oppressed.
  I am half the struggle . . .
    And my companion is the other.

I have come to knock at your door,
  To tell you,
  "NO MORE!"

WE ARE THE REVOLUTION!]

In 1978, La Chrisx wrote "La Loca de la Raza Cósmica" to represent all the facets of what Chicanas could be, incorporating social, sexual, political, and cultural dimensions within the representational politics of identity, attempting to identify the divisions and differences between Chicanas while at the same time emphasizing unity. "La Loca de la Raza Cósmica" is linked with the ideas of José Vasconselos, a Mexican who in 1922 named and identified Latin Americans as a new "Mestizo" race: a people of heroic proportions and power connected, in addition, to the idea of being the chosen people, as the Aztecs believed themselves to be. Chabrám sees La Loca and other early female "yo soy" representations as metaphorically "answering Joaquín and José," constructing a ChicanA identity to speak in ChicanA voices, to answer directly the male "yo soy" texts that had already been written. In particular, she is talking about "Yo soy Joaquín," written in 1976 by Rodolfo Gonzales.

Certainly "La Loca de la Raza Cósmica" is such a contestation: an apt refiguration of the male sociopolitical text that not only inscribes the female into cultural identity but also changes and redefines that identity. As Chabrám points out, however, while "Yo soy Joaquín" "constructed an essential identity for cultural affirmation by means of an epic poem which moved through five and a half centuries of Mexican and Chicano history and linked the common Chicano hero to legendary Mexican and Chicano male figures, this Chicana-centered text roots itself in the present and the contrary experiences of a variety of Chicana prototypes" (Chabrám-Dernersesian, 89).[1]

Soy la Mujer Chicana, una maravilla
    Soy tan simple como la capirotada
and at the same time I am as complicated to understand as the Aztec
    Pyramids.

. . . . .

Soy mujer
soy señorita
soy ruca loca
soy mujerona
soy Santa
soy madre
soy MS.

    (La Chrisx, 6; Rebolledo and Rivero, 84)

[I am a Chicana, a marvel
I am as simple as a capirotada pudding
and at the same time I am as complicated to understand as the Aztec
    Pyramids

. . . . .

I am woman
I am a young lady
I am a crazy broad
I am a big, strong woman
I am a Saint
I am a mother
I am MS.]

Thus La Chrisx identifies both sexual and social constructions of women, intermingling them. Within the 163 lines of the poem, she explains the multifaceted social, political, and folk identity of Chicanas using folk culture, music, and language to further define her position. And at the end, in case she herself has practiced exclusion, La Chrisx inserts the caveat

Con mucho cariño dedico esto a las Locas de la Raza Cósmica,
Y si no te puedes ver aquí hermana, solo te puedo decir
  "Dispensa"

[With affection I dedicate this to the Crazy Women of the Cosmic Race,
And if you don't see yourself here, sister, I can only say
  "I'm sorry"]

In the poem, the lyric speaker fluctuates between the collective and the individual, between occupations and representations, between the radical ("soy la Holy-roller," "soy junky") and the traditional ("soy going out with my brother as chaperone"), between the cultural and the political. She explores the oppression of women in society, in culture, and in the home. She shows Chicanas working, not working, swearing, being respected, being political. It is a representation of everyday women, in their individual as well as collective aspects and roles. There are no great heroines mentioned here. If it is an epic poem, it is because so many women understand it, because it is constituted from the collective notion of everyday life: drudgery, work, childbirth, misfortune, success, and survival. The theme of this "yo soy" text is the merging of the individual into the collective, and the struggle also to maintain individuality apart from the collective.

The pseudonym of the author is a prophetic play on Christ, the martyr, the sacrificed, the victim, yet also the savior, the redeemer. Of course, the narrator of the poem is a "loca" (a crazy woman), a woman who speaks from madness, who speaks outside the norm. The idea of the madwoman in the attic, the deprived heroine who has been the subject of much contemporary feminist criticism and discussion, is refigured here and transformed into a member of a privileged race — a cosmic one — who is speaking to the members of "royalty" — the Chicanas who comprise her group. This humorous poem plays on the juxtaposition of disparate and contrasting elements to achieve its power. And as Chabrám explains, the poem affirms Chicanas in counterdiscourses, "crediting them for their perseverance, creativity, and struggle in the face of racism, machismo, economic exploitation, and the combined pressures of everyday life" (89). Many other "yo soy" texts were written during the early phase of refiguring the Chicana Renaissance — some *were* responses to the male identity narratives, some to negative cultural definitions, but many were affirmative celebrations of being female and Chicana.

While Anglo feminists, our own compañeros, and others may have tried to simplify and label Chicanas as a single, unifying/unified figure, "the

Chicana" (as did Alfredo Mirandé and Evangelina Enríquez in their 1979 book *La Chicana: The Mexican-American Woman*), Chicana writers themselves were trying to articulate the complexities of their struggle for representation. For many, this attempt at articulation reached a crisis as Chicana writers fought to include themselves within the movement context. As Cota-Cárdenas stated in "Crisis de identidad o ya no chingües . . . ,"

Soy chicana macana
o gringa marrana,
la tinta pinta
o la pintura tinta,
el puro retrato
o me huele el olfato,
una mera gabacha,
o cuata sin tacha
una pocha biscocha,
o una india mocha,
(me pongo lentes rosas o negros
para tomar perspectiva,
todo depende, la verdad es relativa)

(*Noches,* n.p.; Rebolledo and Rivero, 88)

[Am I a false Chicana
or a gringa pig
shady ink
or a shady painting,
the very picture
or my breath smells fishy,
a mere gabacha
or a cuata without equal,
a cooky pocha
or a fractured india,
(I put on rose- or dark-colored glasses
to take on perspective,
it all depends, the truth is relative)]

(Translation by Cota-Cárdenas)

This crisis arose from the recognition, and rejection, of the multiply stifling layers that had erased the voices of Chicanas for so long (the truth is relative in "real" and "historical" oppositions), and from the shifting and sliding they had to do in order to survive colonialism and repression. Alarcón, writing about *This Bridge Called My Back* (Moraga and Anzaldúa), explained that from the outset, the writers were aware of the displacement of their subjectivity across "a multiplicity of discourses." "This displacement in turn implied a multiplicity of positions from which the writers tried to grasp or understand themselves and their relations with the real or historical context around them. They were also aware that these 'positions were often incompatible or contradictory, and problematic'" ("The Theoretical Subject(s)," 356).

Thus while Chicana writers were trying to seize their own voices and become speaking subjects, they were at the same time "decentered" and tended to dissolve into the collective and political. The multiple voices that the writers were articulating, what Alarcón calls the "multiple voiced subjectivity" (364), evolved out of the fact that so many competing ideologies or senses of identity called to Chicanas. Where did their self-identification or allegiance lie? Unable to completely unify or ally with one group, Chicanas felt themselves pulled and pushed (and often rejected) by the various representations, a process that Alarcón terms "dis-identification" (366). Chicana writers were slipping and sliding from one representation to the other, what in the 1990s we would see as "positioning." This sentiment was clearly articulated by Pat Mora in "Legal Alien."

> American but hyphenated,
> viewed by Anglos as perhaps exotic,
> perhaps inferior, definitely different,
> viewed by Mexicans as alien,
> (their eyes say, "You may speak
> Spanish but you're not like me")
> an American to Mexicans
> a Mexican to Americans
> a handy token
> sliding back and forth
> between the fringes of both worlds
> by smiling
> by masking the discomfort
> of being pre-judged
> Bi-laterally.

(*Chants,* 52; Rebolledo and Rivero, 95)

After Gloria Anzaldúa published *Borderlands: La nueva mestiza* in 1987, Chicanas breathed a sigh of relief because the tensions, the conflict, the shiftings were finally articulated. And Anzaldúa not only defined what Chicanas had been feeling for some time, but she presented it in a positive way. She recognized the multiplicities we had felt, and the ambivalences we instinctively intuited in going against a unifying tradition. Most important, in many ways she validated the shiftings, seeing them as coming from a position of resistance and the need to survive under colonization, and affirming that Chicanas could position themselves and choose whatever strategy would serve. This reaffirmation also recognized that the lines drawn for the borders were arbitrary and limiting and did not reflect the real world. It was okay to see the limitations and to cross them. Anzaldúa also clearly defined the historical oppression that made women feel they couldn't cross the borders, and the empowerment that occurred when they realized it was their choice. Thus the process of "Mestiza" consciousness was acknowledged. Shortly thereafter, many books and articles appeared that dealt with the concept of borders, including *Between Borders: Essays on Mexicana/Chicana History* (1990), edited by Adelaida R. Del Castillo, and *Criticism in the Borderlands* (1991), edited by Héctor Calderón and José David Saldívar. And in 1992, a conference in Chicago, "Crossing Borders, Creating Spaces," addressed the same issue.

Naming: Creating Identity

To name something, as Anglo feminists already knew, is to have power. But to name is often to accept. Chicanas are very much engaged in an articulation of accurate naming and the acceptance of all the cultural and social premises that lie behind the "names." Therefore, the articulation of a positive notion of Mestiza consciousness and the power of being *mitá y mitá* (half and half), or more, allows the struggle for interpretive power to insert itself forcefully into cultural discourse. It allows for that sense of marginal discourses and creates a space for counterdiscourses that may spring up. The representation of these counterdiscourses is very self-conscious on the part of Chicana writers and often inserts itself directly into the texts.

How we are identified by others as well as how we see ourselves is complex, both symbolically and in representation. The stereotyping of Chicanas is often the subject of speculation by Chicana writers. Society names — "You're a Meskin" — and Chicanas struggle against that reductive naming, endeavoring to represent themselves as the complex creatures they are. For Miriam Bornstein, "el nombre que llevo a cuestas peca por no definirme" (the name that burdens me sins for not defining me) (*Siete poetas,* 1). Bornstein feels that she is defined by all the mythic and cultural roles society imposes on her because of her name "Mrs.": wife, mother—representations that leave no room for her own self. Her complaint is echoed by Lorenza Calvillo-Craig, who understands that she is all that society perceives her to be—in the various relationships to her parents, grandparents, other family members, and friends. This acknowledgment is symbolized through Calvillo-Craig's various representations of her names.

> I am lorenza
>> lencha
>> lorraine
>> wa
>> panzas and
>> daughter

> (1; Rebolledo and Rivero, 83, translation mine)

"Lorenza" is her formal Spanish name; its diminutive, used by family and friends, is "Lencha." "Lorraine" is the English-defined name, "wa" a child/baby-talk name, and "panzas" an affectionate name probably used by brothers and sisters to tease her. All these names are subsumed into a common denominator and therefore not capitalized. However, she ends her poem by strongly auto-affirming her own centrality, doubly repeating her center:

> I am
> I am
> me

> (1; Rebolledo and Rivero, 84)

Cisneros, in "My Name" (*Mango Street,* 12–13; Rebolledo and Rivero, 79), also recognized the importance of naming oneself. In the narrative speaker's litany of naming, she considers and discards all the names that "don't fit." The speaker recognizes the heritage linked to her name "Esperanza," also her grandmother's name, but sees it as the female heritage of being the object, not the subject, of cultural discourse. In addition to the English translation of the name "Esperanza" as "Hope," it also includes the idea of waiting (the Spanish root verb "esperar" means to hope or to wait). That more subtle usage is seen by the narrator as the passive role women often take, like that of her grandmother, who looked out the window all her life. The narrator rejects that role, just as she would like to reject the name.

The name she finally chooses for herself is one imbued with a sort of mysterious, sexual (albeit crude or vulgar) glamour. It is a name that conceals, does not reveal all; yet it is one that implies an active role in life: ZeZe the X.

Naming and the acceptance of names is seen by many writers as a continuing process of self-definition. While the epithet of "Meskin" or "you're a girl" can hurl the full weight of prejudice against Chicanas, people can also insult by giving them well-meaning but prejudiced "compliments." Veronica Cunningham aptly pointed this out in her 1976 poem "ever since" (Rebolledo and Rivero, 101–2).

> ever since
> i kan
> remember
> i have been
> slapped
> with compliment
> after compliment
>
> .   .   .   .   .   .
>
> you're lucky,
> you don't look Mexican.
> you don't act
> like a girl.
> you can make something
> of yourself.
> you don't have
> to tell anyone
> you're a lesbian.
>
> (30; Rebolledo and Rivero, 101)

The "compliments" appear to be such only to the outsider; from the speaker's perspective, she is "slapped," for they are statements that urge her to deny all that she is: her sex, sexuality, color, class, and culture. This denial would extinguish not only her true representation but her total existence — and she asks,

> if i kant
> live
> this life
> as i am

why live it
at all

(30; Rebolledo and Rivero, 102)

For Mora, as for Cabeza de Baca, placing ourselves by name within the long and intimate heritage of our mothers, grandmothers, and great-grandmothers imbues us with a sense of cultural heritage that we must pass on to succeeding generations. In "The Named, the Namer, the Naming," Mora recounts precisely where she is in the genealogy of her family. She is the object, the subject, and the process all in one. The text has no periods, therefore no disruptions, no ends. "I am Patricia Mora, born in El Paso, Texas, daughter of the desert, of the border, of the Rio Grande, daughter of Estella Delgado, who is the great-granddaughter of Anacleta Manguera and Neponuceno Delgado, the granddaughter of Ignacio Delgado y Manguera and María Ignacia Barragan, the daughter of the circuit judge Eduardo Luis Delgado of Cusihuirachic, Mexico . . ." (n.p.). The process of naming is intertwined with family history and events, tragedies and triumphs, and is linked with the flow of the river, "the river that whispers, the river of sorrows, the river of hope, the river of stories."

For Anzaldúa and other Chicana writers, a most important aspect of being able to seize subjectivity and to inscribe oneself into dialogue is acceptance of all that you are, acceptance of those names — Meskin, Chicana, girl, lesbian — and the understanding of the positive and negative aspects, which helps Chicanas break through the oppression and colonialism. We cannot have our culture and ourselves denied to us. La Chrisx presents this clearly in her self-affirming "La Loca de la Raza Cósmica."

Soy Mexicana
soy Mexican-American
soy American of Spanish Surname (A.S.S.)
soy Latina
soy Puerto Riqueña
soy Cocoanut
soy Chicana

(7; Rebolledo and Rivero, 88)

Anzaldúa acknowledges that the acceptance of having "all five races on your back / not knowing which side to turn to, run from" (*Borderlands,* 194) is difficult, but she argues that it is only the internal acceptance of all the divisions and differences that we are that will enable Chicanas to live and survive. We must be, she insists, the crossroads (195). Poet Marina Rivera agrees.

> this Mexican plate cannot be fixed
> because the pieces never took one form,
> each man, each woman comprising a language
> with dictionary loaned solely to listener
>
> . . . .
>
> we are rivers running slowly or fiercely,
> deep or shallow, filthy or clean —
> rivers which are born, cross, die and recross.
>
> ("mestiza," 100)

Thus the naming of ourselves, the acceptance of that name, and the pride we feel in it should lead us from a position of fragility to a crossroads of survival and strength.

Growing Up Chicana: The Search for Self in Childhood

⟨As many critics have pointed out, numerous texts in Chicana literature explore and "remember" growing up Chicana.⟩Traditional male bildungsroman were texts illustrating the journeys and struggles young men went through to become subjects of consciousness. From school years until their acceptance into society, these male growing-up narratives demonstrated how young men were able to integrate themselves into the social system. Most of these growing-up texts "delineate a turning point in the hero's life, that is of both personal, psychological import and social significance" (Annis Pratt, 13). For young women, however, integration at the end of the bildungsroman often meant finding a suitable partner to enter into marriage, and often the marriage led to madness, unhappiness, and the end of any dreams of self-realization. Thus for contemporary females (and particularly minority writers, who are even more marginalized), it has been a particularly difficult challenge to change the heroines' journey and engage in a fruitful struggle for self, and towards consciousness.

One of the main strategies for achieving consciousness — or seizing subjectivity — is through knowledge. As Chicana writers "remember" their childhood, they are witnesses to the construction of their own identities and the development of an understanding of their historical role in their families and communities. Unlike earlier female bildungsroman that ended with marriage, the ideal or end result of the quest of the narrative of development has become self-knowledge and an understanding of the significant events and relationships that shaped them. For women, this could include awareness of sexuality and all the joys and problems that surround it, death and its manifold repercussions, and love and the fulfillment as well as the fetters it brings. One striking similarity in the writing of many Chicanas is the importance of their bonds to female family members, *abuelitas* and *tías* (grandmothers and aunts), and friends. The older women provided that vital knowledge that explained menstruation and the secrets of survival. These women also provided comfort and solace against violence and rape.

There has been real concern among minority writers about understanding the forces and factors that shaped them into the adults they have become. In order to understand the construction of identity, and the ability of Chicanas to construct themselves as speaking subjects, they have had to examine the enabling factors as well as the stifling factors in their lives. Thus writing that looks at childhood, the society around young Chicanas, and their relationship with public institutions such as schools illuminates their personal development and at the same time offers a view of the collective or communal development.

[Many Chicana narrative and lyric voices appear to be those of young girls, as in the work of Gonzales-Berry, Cisneros, Mary Helen Ponce, and Helena María Viramontes] But the voices are always multiply layered with an adult consciousness that intervenes in the remembering. Of course, as we look at works like Cisneros's *Mango Street,* Viramontes's "Growing" (*The Moths and Other Stories,* 31–46), and Gonzales-Berry's "Rosebud," among others, what seem to be simple stories of childhood evolve into complex representations of ethnic social relations. It is often as a result of examining complex situations the young narrators do not understand — situations that often deal with societal rejections — that the narrators begin to understand what it means to be a woman, or what it means to be a Chicana. Often they remember hearing those words that limit their lives, "Tú eres mujer" (You're a woman), and all that implies. Bernice Zamora recalls such an encounter in "Pueblo, 1950," in which she recognizes the stigma and social limitations of being a girl.

I remember you, Fred Montoya.
You were the first *vato* to ever kiss me.
I was twelve years old.

My mother said shame on you,
my teacher said shame on you, and
I said shame on me, and nobody
    said a word to you.

(*Restless Serpents*, 13)

Here, society is quick to assign blame to the girl for even an innocent sexual transgression (a sort of early blame-the-victim perspective). The young girl has herself internalized the shame, which is given added weight because it came from other women, women with authority: her mother, her teacher. But it is in the remembering that the poetic speaker's consciousness has changed, and she is able to assign at least part of the responsibility where it should lie.

It seems that in these texts of self-development, an important ingredient is the realization of being silenced or being marginalized because of ethnicity and gender. An eloquent text in which this is illustrated is "The Gift?" by Sylvia Lizárraga. In this story, a young girl realizes over and over that she is invisible because she is a Chicana. The narrator recounts a series of events in her young life when she is ignored or, as she puts it, "not seen." "When was the first time I noticed I had the gift of making myself invisible? I know it was a gift because it didn't happen little by little and each time it became more perfect; I just became invisible all of a sudden and really invisible. It was as if I erased myself, or was it that I was being erased? I don't know. The only thing I know was that I was still there, I knew that I was there, but nobody saw me" (91).

One time the narrator is invited to go along with her friend Teresa (who is not a Chicana) to visit an older woman who is to help them enter school. Throughout the interview, the woman ignores the narrator, paying attention only to Teresa and not even looking at the narrator. The young girl rationalizes that she must be invisible, although subconsciously she realizes she is being rejected and marginalized. This is the reason for the questioning in the story, directed at herself as well as at the reader.

> Every time they can't see me I feel somewhat strange, as if I'm lacking something. Although I don't know what it could be, the only thing I know is that I'm missing something, because although I can see myself and I can see the people I'm with, they can't see me. At times I wonder, do they also feel something strange when they can't see me? Can they feel the *not* seeing me? Or am I the only one who feels it because I know I'm there; because I am there, aren't I? (92)

The power relationships expressed in this narrative, and the societal construction of identity based on these power relationships, are intense forces that need to be overcome in order to not feel erased. It is with the consciousness of these factors that empowerment to rise above them is facilitated.

Gonzales-Berry explores the impact of racial prejudice on a young child in "Rosebud." Her child narrator is being raised on a ranch with four sisters; all are fairly isolated and sheltered. One day the narrator goes to another town, ironically named Amistad (Friendship), for a 4-H Club meeting at an all-White school. After making biscuits, one boy asks for the narrator's biscuit. She refuses to give it to him, noting that it is the only one left and she is saving it for her mother. The boy looks at her "real mean" and calls her a "Dirty Mexican." Taking the term literally, and bewildered, the narrator runs to look in the mirror.

> He lied. I wasn't dirty. Why did he say it? Why?
> When we got home, I gave Mom her biscuit, and I told her about Tommy Bevins.
> "Ay, M'ja," she said, "forget it. Just turn the other cheek." Mom always said, "Turn the other cheek." "That Tommy doesn't know anything. You're the cleanest and sweetest little Mexican I know." She held me in her arms and kissed away the tears. (31; Rebolledo and Rivero, 320–21)

With our mothers often kissing away the tears, the question in Chicana literature still remains "Why? Why is there so much prejudice?"

As can be seen, many of these growing-up stories deal with the realization of the limitations put upon girls as they become women—and because they are Mexican/Chicanas. Many of these poems and stories are recounted through an ironic eye. Perhaps the stories and poems are even more poignant because the narrator's voice is young, full of innocence and hope. In "Monarquia," Lizárraga narrates the high school "nobility" contest in which the way to become prom queen is to bring in the most used paper to be recycled. All the students at the school, both Anglo and Chicano, are enthusiastic about the contest, which at the outset seems fair. Nonetheless, the girls with cars and other advantages have more opportunities to collect paper. The end result of the contest is that not only do the girls with more money and cars (read White) win, but the disadvantaged students suffer from a disintegration of their grades as well as their shoe leather (R. Sánchez, *Requisa*, 133–34; Rebolledo and Rivero, 329–30).

Cota-Cárdenas also understands this ironic eye when she chronicles the poetic speaker's realization that in spite of youthful transgressions and rebellions, she and her sister now "behave." In "Aay Cucuy. . . !" she narrates how when she was young and daring, she would dance on top of the cement tomb of a relative. Her cousins and sisters and brothers would scream with fright at her sacrilege and desecration while she was "dancing and singing / singing and dancing" (33; Rebolledo and Rivero, 314), yet as a grown woman, when the tormented soul comes looking for her, she denies herself—three times saying no, she is not that same person. In "To a Little Blond Girl of Heber, Califas," she describes her rebellious sister who wore cowboy boots and was always followed by her weenie dogs, even though "once she tried to take a molar from one / with a large pair of mechanics' pliers" (34; Rebolledo and Rivero, 132). During Holy Communion, this rebellious child called the priest "Cabrón," but now, Cota-Cárdenas tells us with nostalgia and some regret (indicated in the word "well"),

> Now
>> well she's a mother wife
>> and she behaves herself.
>
> (34; Rebolledo and Rivero, 132)

Many stories written by Chicanas chronicle the world in which the adolescent hero's expectations conflict with the dictates of the surrounding society. Chicana heroes desire freedom to be themselves, in all of their abilities and aspects, a freedom often denied by a culture that would have them toe strict norms of behavior for young women. They long to find the freedom of the road, to travel, to leave home, to have meaningful work, and especially to be respected for and to use their intelligence. In particular they would like to understand their growing sexuality, have control over their sexual desires, and not be just sexual objects, commented on and "pssst" at in public. These desires often seem overwhelming, clashing as they do with the norms of a strongly traditional family and male-oriented society, and an often-oppressive religious structure. In the growing-up stories, the narrator's voice is often one of guilt felt in the rebellion against these established cultural institutions, the rebellion itself internalized and viewed as "sinning." These dialogues about freedom and sexuality are generally internal ones, self-reflective and not revealed even to female friends and relatives, yet now, surprisingly enough, revealed to us, the readers. These "confessions," if you will, are revealed in an intimate voice that, at first glance, seems directed against the narrative or lyric speaker but ultimately exposes societal conventions that have attempted to restrict the young woman: restrictions that somehow have been overtly, or covertly, overcome.

"In the Toolshed" by Patricia Santana-Béjar explores the world of sexuality in a poignant yet hilarious way (Rebolledo and Rivero, 335–36). A child, caught in the web of her own sensuality intermingled with religious as well as folkloric "old wives' tales" about "sinning" and transgressions, carries on a dialogue with herself about her awakening. The dialogue is poignant and amusing at the same time because Santana-Béjar touches upon all the fears, doubts, and trepidations about sexuality that most young girls experience — especially those who have lived in cultures that are secretive about sexuality. (The extent of the secrecy in this girl's family is shown by the fact that her mother makes her take a bath with her underwear on.)

The success of the story is built around the parallel structures of what the narrator believes about sex and the actuality of sex. For one thing, she wanted to be a nun (a dream of many young Catholic girls) but now believes she can no longer be one because she has fallen into "mortal sin": her transgression is masturbation. She is so afraid, she cannot tell anyone, especially the priest. She is sure she has succumbed to her evil side (her left side), because her mother told her that. Trying to counter the evil in herself by doing everything spiritual with her right hand and crossing herself three times, she is convinced that this will give her more grace. Yet she forgets and can't seem to stop her autoeroticism. Indeed, rather than admit it brings her pleasure, she rationalizes that she only indulges in order to fall asleep sooner. In this narrative, not only does her own sexual oppression appear, but that of her mother as well. The internalization of the "sin" and the guilt leads her to lock herself in the toolshed to try to expiate her sin, but she knows her life is ruined, and there is no one she can tell.

In Viramontes's "Growing," the narrator articulates the confusion between being a child and a woman. Naomi wonders

> why things were always so complicated once you became older. Funny how the old want to be young and the young want to be old. . . . There were too many expectations and no one instructed her on how to fulfill them, and wasn't it crazy? . . .
>   . . . she could no longer be herself and her father could no longer trust her because she was a woman. (*The Moths,* 38; Rebolledo and Rivero, 313–14)

As young women in Chicana literature struggle to deal with and understand their sexuality, so too do they struggle to understand the world in which death and violence play a part. In the process of coming to terms with death, a child's concept of her own life changes as she begins to understand her mortality. In her poem "Velorio" (Wake) (*My Wicked, Wicked Ways,* 3–5; Rebolledo and Rivero, 322–23), Cisneros contrasts a happy, carefree moment of childhood with the stark realization of the finality of death. A group of little girls, laughing, are called inside to witness the wake of the baby sister of one of the girls, Lucy. There is a striking contrast between the girls, who have been playing outside "fresh from sun and dirty," and the cold darkness of the living room, strangely rearranged for visitors,

> The kitchen chairs facing front
> where in a corner is a satin box
> with a baby in it.

The young narrator also feels strange and out of place.

> and I thinking it is wrong
> us in our raw red ankles
> And mosquito legs.

The girls represent a vital presence in the face of death, with the baby "in a box like a valentine." The event is sharpened in memory by the sensations associated with it: the sense of strong color (pink), the sense of temperature ("cold, cold") and the sense of smell ("and your hair / smelling sharp like corn"). In a short story by Cisneros, "My Friend Lucy Who Smells Like Corn," we discover that Lucy is one of nine sisters, living poor with parents who are always working. Underlying the peaceful happiness of the narrator's childhood is the reality of child mortality and living in overcrowded circumstances.

Cota-Cárdenas's young narrator in "Whimpy's Wake" also deals with the instinctive grasping of the idea of death and loss. Whimpy, a Mexican laborer in the migrant labor camps of California, has befriended the young narrator by giving her "funnybooks" because she liked to lose herself in the imaginative stories: he teases her by calling her "Miss Funnybooks." Whimpy dies in an accident attributable to poor transportation conditions and cars in disrepair. Heading the story are news items about the living and social conditions of the *braceros,* or labor camps, and the undocumented Mexican workers staying there. The narrator, who has been told Whimpy is "sleeping," runs to see him when his body arrives for the wake. "He came in a long car, really big, black, and shiny, and we couldn't understand how he could sleep in that long box, which was also black, like our mama had told us" (133). Although not allowed to attend the velorio, the narrator decides to talk to her friend Whimpy, since the news that his brother was also involved in a wreck had just arrived. She thinks the velorio is some kind of a party since everyone is drinking, talking, and listening to music. The child sees Whimpy in his coffin and is surprised because "now, there was another Whimpy, all pale, and his curly hair combed real good, his face the color of the candles that surrounded him and pretending to be asleep" (134).

When she hears that Whimpy is dead, she realizes the truth, and she and her little brother stay there "a long time, thoughtful and trembling in the dark, holding hands tight. . . ." (134). She is sure someone made a mistake "because there were only supposed to be dead people in the funny-books" (134). But imagination, fantasy, and funnybooks have become real. . . . Here reality becomes stronger and more dramatic than funnybook fiction—and even more poignant for the reader because of the narrator's entrance into consciousness and comprehension of mortality. As text after text in Chicana literature shows, these moments remain in the children's memories as turning points in the loss of innocence.

However, growing up is not all sadness and struggle. Many stories chronicle the successful rebellions and the survival of these young heroines, who often are aided and abetted by other female forces in their lives (mothers, grandmothers, sisters, friends). For Denise Chávez, the metaphorical advice in "Tilt-a-Whirl" comes from Emilia, the Mexican Indian servant who "sustains" the poetic speaker on that "fun" machine.

> Sliding down
> Emilia
> I was
> falling off
> that thrill machine
>
> . . . . . .
>
> your great tortilla-hands
> sustained me
> you folded me up
> like dough
> set me back down
>
> . . . . . .
>
> at the gate of death
> without thinking
> you turn me back
>
> . . . . . .
>
> as easily as flipping
> a tortilla from the heat.

This life-sustaining act is connected to the nourishment that Emilia prepares later as she makes the tortillas. She tells her that the survival secret is

> turn and
> turn and turn
>
> .   .   .   .
>
> instead of islands
> you have worlds.

From the tilt-a-whirl that is the thrill machine at the carnival, to the flip-
flopping of the tortillas, the woman Emilia emerges as a sage role model
who counsels adjustment, connectedness, and nourishment.

Alma Luz Villanueva has illustrated the kind of independent stub-
bornness young girls often need to have if they are to endure in "I Was a
Skinny Tomboy Kid" (*Bloodroot,* 50; Rebolledo and Rivero, 333–35).

> and I vowed
>   to never
>   grow up
>   to be a woman
> and be helpless
>   like my mother

Yet at the same time, the child grows to recognize how hard it had been for
her mother.

> but then I didn't realize
>   the kind of guts
>   it often took
>   for her to just keep
>   standing
> where she was.

Bereft of strong examples, the child learns to look to herself, where she finds
sustenance and "self/mothering."

> I grew like a thin, stubborn weed
> watering myself whatever way I could

"Tilt-a-Whirl" © by Denise Chávez, 1975.

> believing in my own myth
>> transforming my reality
>> and creating a
>>> legendary / self

These young women have to believe in themselves no matter what the obstacles, as Demetria Martínez shows in "Elena at 5 Years." Although she is told that a brown egg can't hatch, Elena is determined it will and breathes on that egg every day.

> But at 5, Elena
> Has a good ear for heartbeats.
> Sidewalk cracks cry
> When her tennis shoe touches them,
> Lava chips that embroider
> The yard have names,
> And a brown egg is throbbing
> In the cup of her hand.
>
> (*Turning,* 105; Rebolledo and Rivero, 316)

To become the agents of their own subjectivity, these young heroines have to believe in and assert themselves. These are their strategies and their links to survival. Growing stubbornly, these heroines begin to make their own legends and their own realities as they steadily make their way.

6

Constructing Identities as Writers

As I have stated elsewhere, and as I still believe, "writing, after all, is naming, mapping, and leading, as well as creating. It forms an explanation of the meaning of existence; it can order chaos, introduce reason into ambiguity, re-create loss, call up the past, and create new models and traditions. In sum, it orders existence and invents new worlds. It can denounce injustice and prejudice and may function as a focus for a shared experience" ("Witches," 167). At the time I wrote this in 1984, I felt that writing and writers could be a panacea for many evils. While I still believe much of this, I also see the writers as mediators — between past and present, between cultures — and I believe that even if writing does name, it still struggles at the representation of that naming, and often fails. Of course, I cannot show all the many ways in which writers identify and represent themselves, but I would like to discuss writers as testigos/historians/ethnographers, as translators of foreign mail, as cooks.

The Writer as Testigo/Historian/Ethnographer

When we think of the writer as historian, witness, or ethnographer, we presuppose a discourse of truth, a presentation of facts and details that conform to some mainstream notion of what is "real" and what is truth. Historians and ethnographers assert, or are perceived to assert, that their discourse is without bias. However, Alvina Quintana argues in her essay "Ana Castillo's *The Mixquiahuala Letters:* The Novelist as Ethnographer" that the present historical moment has problematized the ideological implications of such assertions and has led to a reevaluation of the authority of personal experience (73). Because the issues of objectivity, authority, and interpretation have become problematic in the disciplines of history and anthropology, a connection can be made between those disciplines and that of literature.

Quintana believes that imaginary and ethnographical writing

> reflect limited ways of seeing the world; both are influenced by social conditions and the ideology of a particular historical moment. In this light it is interesting to think about feminist writers of fiction, who, much like an anthropologist, might focus on microcosms within a culture, unpacking rituals in the context of traditional symbolic and social structures of subjugation. Yet unlike both the conventional anthropologist and the classical Chicano writer of fiction, the Chicana feminist is also interested in scrutinizing the assumptions that root her own cultural influences, unpacking so-called tradition and political institutions that shape patriarchal ways of seeing. (74)

According to Quintana, "the process of fashioning any kind of marginal identity . . . involves a series of negotiations and mediations between the past and the future — a past and a future which for the Chicana is culturally explosive in terms of women experiences and historical implications because, at this point in history, she attempts to define herself as she maneuvers between two opposing realities that fail to acknowledge her existence" (74).

In her exploration of *The Mixquiahuala Letters,* Quintana sees Castillo as a modern ethnographer and the voice of Teresa, the novel's narrator, as her "informant." The letters, which systematically observe, record, and describe experiences of daily life, comprise a novel that "reflects the historical forces of the eighties, as well as an incredible diversity of concerns, literary and otherwise, from what has been previously recognized and legitimized by canonical structures" (74). Teresa describes institutions and religious rituals to emphasize how women are viewed differently in Mexico and the United States, thus becoming a sort of ethnographer. Although Quintana also sees the novel as a "parody of modern ethnographic and travel writing" (79), she claims that it answers ethnography's dilemma of the contradictions of the fieldwork process and personal engagement. It is "a personal narrative which mediates between objective and subjective narratives" (79). Furthermore, since each letter can be read as a whole or scrambled according to the reader's desire, in good Cortazarian fashion, the reader's subjectivity or objectivity is also called into play.

Moreover, when colonized subjects decide to seize their own representation, they may decide to represent themselves by engaging with the colonizers' own terms, what Mary Louise Pratt calls "autoethnographic expression" (7). This form of expression is one that "involves partial collaboration with and appropriation of the idioms of the conqueror" (7), but which at the same time functions as a form of resistance. To further complicate this attempt at auto- or self-representation, we have the *testimonio,* or testimonial narrative, a form whose contemporary outpouring has arisen from political terror and subjugation in Latin America. Social struggles will not lead to change without the documentation and narration of that struggle. And while the social struggle that has taken place within minority communities of the United States may not have reached the same level of political and social repression that exists in Latin America, it nevertheless very much exists and is part of the contemporary Chicano experience. Thus, testimonio also acquires authority as it is the personal witnessing, the personal narrative which gives it validity. Much of the traditional testimonial literature is in the form of prose, but the tradition also extends to drama and poetry, for example, the testimonials in *Canto general* by Pablo Neruda and in the poetry of Ernesto Cardenal of Nicaragua. Thus the connection between creative writing and historical representation is clearly accepted by the tradition.

Chicano literature is a border literature enriched by various literary traditions, the Latin American as well as the U.S. American (with all its ethnic manifestations and components). The testimonial tradition so prevalent in Latin America is one that, Amy Kaminsky argues, feminist critics especially need to pay attention to. For Kaminsky, this awareness of the importance of testimony lies in the notion of "presence." This powerful idea is seen in the honoring of victims of repression in Latin America, when "their names are called out as if in the rolls and the collectivity responds 'Presente'" (24). Kaminsky interprets presence as making visible "the invisible, the continued life of those who have been murdered, the appearance of the disappeared, the testimony that makes whole the body of the tortured. . . . it is presence in the face of erasure and silencing" (25). In addition, this awareness is a way of reminding ourselves, as writers and readers, of the responsibility of remembering. Because Chicana writers also function within cultures that have silenced and erased them (although not to the extreme of the political repressions of Latin America), this notion of testifying and remembering in order to achieve "presence" is seen throughout their writing.

From the perspective of these arguments about modern fiction writers functioning as ethnographers, one could include such narratives as Margarita Cota-Cárdenas's *Puppet* and Lucha Corpi's *Delia's Song* within the same vein. Moreover, I would argue that these writers are historians of their times as well as *testigas* (witnesses) to the social and political happenings around them, and that it is possible for writers to fashion themselves as objective interpreters of these events even though, at the same time, their narratives are clearly subjective, and often emotional.

As discussed earlier, Chicana writers, in their discussions of growing up Chicana, seek to understand the historical and political forces that shaped them, and their participation in the larger sociocultural scheme. They do this also in other texts. In *Puppet,* Cota-Cárdenas recounts the story of a young Chicano victimized first by society and later the police, and she examines the relationship of the young man to Petra, the novel's protagonist. In so doing, she is acting first as a witness to actual happenings, and later as a historian in documenting them. One way in which this occurs is the constant shifting between the personal and the political.

> Petra, habla Loreto. . . . Oye, este relato del muchachito que mataron. . . Tienes que seguir adelante con esto . . . Mira, tiene mucha, pero mucha garra . . . No, qué miedo ni qué miedo . . . no te rajes, sí yo sé que no te gusta esa expresión, pero olvídate por ahora y escúchame . . . el pueblo tiene que saber esas cosas . . . No, sí está bien así, está bien fuerte . . . El escritor tiene que ser testigo . . . (23)

> [Petra, this is Loretto . . . Listen, that story about the young man that they killed . . . You have to go on with it . . . Look, it has a lot, but really a lot of relevance . . . No, what fear . . . don't screw yourself, yes I know that you don't like that expression, but forget about it for now and listen to me . . . the people (the community) need to know these things . . . No, yes it's fine the way it is, it's real strong, the writer has to be a witness . . .]

To remain true to that calling, Petra continues,

> "Sigues, ciegamente, coleccionando historias, incidentes del barrio, de la comunidad de . . . Escribes fragmentos desorganizados, confusos." (40)

> [You continue blindly to collect stories, incidents of the barrio, of the community of . . . you write disorganized, confused fragments.]

The narrator of *Puppet* documents drug use, life in the barrio, Chicano history and literary history of the '70s, and her involvement in the community. *Puppet* is a call to action and to involvement. It is a call to the writer to be a historian, to record not just the positive evolution of the community but also its evils. The narrative indicts the Chicanos who pass drugs, the police who victimize the community, and the fears Chicana writers have about writing alternative discourses. Throughout the novel, the narrator not only engages in dialogue with her Chicana self and her readers, she also self-consciously interpolates an ironic commentary, calling herself "tuerta, chueca" (one eyed, crooked). She often cautions herself,

"Te estás saliendo del papel" (You are going outside the paper), metaphorically calling attention to her own role as writer. At the end, she looks in the mirror and sees not only her own eyes reflected, but also those of the character Puppet (134). Thus she assumes communal responsibility as well as her own personal responsibility. In remembering Puppet, she calls him into presence.

In *Delia's Song,* Lucha Corpi is the witness to changing events in Chicano and American history of the 1960s. The book is dedicated "to all the Chicano students who participated in the Third World Strike, at the University of California at Berkeley, with my deepest gratitude. Without their courage and determination my son, Arturo, most likely would not now be a senior and a Regents' Scholar at U.C. Berkeley" (3). The novel documents not only the strike and struggle that took place but also the positive changes for Chicanos it was able to bring about.

The text begins with a dream about the violent events during the strike. However, the time frame fluctuates between those events — which occurred in the narrator's youth — and the present, when she has finished her doctorate but still does not know who she is. The consciousness of the narrator therefore fluctuates between memory and dreams of the subjective world, and the "objective" reality of everyday life. As Corpi documents the events of the Civil Rights movement, the Third World Strike, and Delia's participation in both, the narrative goes beyond oral history and testimonial and becomes the agent for self-figuration. Having come from a traditional Mexican American family to Berkeley in the tumultuous late 1960s, Delia seeks understanding of her role in the strike, and through this understanding, she is able to achieve the power to give herself her own shape, to control her own identity.

As a young, unformed woman, "she had always managed to avoid discussing any issue that would require a strong position on her part" (17). Nonetheless, as the strike progresses, and as she becomes more involved in the issues, Delia is given the task of "chronicling the events."

> Rallies, riots, the arrival of the National Guard for the first time on campus, the chancellor's constant refusal to meet with any of them, the support for the strike vote by the American Federation of Teachers and the American Federation of State, County and Municipal Employees, the Regents' vote for immediate suspension of all students who violated rules, the 150 people arrested, 38 students placed on interim suspension, 18 of them falling under the Regents' ruling. With a steady hand, Delia entered all events and dates in the chronology during the weeks to follow, but she stopped writing in her journal. (50)

Eventually, however, Delia begins alternating her writing between two texts: the journal, which represents Delia's personal experiences, and the chronicle, which represents the historical and cultural context. The one feeds and nourishes the other and vice versa.

Along with the Third World Strike, which symbolizes the individual's responsibility to act on behalf of community, Delia needs to seize her subjectivity in terms of her own family. Her two brothers have died young: one in Vietnam and the other from drugs. Her mother seems to pay more attention to the dead than to the living. It is through her chronicling of these more personal events that Delia is able to understand, and to come to terms with, her family and her past. This occurs even though she is told by a friend, "You're not responsible for your father's weakness or for your brothers' deaths or for anyone else's failures . . . There's only so much you can do for other people. You can't let their ghosts rule you. You have a lot of living to do yet" (76). But Delia responds, "Chicanos can't afford not to be ruled by their ghosts. We're like ants who carry the dead on their shoulders" (76). Indeed, the novel is structured around the dead and death, particularly a Day of the Dead party where Delia meets a man, dressed as James Joyce, who brings her back into life. The themes of death, loss of innocence, and regeneration all vibrate against that Mexican tradition of honoring the dead.

It is in the writing and the chronicling that began with the Third World Strike and which continues to the present, however, that Delia is able to find herself, to understand the past, and to find a positive meaning in it. Suffering from a series of nightmares, she tries to exorcise them by writing them down every night in search for a pattern. Soon, it is the writing that begins to take over. "It was the writing that had become important. She alone lived in that world, had control over it, created chaos or order as she pleased, at times. At other times it controlled her, demanding every inch of space in her mind. She would curse it then, busy herself with other things, uselessly, because she knew that eventually she would get back to it" (108). Throughout the novel, she continues to ponder the most violent nightmare she had, and it begins to acquire a clearer and clearer shape. "I couldn't begin to describe the horror of it all. This time it was clearly a man, and he sliced my tongue. Who is he? Why did I have to be punished? What frightens me most is that I didn't fight him. I let him maim me. He took away my tongue. My tongue! The very instrument of voice" (127). We discover later that her dreams involve an earlier episode with a man who abused her, and whom she threatened with a Spanish dictionary. But as she begins to understand the dream, so too is she able to finally recognize the complexities of her relationships with men, with her family, and with her culture. Silence, and overcoming it, are significant concerns in Chicana literature, as María Herrera-Sobek reveals in "Silent Scream."

There is
So much pain
Inside our throats
We are afraid
That if we speak
We'll yell
We'll shriek
We'll moan
We'll scream
We'll cry
And so
We stay
Quiiiiiiiet.

(*Naked Moon*, 87)

So, too, does Delia come to recognize her own silencing, which comes from an internalization of guilt and anger: it is *"the code of silence Silence Silence I sliced my own tongue"* (Corpi, *Delia's Song*, 145). This discovery, then, is the vehicle by which she is able to free herself from guilt, colonization, and oppression. In a very powerful way, she describes the process that silences women.

I learned silence, painfully, slowly, as one learns to write, stroke by stroke until the letters form and sound is etched on the whiteness of the paper, and voice uncovers its reason for being.

Silence then is simply the pause between words, the breath that keeps them alive, the secret element that spans the territory between them.

I have feared you so, Silence, my oldest enemy, my dearest friend. I surrendered my tongue to you once, freely, and I learned your secret. I learned to write. (150)

At the end of the novel, the narrator is able to say, "I want my life. I'm tired of being what someone else wants me to be. I want to stop living my nightmares, being afraid of myself, always asking for forgiveness" (190). Like the narrative speakers in Cota-Cárdenas and Castillo, Corpi's narrator is involved with politics, history, and culture. Community and individual are inextricably intertwined and the personal and the political nurture and feed each other.

That Chicana writers clearly see their destiny and representation as historians, ethnographers, and witnesses is also evidenced by Inés Hernandez's poem "Testimonio de memoria," in which she discusses the role of Chicanas in *movimiento* politics and concludes,

> y doy gracias que mi lengua es mía
> y es libre
> y grita
> y llora
> y canta
> y demanda
> y reclama
> > por la justicia verdadera
> > y por la justiciera paz

> [I give thanks that my tongue / language is mine
> and it's free
> and it screams
> and cries
> and sings
> and demands
> and claims
> > true justice
> > and a just peace]

This awareness of being a witness can also be seen in "Mirror Image: Womanpoetry," by Elba Sánchez.

> this one
> this one comes
> to give testimony
> to express her pain
> opening the door
> to her reality
> shouting truths
> firmly embracing
> her passion
> > (50)

124

The Writer as Translator of Foreign Mail/Male:
Or, the Writer as Malinche

Complications, multiplicities, triple cultures or more are not easily understood and must be explained. In addition to multiple cultural levels, there are multiple language levels and perspectives. The borders, the limits, the center, the margin — all must be understood, and constantly translated. We are Malinches all.

It is Malinche, known as *la lengua* (the tongue) who is symbolically understood to be the first indigenous woman to speak not only native languages but also Spanish. She was an intelligent woman who rapidly learned Spanish and who spoke more than one indigenous language (Maya and Nahuatl and perhaps more). She was able to use words to communicate culture, to integrate culture, to assimilate, to not assimilate, to start a new race, and to forge a new culture. Because we have so little knowledge of her private life, we do not know if she spoke Nahuatl and Spanish with an accent, whether her translations were accurate, whether she resisted or embraced assimilation. Because she was central in the communications between natives and Spaniards, she is considered the first translator of the foreign male/mail (patriarchal communication), and because she is so problematic, she has remained an enigma to both Mexican and Chicano literary critics.

As previously stated, Malinche/Doña Marina is a complex and ambiguous figure for many writers. She is seen as the betrayer of her culture and of her race. At the same time, taken by violence she is *la chingada,* the forced one, the violated one. She was sexually violated and had the violator's child. This child, created in her body, was a male child, who in turn denied her because she was Indian. She was also violated in language and by language: language which she did not deny, language which she used and assimilated. Thus through both her body and her tongue, she accepted the foreigner. And in turn she was rejected by patriarchy. (One wonders how Malinche's daughter would have fared. . . .)

This complex and mysterious woman creates fertile inspiration for Chicana writers. She is enough of an enigma that she offers endless possibilities for exploration of her ambiguities and her complications. Chicana writers are also translators as they shift from one culture to another, from one perspective to another. And being a translator has levels of perspectives and depths that are endless. Their private space may be Spanish-centered; it is at home with their peers where they may feel centered. When they shift to a public space that is English-centered, they may feel slightly uncomfortable, no matter how assimilated they are. Or they may try to imprint their own identity on both public and private spaces. The Chicano movement was one of preserving Chicano culture and imprinting it on Anglo culture. Additionally, Chicanas must imprint themselves on both Chicano and Anglo male culture. Thus the translations are never ending.

As we have seen, these cultural, social, historic, and linguistic borders are not new for Chicana writers. In the written literature, as early as 1885, María Amparo Ruiz de Burton wrote *The Squatter and the Don* as a denunciation of the violence and fraud experienced by the Spanish/Mexicano settlers of California as the Anglo-Americans took away their land. Ruiz de Burton explores and documents the clash of two different legal systems, two different ways of doing business, two different cultures. In the 1930s, when Cleofas Jaramillo wrote her autobiography *Romance of a Little Village Girl* in English, she tried to understand the changes in her life in New Mexico. And although Jaramillo reconstructs her life in English, throughout the narrative she is jarred by inconsistencies and the feeling of being alienated through language and in culture. These very themes are repeated in other texts written throughout the 1950s by Nuevomexicanas, including Otero-Warren's *Old Spain in Our Southwest* and Cabeza de Baca's *We Fed Them Cactus* (discussed in chapter 1, "Early Hispana/Mexicana Writers").

Other writers continue to explore the feeling of alienation through language, but perhaps Lorna Dee Cervantes best captures the confusion generated by slipping across multiple borders in "Beneath the Shadow of the Freeway" (*Emplumada*, 11–14; Rebolledo and Rivero, 116–18). In large urban areas, freeways were often built in the barrios — the Chicano residential areas — destroying not only older houses and sections but cultural traditions as well. In the poem, Cervantes sees the boundaries between dominant and minority cultures, but she also recognizes that perspectives differ along generational borders as well. The narrator jumps across the link of the mother to connect back to her *abuelita* (grandmother), who represents language, continuity, and tradition, while she herself is the connection to the future. The mother, in turn is the one who has had to shift back and forth with an ambivalent perspective. The narrator becomes the translator between the private space of her grandmother and the public space of the patriarchal world. Unwilling to take sides between her mother and her grandmother, she turns to books (which she accurately identifies with the male perspective).

> I became Scribe: Translator of Foreign Mail,
>   interpreting letters from the government, notices
>   of dissolved marriages and Welfare stipulations.

>   (11; Rebolledo and Rivero, 116)

This mail represents a patriarchal, bureaucratic world in contrast to the female-centered world of her mother and grandmother. Her mother is lost in that male world because she is too trusting, too soft. The translator not only has to learn to function within the public world (and to write) but she learns to rely on a new, yet old, form of female resistance, to trust "only what I have built / with my own hands." (14; Rebolledo and Rivero, 118). Although her grandmother also trusted what she built with her own hands, she was unable to cope with the new world because of language, her inability to understand. The new Chicana must learn to function through language, and also through an understanding of the old ways.

Even as she translates, Cervantes has always felt that she has relinquished part of her communicative heritage. She decries that she was brought up with "no language," meaning she has lost her Spanish / Indian roots. Her perspective is a self-reflective consciousness and desire for her ethnic culture; like Malinche, she is in the process of creating a new Chicana culture. However, at critical moments in her poetry, ambiguity strikes. She may be independent, she may build her own house by herself, she may function in the public world — nevertheless she is wounded.

> My own days bring me slaps on the face.
> Every day I am deluged with reminders
> that this is not
>   my land
>
>   (36–37; Rebolledo and Rivero, 287)

The struggles and complications of trying to live in multiple cultures are also articulated by poet Pat Mora. Two of these cultures are male and female cultures, but she is also acutely conscious of the suffering caused by class differences. As an American Mexican she is invited into a friend's living room where she sits drinking coffee while the Mexicana Mexican servants are working in the kitchen. The soft voices of the women speak to Mora in whispers. And while she recognizes their exclusion from the "big house," she also wonders about their secrets, dreams their dreams (*Borders*, 23–24). She sees that she is placed in a position of "opposition" to the women "from over the border" yet she recognizes her sense of kinship and sameness with them. In the world of the narrative speaker, she is never quite at home: there is always a pea under the mattress, a cactus thorn in the flesh. Nonetheless Mora's consciousness about class and privilege form the background for a new order that Mora would create — a place where all women could feel secure, could realize their dreams and bloom.

Mora's desert landscapes are harsh, richly illustrative of an environment of struggle. The sun beats fiercely. There is little rain. Mora compares Chicanas to desert cactus, showing their survival skills, their ability to adapt. Even when there is little water and poorly nourished soil, these desert women *are* like cactus: at the first sign of water, "of softness in the air," they bloom, and in so doing they are so extravagantly, so astonishingly beautiful, they "stun" (80; Rebolledo and Rivero, 107). Oppression, pain, alienation, and disappointment are first suffered in silence, then expressed in language, and eventually transcended through writing.

Gloria Anzaldúa has perhaps most directly articulated the perspectives of the border. She has defined the limits and boundaries of mestizaje, sexuality, tradition, and myth. While for some, borders have been limiting devices, Anzaldúa and other Chicana writers find the state of being *mitá y mitá,* half and half (in whatever form you prefer to define it) a powerful and empowering one. This may mean being Mexican American, lesbian, or any of the other possible border states in which we find ourselves. It is no longer "a duel between the oppressor and oppressed" (*Borderlands,* 78). No longer is it a struggle to reconcile opposites, but instead it is a search for a new type of consciousness. For Anzaldúa it means we must consciously be on "both shores of the border at once" (78).

Dealing with multiple cultures and their differences can at times result in confusion and extreme perplexity, but at the same time these multiplicities of cultures, perspectives, and languages allow Chicana writers (and their readers) to pick from among various survival strategies. Just as writing their silence is a sensuous act, it also allows writers to endure and to create their own images, their own souls. In fact, in Anzaldúa's *Borderlands,* an entire section is entitled "Crossers y otros atravesados." The section honors all those who have been able to discard their boundaries and limitations and to connect to others in a loving way, and it documents the tragedy and violence against those who have had the courage to cross limitations. The final poem, "Interface," is an exploration of a formless "other" who is transformed into a formed being with a yet fragile skin.

At first it was hard to stay
on the border between the physical world
and hers

(148)

As "the other," with the lyric speaker's complicity, takes form, she is "able to pass" (as heterosexual, as Anglo, as a person). This remarkable poem is

about formation, transubstantiation, adaptability, and the acceptance embodied in change. For Anzaldúa, coming into a new sense of Chicana
consciousness, collective and yet individual, signals the transformation of
the border state into something empoweringly positive. It is a sentiment
echoed by Chicana writers everywhere, including Alicia Gaspar de Alba,
who notes that Chicana writers, "like the curandera or the bruja," are en-
dowed with the ritual and spiritual responsibility to keep the culture, the
memories, the rituals, the stories, superstitions, language, and the images of
their (specifically Mexican) heritage. "She is also the one who changes the
culture, the one who breeds a new language and a new lifestyle, new values,
new images and rhythms, new dreams and conflicts into that heritage,
making of all of this brouhaha and cultural schizophrenia a new legacy for
those who still have to squeeze into legitimacy as human beings and American citizens" ("Literary Wetback," 245).

As we have seen, the borders (for they *are* multiple) have inspired
Chicana writers to find multiple strategies for survival and for expanding
their limitations. Another "border" novel, Sylvia López-Medina's *Cantora,*
explores the condition of being a Mestiza translator for its transformative
values. López-Medina uses what she calls "the dreamsongs of oral tradition" to trace the survival of the women in her family (viii). As she says, "to
grow up mestiza in California . . . was to grow up living on the edge of
irony. It meant growing up in a vise — caught between the pride and aloof-
ness of my Hispanic grandmother and the humility and love of my Mexican
grandmother. . . . Being mestiza means that by being set apart, we have
become the observers, thus, we are not lost in the tangled forest of U.S.
culture, we are not lost at all" (viii). Throughout the narrative of four
women's lives, told through each of their voices, the women survive domi-
neering fathers, revolutions, immigration to a new country, and dark family
secrets.

López-Medina's narrative hero reconstructs a history of her family as
well as an identity for herself. Her name, appropriately, is Amparo, from the
Spanish *amparar,* meaning to help, to assist, to shelter. It is through her
"translations" of the not-said, of the silence in the stories told to her by her
great-grandmother, grandmother, and mother that she comes to understand the family secrets — to identify and name them — thus liberating herself as well as the women who have preceded her in the family chain. She
herself is about to give birth to a child, a girl, who she says "will not be
born with a shadow on her soul. I don't know who her father is, but then,
it doesn't matter. I know who her mother is, and so will she" (306). Thus
the Mestiza has finally come into her own, without shadows and without

blemishes. She has claimed her voice and challenged and learned from her silences.

Writing, then, has become the symbolic border that writers cross at will. They have conquered the linguistic oppressions that kept women silenced for so long, and they have learned the survival skills to opt for their culture and more. They have turned the linguistic talents of La Malinche into the art of writing. They are in the process of articulating the various translations they live, and they have become expert translators of foreign as well as domestic mail.

Salpicando la Salsa: The Writer as Cook

In the process of formulating an identity both ethnic and female, one area that is distinctly original is the concept of the writer as cook. It seems that one way to express individual subjectivity (while at the same time connecting to the collective and community) is by reinforcing this female identity as someone who cooks. One of the spaces traditionally construed as female is the kitchen, and Chicana literature is filled with images of active women preparing food. These images are a far cry from the anorexic Victorian heroines of nineteenth-century Anglo-European novels, who sublimated their hunger as well as their sexuality (Michie).

Chicano kitchens are filled with abuelitas, mothers, wives, and daughters mixing ingredients and making meals. Women are imaged as nourishers both physically and symbolically; therefore, it is only natural that Chicana writers have seized that nourishing space and have linked writing and cooking. Furthermore, there has been recognition recently that cooking is linked to women's way of knowing (see Leonardi, Goldman). This women's culture is just beginning to be seriously recognized as an intellectual tradition. The bestseller by Mexican writer Laura Esquivel, *Como agua para chocolate,* is an exemplary case.

In *Como agua para chocolate,* Esquivel structures the narrative around recipes that are so central to the narration, they cannot be separated. The recipes, household remedies, and other strategies of domestic agency become the central icons for "seeing" and "knowing," freedom and repression. Meaning and authority are incarnated in the "recipes" and their cultural context. As Susan Leonardi explains, just giving a recipe is not enough: "Like a story, a recipe needs a recommendation, a context, a point, a reason" (340). This context is particularly important, she says, because this knowledge or tradition is one that has not been respected as intellectual and serious. "Women professionals who can cook should never admit it if they want to maintain credibility. This cooking can be a dangerous thing for a woman" (347).

As discussed in the introduction, Debra Castillo's *Talking Back* elaborates a theory of feminist praxis towards Latin American women writers, including Chicana writers. As Castillo states, often-contradictory strategies for an evolving critique are formed around the central metaphors of the recipe and cooking, which I will paraphrase as "cooking the texts." The recipe, which stands for the theoretical basis underlying the textual analysis, is represented as a loose format around which things may be added or taken away.[1]

Castillo envisions this theoretical basis to be a reciprocal one, and she sees Chicana writing as the type of writing that challenges a monumentalizing or totalizing view of literature. The theoretical basis, like the recipe's discourse, is "a model precisely and exactly handed down, but allowing for infinite variation, an archetypal form and a metaphorical description of a gendered discourse. Furthermore, a good recipe book . . . reproduced the social context of recipe sharing — a loose community of women that crosses the social barriers of class, race, and generation" (8).

Several other metaphors can be added to that of the recipe: the "salpicón de la sopa," or the flavoring of the soup, that writers and critics choose to spice up their work; women's hunger, which is spiritual as well as physical; and the idea that the cook is always nourishing the family, but at times that means denying nourishment to herself. Prime examples of metaphysical anguish translated into hunger are the poems by Lorna Dee Cervantes included in *From the Cables of Genocide: Poems on Love and Hunger*. In "On Love and Hunger," she elaborates on Marguerite Duras' "Leek Soup," in which Duras says, "You can want to do nothing then decide instead to do this: make leek soup, I mean. Between the will to do something and the will to do nothing is a thin, unchanging line: suicide" (quoted in Cervantes, 32). Cervantes envisions this thin line in terms of hunger and denial.

> I feed you
> as you hunger. I hunger
> as you feed
> and refuse
> the food I give.
>
> (32)

Another related metaphor is that of the work space being the kitchen table. Virginia Woolf, with all the privileges of her class and European heritage, could see the necessity for a room of one's own, with the quiet that such a room allows. Chicana writers also long for that space for their writing, "only a house quiet as snow, a space for myself to go, clean as paper before the poem" (Cisneros, *Mango Street,* 100). However, it may be that Chicana and other minority writers cannot afford to wait for such a room. It may be that given our cultural heritage of closeness to family and friends, we do not even want such a room. Our work space is the kitchen table and all the work, ingredients, and chitchat that revolve around such a space. If we wait for rooms of our own, we may never write, and as Gloria Anzaldúa has emphasized, you can write anywhere when you have to.

> Forget the room of one's own — write in the kitchen, lock yourself up in the bathroom. Write on the bus or the welfare line, on the job or during meals, between sleeping or waking. . . . No long stretches at the typewriter unless you're wealthy or have a patron — you may not even own a typewriter. While you wash the floor or clothes listen to the words chanting in your body. When you're depressed, angry, hurt, when compassion and love possess you. When you cannot help but write. (*This Bridge Called My Back,* 170)

We must continue *amasando la masa* (kneading the dough), putting the salpicón into the sopa, and cooking the texts.

Another metaphor is that of the cook as the "knower," the one who remembers the recipes, who knows how to put them together, who knows what to serve when. The cook represents the oral tradition; she is the nexus to the female tradition, which in some instances is being lost. Certainly, when these cooking discourses are embedded in creative texts, they become clearly gendered discourses with their accompanying feminine meanings. Esquivel illustrates consciousness of and respect for this kind of female knowledge when she writes about the protagonist / cook in *Como agua para chocolate:*

> Gertrudis lanzó una plegaria en silencio y con los ojos cerrados, pidiendo que Tita viviera muchos años más cocinando las recetas de la familia. Ni ella ni Rosaura tenían los conocimientos para hacerlo, por lo tanto el día que Tita muriera moriría junto con ella el pasado de la familia. (182)

> [Gertrudis launched a prayer in silence and with her eyes closed, asking God to allow Tita to live a long time cooking the recipes of the family. Neither she nor Rosaura had the knowledge to do so, and so the day that Tita died, all the past of the family would die with her.]

How then do Chicana writers identify themselves as cooks, and how is this concept connected to their writing? One way for Chicana writers to have a gendered self-representation is to claim authority — and what better way to claim authority is there than by talking about your work? In an interesting inversion, the art of cooking, since it is generally passed down through the female line, also allows the writers to claim that voice of authority found in the cooking or "recipes" of their mothers and grand-mothers. Thus the cooking and the recipes become metaphors for life — for connectedness to tradition, for understanding "how to put things to-gether," for penetrating secrets, for coming to consciousness as you under-stand "the art." Cooking, with its networks of meaning, becomes the oppor-tunity to interrogate life and its manifestations.

In the Mexican literary tradition, we find many examples of women writers who identify with the metaphor of cooking. As previously dis-cussed, the seventeenth-century erudite nun Sor Juana Inés de la Cruz, when forced to put away her books, kept her mind and intellect alive by contemplating chemical interactions, physics, and even philosophy while cooking. She recognized the importance of cooking to women's intellectual as well as spiritual hunger, ironically commenting that if Aristotle had known how to cook, he might have been a better philosopher. In terms of intellectual hunger, she writes in her *Respuesta a sor Filotea de la Cruz* that as a child she had heard that eating cheese made one stupid, therefore she abstained from eating it so it would not inhibit her intellectual progress (4–13 passim).

Twentieth-century Mexican writer Rosario Castellanos, in her short story "Lección de cocina," uses the act of cooking and the narrator's inability to "know" how to cook as symbols for the narrator's consciousness-raising. What the protagonist discovers is that the act of reading a recipe does not really tell you how to cook a dish, especially if you have no knowledge of the tradition. As she personifies the piece of meat she is trying to roast (and is burning), the agency she comes to recognize is her own transformation into a piece of meat, an object, and the loss of her sense of self by having married (*Álbum de familia*, 7–22).

All of these metaphorical aspects are expressed in the concept of Chi-cana writers as cooks. In Chicana writing, the recipes use traditional Mex-icano/Chicano/Indian foods. The ingredients become the symbolic sub-stances that make up "ethnic" identity. Cooking thus expresses an identity politics, coming to represent tradition, the breaking of tradition, the under-standing of that tradition. It is a way of inscribing oneself into the collective representation of women's work. It also represents work, sexuality, and women's spiritual and cultural hunger. Thus the idea of cooking and au-thorship are connected. Both are the agents for the "text" and control the ingredients. In commenting on and repeating the recipes, the authors convey a sense of the comfort of familiar ingredients while at the same time opening up a sense of "difference."

As discussed earlier, among the earliest cookbooks written by Hispanic women in the United States are *Historic Cookery* (1939) and *The Good Life* (1949) by Fabiola Cabeza de Baca, who later wrote an ethnoautobiography, *We Fed Them Cactus*. In her cookbooks, Cabeza de Baca, a home economist, saw clearly that food and the women who prepared it were central to an integrated social system. She not only included recipes but also imaginatively depicted the integrity and vitality of Hispanic culture as it was reflected in the preparation of the food—in the cooperative spirit of the women and in their close relationships. Thus the conditions, social and historical, that informed the production of food were paramount to the text. Moreover, she had a deep respect for native ways and for traditional preparation of foods. Although she recognized the value of canning, which was just coming into its own for home economists, her recipes were full of the "old way" of doing things, such as drying corn and chile. Once, discarding her impersonal professional mask, she proclaimed, "New Mexico is well adapted to chile culture and therefore we have become accustomed to the pungent flavor which it gives to our foods" (*The Good Life,* 45). Later, describing dishes made of blood, she comments, "please do not shudder at the thought of eating blood—it is a delightful dish which has no identity with the raw product" (46). Fabiola lingers over what she considers to be the most important facet of food, its cultural positioning within the social context.

Another early writer, Cleofas Jaramillo, also contributed to the collection of "native" recipes and the folklore associated with them. She wrote *The Genuine New Mexico Tasty Recipes* (1939) in response to what she considered to be inaccurate portrayals of recipes she saw featured in *Holland Magazine*. Anne Goldman sees Jaramillo as resisting this cultural appropriation of "Spanish" food by asserting her cultural history and tradition of food knowledge. Jaramillo maintains that a true or historical authority comes from the testifying or knowledgeable cook (Goldman, 179–81). The loss of cultural integrity and authority is articulated through a parable about the devaluing of "traditional foods." Jaramillo's cookbooks resonate with her insistence on the authenticity and antiquity of her collection, and "the generational focus here suggests that, like the Spanish colonists themselves, food can have a lineage" (Goldman, 181). Thus Cabeza de Baca and Jaramillo, in addition to affirming the ways of knowing and cultural practice of their ethnic groups, also continually emphasize "the struggle involved in the process of self-assertion, an affirmation that is as much the task of family and community as of the subject herself" (Goldman, 194).

Clearly, for these writers, the cultural production of food preparation — including the domestic work that surrounds that preparation and the class differences of and between the women who prepare the food — becomes a metaphor for the struggle in the political and social sphere. It is a struggle that is camouflaged, however, since as Goldman points out, "presenting a family recipe and figuring its circulation within a community of readers provides a metaphor nonthreatening in its apparent avoidance of overt political discourse and yet culturally resonant in its evocation of the relation between the labor of the individual and her conscious efforts to reproduce familial and cultural traditions and values" (172).

All of these aspects — the seizing of authority by means of the recipe, the resistance of assimilation by means of emphasizing traditional cultural values, the creation of a community of sympathetic readers, the definition of an ethnic identity by means of food preparation, and the construction of a conscious self by means of cultural food icons — inform and give agency to the cook. The mingling of these factors has continued to be important in Chicana writing, as the surprising number of texts that incorporate food as a representation of one or another of the facets named above shows.

These ideas are seen in Ana Castillo's *So Far From God* in the section titled "Three of La Loca's Favorite Recipes Just to Whet Your Appetite," in which advice, character development, cultural nuances, and family relationships are all tossed in together with recipe giving. "'If you want to be a good cook,' Loca started out in a solemn tone with her sister (who Loca was sure must have found it pretty hard not only to admit that she didn't know how to do everything perfectly but that furthermore, Loca could do at least one thing even better than her), 'you have to first learn to be patient.' Loca believed in doing things from scratch" (165). The origin of the recipes in this section is a source of contention among the women gathered to prepare them, a contention prevalent also in identity politics. In addition, the narrator/author interfaces and "butts" into the text, giving us her authorial knowledge as cook.

> Biscochitos are Spanish cookies or Mexican cookies, depending on who you talk to. Doña Felicia, for instance, would tell you they were dreamt up by Mexican nuns to please some Church official, like mole. Sofia, on the other hand, was told by her grandmother that the recipe came from Spain. In any case, they are made from rich pie pastry dough, to which you add baking powder, sugar to sweeten, and — here's the trick, there's always a trick, you know, Fe — a bit of clean anis seed. Next, you roll it out on the board to

about a third of an inch thick. (Loca would not say a third of an inch, of course, but for our purposes here, I am adding specific measurements myself.) (167)

Another text using recipes and portraying the Chicana writer as cook is Cordelia Candelaria's "Haciendo tamales."

Haciendo tamales mi mamá wouldn't compromise —
no mftr chili, no u.s.d.a. carne
nomás handgrown y home-raised, todo.
Oregano had to be wildly grown
in brown earth 'bajo la sombra.
Tamale wrappers had to be hojas
dried from last year's corn
nurtured by sweat — ¿cómo no?
Trabajos de amor pa'enriquecer el saborcito.
To change or country
she wouldn't sacrifice her heritage.
Entonces, como su mamá antes y su abuelita
she made her tamales from memory
cada sabor nuevo
como el calor del Westinghouse where
she cooked them with gas under G.E. lights —
bien original to the max!

(*Ojo de la cueva*, 18; Rebolledo and Rivero, 115)

That the female metaphor of making tamales is connected to ideology is indicated by various signifying agents: the home-raised food, the brown earth, the work involved in the growing, the idea of not sacrificing her heritage to change nor country, and finally the making of tamales from memory. This is also the stuff of Chicana writing. The technology of cooking is, however, of American origin: the Westinghouse, the G.E. lights. Thus we see a clear connection to the mixture of things — old ingredients, new technology.

The writer's identification with the long line of mothers and grandmothers connects to a cultural construction of identity. Mora reinforces this idea in "Mothers and Daughters," a poem in which the relationship is intermingled with food and cooking metaphors.

Sometimes they feed one another
memories sweet as hot bread
and lemon tea. Sometimes it's mother-stories
the young one can't remember:

"When you were new, I'd nest you
in one arm, while I cooked,
whisper, what am I to do with you?"

. . . .

always the bodytalk thick,
always the recipes
hints for feeding
more with less.

(*Communion,* 79)

However, not all Chicanas feel the pangs of nostalgia for tradition—indeed, changing the recipe can be the blueprint for juxtaposing a sense of contemporary, time-saving living into the traditional lineup. In Barbara Brinson Curiel's "Recipe: Chorizo con Huevo Made in the Microwave," the narrator prepares this traditional dish in the microwave, acknowledging that,

It's not the same.
When you taste it
memories of abuelita
feeding wood into the stove
will dim.

(*Speak To Me From Dreams,* 64)

She continues eating, well aware that her grandmother, who in her time prepared the chorizo on an outdoor stove, would disapprove of both the method of preparing the food and the food itself.

You can turn away
from that eyebrow,
but there's no escaping the snarl
grandma will dish out
from her photo on the mantle.

It's the same hard stare
you closed your eyes to
on the day you brought
that microwave home.

(65)

Thus at times, the invocation of food also signals change and difference. In "Grandma," Cervantes contrasts the generational gap between herself and her grandmother, again using the tortilla and chorizo motif to note
the close connection between the women. "I eat her tortillas speaking fragmented Spanish / We are friends" (23). Communication, however, is in-
complete since not only does the lyric voice speak "fragmented" Spanish,
but there is also a disjunction connected to her grandmother's inability to
understand the speaker's resistance to cultural norms. The speaker refers to
this disjunction three times: "I am a mystery to her," "to her I am a Puzzle-
ment," and finally, "Abuelita / you don't understand" (23).

Class differences can also be connoted by food, as in "El Burrito Cafe"
by Bernice Zamora.

I watch you taste
the menudo you
Prepare for drunks. Somehow, Agustina
Godiñez, the title *Chef* does not suit
your position

(*Restless Serpents,* 60)

As stated, cooking is often symbolic of life's experiences and is equated
with achieving consciousness. In "The Philosophy of Frijoles" by Gaspar de
Alba, the lyric speaker is taught to separate the "good" beans from the "bad"
beans, which are the dark, old, and broken ones. The grandmother only uses
the "perfect pintos." The rebellious child, however,

always wanted to taste the dark
ones and imagined the wrinkled ones
would boil like the rest.

When she confronts her grandmother on the issue, her grandmother answers, "Don't argue. What do you know about life?" silencing the child
with the weight of her perspective and experience. In the last stanza, the

philosophy of frijoles is quickly transformed into a philosophy of ethnic identification.

> When we got to grammar school
> we didn't know we were experts
> in the Philosophy of frijoles
> but only the perfect pintos
> could be our friends.

Thus the lesson received on food, specifically pintos, a basic nutrient in Mexican diets, is converted into an elitist selection process that becomes ironic in the lyric eye.

In another complicated poem, "Caldo de pollo" (Chicken soup), Gaspar de Alba links the recipe to psychic vision. The poem is composed of five sections: "Recipe," "Memory," "Photograph," "Prediction," and "Truth." Intermingled with the soup on the eve of her thirtieth birthday are the predictions or visions of a drunken woman, one literally so or one out of control. The boiling caldo (or cauldron) predicts death, as does the visual memory of the lyric speaker/cook who remembers a photograph of herself and six other people, three of whom are dead. A woman who fancied herself psychic predicted that the speaker would die at thirty and join the others, a prediction unrealized. Yet it is true in terms of the death of consciousness, since "the girl died" and became the drunken woman—a woman who in turn goes away and metaphorically dies. The soup, which at the beginning of the poem represents death, becomes the source of nourishment. From the memory, the photograph, the prediction, and the truth that are stirred into it, the soup becomes a tonic that cures: the blood spice with rosemary standing for remembrance, basil for possibility, and rue, onions, and garlic for "becoming" or transformation. The lyric voice confesses "29 skins ago, I did not know the recipe." This text acknowledges the changes, the transformation, the dying, and regenerations of life—all implicit in the curative, ubiquitous caldo de pollo. The recipe is one learned though life experience, and the soup made from the recipe is restorative, as is the writing of the poem. Thus the writer/cook assimilates all the ingredients life offers into the stew that nourishes and cures.

Gaspar de Alba's view that recipes are icons for cultural identity and life is also revealed in "Making Chocolate Fondue," a poem about letting go. She says that "the most difficult part / is melting the chocolate," an appropriate metaphor for the letting go or mixing of oneself with other *ingredientes,* since chocolate was an Aztec food unknown in the Old World. But,

> you've got to melt
> that stuff down.
> Otherwise this recipe won't work.
> And you'll never get on with your life.
>
> *(Beggar on the Córdoba Bridge,* 41)

Marina Rivera, in "Mestiza," also explicitly connects writing with cooking, and with sewing as well—all women's work. She says,

> they send word
>
> . . . . . .
>
> invite me to read
> but there is this matter
> of more poems to be
> constructed in shape of tortilla
> lined like a serape
>
> (97)

Later in the same poem, Rivera connects food with spiritual as well as physical hunger.

> to be eldest of ten poor children
> is to shine for one cup of chocolate
> with one piece of French bread.
> having no meat, having no shoes
> you ate your dreams, learned to walk
> on your longings until they wore out.
>
> (99)

Food and its preparation, which can function as a symbol of nourishment as of want, could also be assessed in a real way as a hindrance to women's writing. In "Protocolo de verduras" (The protocol of vegetables), Corpi discusses the problematics of finding time to write poems within the busy work day of women.

> The world demands
> impeccable diplomacy.

Protocol exists,
or so they say,
even among vegetables;
and in my house
there's no time any more
even for melancholy,
that is loneliness laid bare,
because I must tend
to the affairs
of ironing day,
and write poems
when I can
between the shifting winds
of the tempest
in the laundry.

So don't reproach me
if I recall you
in wash water,
or among the leaves
of thirsty houseplants,
or between cabbage and pepper
at dinnertime;
if I read you between the lines
of *Civilization*
and Its Discontents.

(12, translation by Catherine Rodríguez-Nieto; Rebolledo and Rivero, 280–82)

María Herrera-Sobek expresses similar thoughts in "Mi poesía."

My poetry
follows me
between tin cans
between chiles and tomatoes
apples and peaches
brooms and garbage
that on another day
were my only song.

(*Chasqui,* 114; Rebolledo and Rivero, 298, translation mine)

For Chicana writers, then, recipes and cooking are used as metaphors for life and its lived experiences, including other tasks that interfere with writing. And behind the symbolic aspect is the physical reality of time-consuming food preparation and domestic duties that emphasize the cook and take away from the writer. Thus the interconnection between writing and cooking in its aspects of nourishment and deprivation is real as well as symbolic for Chicana writers.

Chicana writers also associate food with love and sex, as in Beverly Silva's "Sin ti yo no soy nada" (Without you I am nothing).

> You are
> The salsa in my enchilada
> The meat in my burrito
> The olive in my tamal
> The chocolate in my mole
> The chile in my beans

> (*The Second St. Poems,* 74; Rebolledo and Rivero, 359, translation mine)

Silva humorously indicates her love as the person who adds something to the basic ingredients. Her love is that "extra spice" that enhances the food—such as the salsa, the olive, and the chile—as well as being the essential ingredient, one without which the dish could not be itself—the meat in the burrito, the chocolate in the mole. The part that belongs to her is the substance that wraps itself around the ingredients.

In "La enchilada," M. Alvarez plays on the relationship between chiles and sex. "La enchilada" could refer to the dish, or to the person who has become "enchilada" or hot, taken with an idea. The various types of chiles are likened to various lovers,

> the green ones
> vine ripened
> ready for salsa

But the tiny red ones are her favorites.

> Piquín / Jalapeño /
> Manzano / Serrano
> What magnificent lovers you are!
> Oh, ever so satisfying!
> How eagerly I long to taste you once more!

> (72)

Although the chile represents the penis in much food iconography, here Alvarez uses the chile analogy to personalize female genitals, subverting traditional symbolism.

As evident in this writing about food, Chicana writers continue their strategy of identity politics, since all of the dishes mentioned are Mexican. Thus food and women's bodies, and food and sexuality, are interconnected, as they have been in literature throughout the world. Whether within homo- or heterosexuality, Chicana writers inscribe their sexuality within cultural practice.

Gaspar de Alba's erotic recipe for "Making Tortillas" equates the making of the tortillas with making love. It should be noted that *tortilleras* is a slang term for lesbians, thus the double erotic message.

> Sunrise is the best time
> for grinding masa,
> cornmeal rolling out
> on the metate like a flannel sheet.
> Smell of wet corn, lard, fresh
> morning love and the light
> sound of clapping.
>
> .   .   .   .
>
> Tortilleras, we are called,
> grinders of maíz, makers, bakers,
> slow lovers of women.
> The secret is starting from scratch.
>
> (*Beggar,* 44–45; Rebolledo and Rivero, 355–56)

As we have seen, the writer, like the cook, is able to fashion her text from various traditional ingredients represented by women's work, history, and culture. They are traditional texts in terms of symbolically equating and allying the contemporary writers (or cooks) with the line of female recipe givers and cooks that came before her. Along with the recipes, we are given the social context, life philosophy, and folklore — the cultural circumstances — that shaped them, as well as the writers' contemporary positioning and attitudes towards them. In the cooking, we see admiration, contempt, understanding, and rebellion. Most of all, we see the importance of the articulation of food, its essence, and its preparation with the gendered self-representation of the writer. Thus does the subject, the cook, fabulate herself within the collective identity of Chicanas and the processes of women's work. In a way, any recipe can change and be changed by the next person who tries it. The process is analogous to the rewriting of a text, or the retelling of a tale that was never written down. It is nourished by all the ingredients that constitute it, while constantly also bubbling back upon itself. It is a representation in which the cook makes the choices, is in control, and exhibits power. The authority is vested in her by her predecessors, and the representation of that agency is based on ethnic foods and politics — it is an agency central to identity.

I close this chapter with a piece of advice, of solace to the silences, to the erasures, from Gloria Gonzales, a New Mexican poet.

> There is nothing
> so lonesome
> or sad
> that
> papas fritas
> won't cure.

1

Women Singing in the Snow

the problematics of writing

In 1984, I published an article titled "Witches, Bitches, and Mid-wives: The Shaping of Poetic Consciousness in Chicana Literature," in which I began to explore the roles and delineations that Chicana poets saw for themselves as writers. I discussed the consciousness of what it meant to be a Chicana poet, and what relationship it had to cultural values and tradition. A large number of texts seemed to address themselves directly to pondering the role of the poet within the larger society, and I concluded that "the poet's role is not just an intellectual concern abstracted from social and cultural reality; it gives direction to the structure of their poems as well as defining the meaning of what it is to write" (167). I discovered that poets imaged themselves as spinners, as painters, as singers of Mexican corridos, as self-transformers, as midwives, and as storytellers. They also saw themselves as witches, and finally as bitches, a role not viewed as negative since it was a form of resistance. Chicana poets, I found, were very much linked to social and political concerns within their community.

Ten years later, this ongoing dialogue with their self-images as writers has heightened and become much more clearly defined. In 1984, the debate about writing and its meaning was embedded within the creative texts themselves: in poems and stories, *ars poética, ars genética* texts. More recently, there has been an emergence of the personal essay in which the writers discuss how they became writers, what they are trying to do in their writing, and what their role as writers should be. And as Chicana writing has come into its own, these texts are evidentiary of intellectual thought and growth and are testimony to the quest of writing as becoming.

Eliana Rivero, writing about Chicana writers and their texts in *Infinite Divisions,* noted:

It has been said that one of the most characteristic traits of contemporary literature is that it "speaks" about itself; that is, the poetic or narrative *personae* of the authors address the subject of writing in their writings. This they do as a way of exploring not only the meaning of language written on the page, but also the significance of the literary act itself. In this sense, Chicana literature is indeed a child of the present. Text after text, whether poem, short story, essay, or novel, comes back to the expression of a creative consciousness that acknowledges its creation, its doings with a pencil, a pen, a typewriter, or a computer. (Rebolledo and Rivero, 273)

Thus in that anthology of Chicana literature, we included an entire chapter on those texts that concentrated in some way on the significance of the literary act. This chapter is an extension of the considerations with which we began, and an elaboration of these texts within their cultural context. I also want to consider the question of language: texts written entirely in English, texts written bilingually, and texts written in Spanish, and what that might mean for the authors in question. In chapter 8, I will explore the problematics of writing in Spanish.

As I pointed out in chapter 3, Chicana writers have struggled to insert themselves and their sense of subject into contemporary discourse. Foremost in their process of identification is a sense of being a split or multiple subject, with all the negative and positive attributes attendant on that concept. Part of the traditional concept of the split subject, in terms of analytical psychology, has been that when the subject is split, part of it becomes absent to itself as it tries to enter the symbolic. For this reason, the split subject is always searching for a retrospective unity. That may explain, in part, why the need to connect with one's ancestral collective consciousness, and with history, has become such a necessity for Chicana writers. As Pat Mora explains, she wants to feel that sense of connectedness to fill the void, the absence (*Nepantla,* 38). There is also a need to feel as if you belong, especially when you are told time after time that you do not.

The seizing of the speaking subject needs a stable space, even if only a temporary one, from which to speak. Julia Kristeva has stated that the idea of consciousness is a series of breaks in process, over time. The moment of speaking serves to rupture the process to establish a stable position from which one may speak. It seems not to matter if the process continues, because the stable space is continually captured over time. For those who learn to manifest within these multiple stable spaces, what appear to be multiple speaking spaces, or multiple positionings, may indeed be part of the process. Writing and speaking form a nexus between the subjects and become part of the concept of self and language. When poets speak about writing as a way of organizing the chaos, I believe they are talking about that moment when a nexus is found. The creative praxis, and the exploration of the creative source within and through language, become for the writer an attempt to articulate her multiplicities.

Representations and Significances

To begin this exploration of the problematics of writing, I would like to examine the idea of women singing in the snow, the image that forms the central theme of this chapter. I believe that the idea of snow as expressed in Alma Villanueva's poem is indicative of a multiple image of women's creativity as well as of the factors that can stifle such creativity. Both the idea of the white page and of the instrument, as well as the fluid used to write on that page (in the case of women it might be blood), will be examined here.

In her article "'The Blank Page' and the Issues of Female Creativity," Susan Gubar examines the images of the blank page and women's blood in relation to the idea of female creativity in Isak Dinesen's short story of the same name. To sum up the story, the nuns of a Carmelite convent grow flax to make the finest linen bridal sheets in the world. These sheets are used by all the noble houses of the region. After the wedding night, the sheet is reclaimed by the convent, where it is framed and hung in a gallery. The virginal blood markings on the sheet are viewed by female pilgrims and nuns with interest. However, also hanging in the gallery is one blank sheet; the sheet that most fascinates the women observing it. The other sheets were hung with the stains of nuptial blood to prove that the women had been virgins upon marriage (296). Nevertheless, the blank sheet is also hung up by the nuns and is, of course, the subject of ruminations. Was the woman not a virgin? Why did the nuns hang the sheet up anyway? And it is the questioning in the realm of possibility that gives the intrigue. The sheet then becomes the image that contains all possibility, fulfilled and unfulfilled.

For Gubar, the idea of the blank page becomes a central metaphor for the issues of female creativity. She argues that women who have been silenced and limited in their creative endeavors experience their own bodies as the only available medium for their art. Gubar also argues that the primary metaphor for women's writing is blood—that women experience creativity as a wounding (300), and she says that "by reading the stains as if they were hieroglyphs, they imply that we must come to terms with the fact of blood before we can understand the nature of female art" (300). Also indicated by the metaphor of the blank page (or any other surface that might be receptive to imprinting ideas or words) is the possibility of creativity. For example, for Delmira Agustini, an early Uruguayan author, the surface was a crystalline lake ("El cisne," 78).

The white paper, fraught with possibilities and impossibilities, is a universal image for writers. In "Paradox," Ana Castillo says,

> i cannot write of the unspoken
> poem created in shadows
> as dusk turns a flat into a place
> for ghosts and one, so white
> next to my obscure origin as when
> virgins' hearts were torn pulsating
> in fear of immortality.

(*Women Are Not Roses*, 14; Rebolledo and Rivero, 303–4)

And Mora says, "It is frightening . . . not to know where I am going in the mesh of words. On the other hand, a blank piece of paper is a way of giving myself space, to explore what will happen. Poetry is both an act of faith and an act of hope" (*Nepantla,* 136). Chicana writers embroider, delineate, transform, and overlay the paper with personal images springing forth from their own cultural heritage. Mora says that she wants "to learn from that world of women and men who have a strong sense of place, who daily work at their craft, choose a reliance on former community artists, seem to embed in their work patterns from the past, struggle and delight in bringing to those around them works of both use and beauty. Maya women weave designs that echo on cotton cloth, their white space; mine is paper" (*Nepantla,* 28).

Central to this idea of women's creativity is Villanueva's poem "Siren" and its image of a woman "singing in the snow" (*Life Span,* 65). This image is intriguing and challenging because as stated in the preface, we have a more traditional image of Chicana writers singing in the desert (although it can also snow in the desert). However, as will be examined further, the image of snow stands for that blank page, for that realm of possibilities and impossibilities, for the quiet before the storm.[1] Because snow is cold, it can also represent that which is inhospitable, that which is a struggle, that which comes forth only in painful circumstances. Minority women writers have had to struggle to write, to articulate that which had never been articulated, to speak the unspeakable and unacceptable. The snow is an all-encompassing paradoxical environment that can be hospitable and inhospitable at the same time.

For women, the idea that the stains upon the blank sheet are made of blood is almost a certainty. This is an image often used by women writers: writing is a wound, it comes from the womb, it is like giving birth, the ink they use is red, painful, it comes from the very interiors of being. Villanueva speaks about writing as giving birth in *Mother, May I?* and Mora also describes the birthing process in "Dar a luz." It is her birthing of "stories wise as old bells tolling in my blood, swelling silence — hard, bitter green, that ripens, glows" (*Communion*, 91). This giving of light, the Spanish metaphor for giving birth, comes from gathering light from within. The birthing images connected to Chicana writing, as well as the wounding images, portray this writing in both its negative and positive aspects.

María Herrera-Sobek, for example, sees writing as a journey, the map marked with blood from the umbilical cord.

> Don't pretend
> you don't know the destination
> the map is marked
> the blood is dripping from the cord.
> Imprinted in your bones
> The route is straight and clear
> No detours
> or stopovers.
> The journey is on.
>
>   (*Naked Moon*, 94)

Sandra Cisneros takes the blood image even further in her poem "Down There," asserting that it is menstrual blood that is the ink in the writing, and that instead of a pen, she might dare to use a tampax. She equates writing with sexuality, expression with desire, joining a long line of women who believe that writing comes from the female uterus.

> In fact,
> I'd like to dab my fingers
> or a swab of tampax
> in my inkwell
> and write a poem across the wall.
> "A Poem of Womanhood"
> Now wouldn't that be something?
>
>   (23)

149

The writing of the early Nahuatl peoples and the Aztecs was signified by the colors red and black. Gloria Anzaldúa incorporates and blends these images in her writing, equating them with plumes and feathers. "I look at my fingers, see plumes growing there. From the fingers, my feathers, black and red ink drips across the page. *Escribo con la tinta de mi sangre.* I write in red ink. Intimately knowing the smooth touch of paper, its speechlessness before I spill myself on the insides of trees. Daily, I battle the silence and the red. Daily, I take my throat in my hands and squeeze until the cries pour out, my larynx and soul sore from the constant struggle" (*Borderlands,* 71– 72). Although the black ink is present, the emphasis is on the red. Thus another cultural context, that of ancient Mexican tradition, lies thinly below the surface of her writing, enriching it.

Like speaking, singing is a significant act because it begins within the throat, the first place where words are articulated. The singing then creates a space where both silence and language are produced. Singing can be celebratory or mournful, challenging or comforting, sad or joyful. Women who sing are cantoras, sirens, corrido singers, gypsies, ritual singers, nuns. They sing in praise of God or sin, they articulate the notes, they feel the rhythm. This is a central image in Villanueva's poem "Siren."[2] She begins by questioning,

Who is this woman with
words dangling from
the ends of her
hair? leaping
out from her
eyes? dripping
from her
breasts? seeping
from her hands? Her
left foot, a
question mark.
Her right foot, an
exclamation.
Her body a
dictionary dying
to define life,
growth, a
yearning.

(*Life Span,* 64)

From the beginning of the poem, the woman is infused with language, with words that have penetrated her innermost interiors and then dangle, leap, drip, and seep from her body. The punctuation exuding from her is emphatic, and it questions, exclaims. The rotundity of her body is ripe with language, its meanings and explanations. This is not a question of merely writing the body; it is a question of the body containing all that language knows. Language is transformed into the entrails of the body, to articulate with the secretions and fluids the body contains. Villanueva explains,

> She
> is a woman
> singing to her
> death . . . love's
> lost beauty
> always found
> at the edge of silence.
>
> (65)

As language and the voice sing, they find their exteriority and become their own things, things that ultimately signify death for the body. Villanueva concludes,

> She is a
> woman singing
> in the snow . . . We are her
> echo.
>
> (65)

Elizabeth Ordóñez has noted Villanueva's symbiotic corporeal and textual generation, and she sees Villanueva's poetic voice as "cultural transgression. Clearly the siren, as a woman singing for her life in a frozen landscape . . . inhabits a text which privileges the voice" ("Body, Spirit and the Text," 70). For Ordóñez as well as for Hélène Cixous, the singing of the siren is linked to the time before hierarchal separation. What Ordóñez concludes is that self-expression (consciousness and unity with the split subject, the body, intellect, and desire) and language or the seizing of voice, language, and subjectivity are "inseparable" for Alma Villanueva (71).

This extraordinary image captures the desires of Chicana writers, all of whom can be said to be women singing in the snow. Yet others find the task more chaotic, more mundane, more painful, and even more prosaic. Let us now look at this multiplicity of perspectives as we examine how the problematics of writing evolve for Chicana writers.

The Struggle for Voice

The central problem associated with the desire for expression is the struggle for voice. None of the other problematics of writing would begin to concern Chicana writers if they were unable to voice their desire. In order to begin to voice this desire, Chicanas need to first insert themselves into subjectivity. They need to become subjects and not mere objects of discourse. While some of this struggle is discussed in the chapter on identity, other aspects of coming into voice deserve consideration.

To begin, Chicanas had to be able to name: name themselves, their ancestors, their environment. As stated before, a surprising number of "yo soy" or "I am" texts exists in Chicana literature, texts that name in an attempt to articulate who Chicanas are, what they stand for, what they are made of. There is also a surprising number of texts that deal with individual naming. Cisneros explores the nuances of a name in "My Name" (*Mango Street*, 12–13; Rebolledo and Rivero, 79); Herrera-Sobek tries to define how she is shaped by her naming in "María," (*Naked Moon*, 72–73); and in another "María," María Dolores Gonzales explores the sadness of being named Dolores, searching for her image among other Chicana writers.

> María. Te busco
> entre las voces de
> Cota-Cárdenas
> entre los colores de
> Cisneros
> entre las imágenes de
> Vigil y de Hoyos.
> Te encuentro aquí
> entre las hojas
> en blanco llorando
> de tantos, dolores.
>
> (186)

[María, I look for you
among the voices of
Cota-Cárdenas
among the colors of
Cisneros
among the images of
Vigil and de Hoyos.
I find you here
among the white
leaves (blank pages) crying
from so many pains.]

Not only do Chicana writers explore their individual naming, they insert the names of their mothers, grandmother, sisters, aunts, friends, and role models into their texts and as titles of their stories. Thus we have Apolonia, Ciprianita, Virginia Chávez, Lobo, Juana Inés, and many Esperanzas. It is as if this naming of our *antepasadas* (the women who came before us) also inscribes them into subjectivity.

Often this naming is a reinforcement of the collectivity as well as of the individual, and the naming is done in Spanish: mujer, lesbiana, mamita, la llorona loca. Women in their totality, in the orginatory state, are also inscribed into the subjectivity. One facet of cultural erasure in the Americanization process was to change Spanish names, which Anglo teachers found unpronounceable, to more English-sounding names. Thus Carlota could become Carlida, and Sofronia would become Flossie (Gonzales-Berry, "Carlota Gonzales"; Santillanes). The Americanization process contributed to the sense of being silenced or erased, and to the split subjectivity of a Chicana going through life "with two names: her private Spanish name and her public English name" (Gonzales-Berry, "Carlota," 35). To reinscribe our Spanish names is one way to seize subjectivity. Yet there are many silences and many unnamed women in Chicana literature. In much Chicana lesbian writing, for example, the "I" has seized its subjectivity, but the other, the lover, is often not named—out of respect, out of fear.

The cognizance of having a voice limited by an oppressive society is another step in the struggle for voice. As Gonzales-Berry has noted, "In English I always felt . . . spied upon, on the verge of being judged: Did I or didn't I measure up?" ("Searching for a Voice"). This idea is reinforced by Cervantes when she talks about her

"excuse me" tongue,
and this
nagging preoccupation
with the feeling of not being good enough

(*Emplumada*, 36; Rebolledo and Rivero, 287)

Other feelings of inadequacy arise when Chicanas sense they do not fit the dominant culture's standards of body, beauty, behavior, culture, or religion. Herrera-Sobek understands the constraints of that struggle for voice; in her poem "Amoebas," she writes,

You really should not let
that blue sky
intimidate you
beyond the dome
of triple-celled amoebas
roars the silence
of the universe.

(*Naked Moon*, 90)

If we read the blue sky as white American culture, and the triple cells as the triple oppression that Chicanas face, the poem becomes much clearer. And Cota-Cárdenas reinforces this idea when she wonders in "Watercolors,"

Could all the blue eyes
of the world fit into Lake Mead?
The brownness is contained
neatly at the edges.

(*Marchitas*, 45)

The struggle for voice needs to take into account all the reasons that Chicanas have been silenced, erased, made invisible. This struggle and, finally, triumph are eloquently articulated by Dorotea Reyna in "Voice."

I.
For a long time
I held
my breath;
the pressure grew

but somehow did not kill.

.   .   .   .

Voice?
I had none.
Imagining that such a gift,
like so many others,
was the providence of them.

.   .   .   .

II.
So I tried to look
like them. Walk and talk
and ride like them.
The black flower
I learned as a girl,
I traded for the lily.
For someone with no
voice, I gave away my own
quickly enough. Black bull,
vernacular, precious native seed.
I gave it away just like that.
Like Malinche, and for
her reasons.

IV.
To have a
voice . . .

.   .   .

V.

.   .   .

Sometimes I sit
in my room and think about voice.
Wondering how to bounce it.
How to catch it. How to sew
it to my skin so it can't stray.

Sometimes language,
sounds, my voice, comes up

to my ears and I feel it
tilting like water
in a cup —

    (174)

The advice most frequently given by Chicana writers about finding a voice is that they must find it within themselves, whatever that signifies. That they must accept sexuality, culture, and self in order to speak. In "Marchitas de Mayo," Cota-Cárdenas says,

No escribas para otros.
Así no encontrarás
tu sentido.

Búscate allí. En tu roperito.
Donde dejaste
el pedazo de ti
que te hacía falta,
polvoriento y sano,
apenas latiendo
en el rinconcito.

    (*Marchitas,* 1)

[Don't write for others.
If you do you will never
find your own meaning.

Look for yourself there. In your little closet.
Where you left
that piece of yourself
you needed
dusty and healthy
just barely beating
in a small corner.]

    (Translation by Cota-Cárdenas)

One way of overcoming hate, prejudice, fear, and insecurity is to ally oneself with other women and with the community. Anzaldúa exultingly declares, "I will no longer be made to feel ashamed of existing. I will have my voice:

Indian, Spanish, white. I will have my serpent's tongue—my woman's voice, my sexual voice, my poet's voice. I will overcome the tradition of silence" (*Borderlands,* 59; Rebolledo and Rivero, 294).

The Struggle for Language

In addition to the struggle for voice comes the struggle for language. Because of the English/Spanish language question that subsumes Chicano culture, no matter what language they speak, Chicana writers always feel a void, an exile from language. If they are English speakers only, they feel they have been denied Spanish, and they cannot speak in the language of their forbearers. Cervantes recalls that "Mama raised me without language / I'm orphaned from my Spanish name" (*Emplumada,* 41). If they are Spanish speakers, it is the shame of having to give up that language to communicate in English, or it is the struggle to learn a new language. (Often children were punished at school if they spoke Spanish, and punished at home if they spoke English.) If they are bilingual, it is perhaps the most satisfying, and yet many writers then feel an ambivalence about which language to use. Thus the struggle for language for Chicano writers carries a very complex multiplicity, a sharpened awareness of it, within which is a sense of exile, as Cisneros writes in her introduction to Mercé Rodoreda's book *Camelia Street.*

> For two decades when she lived exiled from her language, Rodoreda does not write. At least, she does not publish. I know she has said during this time she couldn't bear the thought of literature, that literature made her feel like vomiting, that she was never as lucid as during this period when she was starving. I imagine myself the months I lived without English in Sarajevo, or the year I lived without Spanish in northern California—both times not writing because I could not brave repeating my life on paper. I slept for hours, hoping the days would roll by, my life dried and hollow like a seed pod. What would a writer do not writing for a year? For twenty? (ix)

Alicia Gaspar de Alba, in "Literary Wetback," says,

> English . . . the forbidden tree of knowledge that I could diagram with my eyes closed, was a reward that my family could never give me, and therefore, a rebellion. My brother and I used to sneak conversations in English, even swear words, behind my Grandma's back. I would write hour after hour in my journal/portable confessional, playing with the forbidden words and sentences as if they were a hieroglyphics that only I could read. (243; Rebolledo and Rivero, 289)

Thus the struggle for language is primal for Chicana/o writers. As Anzaldúa states, we live with the feeling that we are "deslenguadas. . . . Racially, culturally and linguistically somos huérfanos—we speak an orphan tongue" (*Borderlands,* 58). And she calls for an acceptance of all the languages that Chicanos speak, declaring, "I am my language" (59). The problematics of the struggle for language are resolved individually by most authors, but the reality of the situation, and the desire for communication, for readers, and for expression lead most Chicana writers to write in English, with some code switching (sometimes translated, sometimes not). Many writers probably cannot write entirely in Spanish. Nevertheless, it cannot be denied that the ideal reader would be someone who is bilingual.[3]

Embarking on the Mysterious Process

As Chicana writers embark on that process of writing, finding and giving voice—a process often viewed as otherworldly, mysterious—the first question that comes to mind is "Why? Why write at all?": a good question in light of the often painful and difficult process involved in writing. As discussed previously, part of the answer lies in the fact that writing, for many Chicanas, is a political struggle. It is a struggle not to let oneself be dominated and colonized. It is a struggle to bear witness. It is a political and social act experienced by many writers, although at times reluctantly.

> I am not a revolutionary.
> I don't even like political poems.
>
> . . . .
>
> I do not believe in the war between races
>   but in this country
>   there is war.
>
> (Cervantes, *Emplumada,* 35; Rebolledo and Rivero, 286–87)

Writing can flush anger about prejudice and social injustice.

Another reason for writing is the universal desire to tell the stories, to inscribe our personal and collective histories. Certainly for early writers such as Fabiola Cabeza de Baca and Cleofas Jaramillo, this was as pertinent as it is for more contemporary writers such as Mora and Anzaldúa. The fear of forgetting, being forgotten, and becoming disappeared in a cultural and social sense are part of the desire to remember, to be remembered, leading Mora to wonder,

How do I tell my children
there is more than pain.

. . . .

There is worse than pain.
There is forgetting
those are my eyes in the mirror.
There is forgetting my own true name.

("Tigua Elder," *Communion*, 61)

Just as the writer is the scribe and historian of her personal experience as well as communal experience, she is also the journalist, sociologist, teacher, and activist (Gaspar de Alba, "Literary Wetback"). Mora argues that minority writers have a special burden when they write, that they "perhaps feel a particular kind of discomfort, sensing that their words may either be subjected to particular scrutiny or scanned with indifference, that the many whom they are thought to represent deserve a more effective voice. We also worry about serving our community" (*Nepantla*, 150). Yet for Mora, the frustration endured in writing also pushes her to discoveries and fulfillment as she listens to her inner voice ("A Poet for President," *Nepantla*, 172–81).

Sometimes writers write because, as Bernice Zamora has succinctly put it,

. . . Lyrics,
lyrics alone soothe
restless serpents, strokes
more devastating than
devastation arrived.

(74; Rebolledo and Rivero, 279)

And sometimes they write to feel connected with nature and the universe.

Writing poems
sitting in the deep end
of an empty Tucson swimming pool,
I cup the algae
in my free hand
and smear it on my face
for inspiration,

feeling life connecting
glowing kinship
in this desert Atlantis.

(Cota-Cárdenas, "Dedicated to American Atomics II," *Marchitas*, 51;
Rebolledo and Rivero, 298–99)

There is a great deal of evidence that once someone begins writing,
it becomes a compulsion. And even when it is painful and difficult, it is
like being out of control or out of self, and the writer cannot stop. Cota-
Cárdenas says,

I speak to you seriously
      poetry
   if you don't leave me alone
      the dishes won't get washed
      nor spoiled little faces
      work won't get done
      nor meals cooked
You're undoing me
   you despot
      leave me for a few days.

("Lírica fanática," translation by Cota-Cárdenas)

Evangelina Vigil, in "Como embrujada," marvels at the demands of
writing.

How strange
to have this compelling urge
to write to ghost readers.
I spill my whole life on you
and don't even know who you are.

(1, *Nade y nade*)

And Herrera-Sobek describes poetry following her "between chiles and
tomatoes," bursting out

between cries
of children
and husbands hurt
by the explosion

160

of a pen
that bleeds

and assaulting her

among the rivers of embraces
I receive
from impatient lovers
in desperate competition
with my pen.

("Mi poesía," Rebolledo and Rivero, 298, translation mine)

Thus creative energy is violent and despotic and all-encompassing.

At times, creativity can also be elusive, like *la bella dama sin piedad,* the beautiful, mysterious woman without mercy so often cursed in literature; the inspiration that flits away when one most needs it, leaving the writer to search for the exact word, phrase, description. Sometimes, Herrera-Sobek says,

The words
Slip
In and out of my fingers
Like rosary beads
Refusing
To yield
An answer
To my prayers.

(*Naked Moon,* 86)

Then writing is not violent nor aggressive; it becomes quiet, recalcitrant, frightening.

The sound of the poem
knocking at the door
escaped me.

Asleep
without breath
I let it go
and it went away

forever
lost
among the folds
of memory.

> (Herrera-Sobek, "Poema inédito," translation mine)

In "Como la semilla" (Like the seed), Lucha Corpi experiences lack of inspiration as a threat.

. . . .

my thirsting poem is silent.
Its quietude scatters
inside me and I am frightened
by its withered whiteness.

> (*Fireflight,* 47; Rebolledo and Rivero, 280, translation by Catherine Rodríguez-Nieto)

For some writers, the process of writing enables them to control chaos and put things in order; for others, such as Mora, writing is ambivalent and messy,

> untidy and disconcerting. No successful ad company would want to market it. It's not fast, it's not predictable, it's not sweet. First we fantasize about that hushed moment when we'll be wonderfully alone with all our familiar, comforting writing implements at hand. . . . We savor the moment when, bursting with inspiration and wisdom, we at last lift our pen or start our computer and begin a new work. And work it is, though we forget that aspect in the amnesia necessary to bring us back to the blank page. (*Nepantla,* 149)

Once the writers are enmeshed in the process of writing, the experience can become otherworldly. Naomi Quiñónez writes of it as if she were separated from the planet both physically and mentally.

I must confess
I have been off the planet earth
for 3 days and 3 nights

And the destination of her journey was poetry:

I have been caught
writing poetry
instead of monthly reports.

> (300–301)

She describes the journey as one into madness, which as process and praxis is her lover. Writing as an act of *La Loca* is described also by other writers, including La Loca de la Raza Cósmica. However, calling it an act of *La Loca* is not negative, but an acknowledgment of being swept up in the process.

Searching for the Source

Octavio Paz wrote that "magicians and poets, unlike philosophers, technicians and sages, draw their powers from themselves. To do their work is not enough for them to possess a body of knowledge, as is the case with a physicist or a chauffeur. Every magical operation requires an inner force, achieved by a painful effort at purification" (42). Although Chicana writers would probably agree that an inner force is necessary to produce a work, they describe it not so much as a purification (although it is that also) but more like a wounding. This is because they are also involved with bearing witness, with testifying, with involvement in the political and social world around them, and they cannot always purify or ally themselves with the aesthetically pure, as Paz was able to do. Angela de Hoyos directly addresses the fact that poets like Paz expect women to be silent, "sin palabras," but once women have words, they cannot be expected to behave as Paz would like. In "Reply of the Words, II" she says,

> words are like mares
> (my dear amigOctavio)
>
> :treat them
> gentle
> — with a loose rein —
> if you
> want them
> to behave
>
> (*Woman, Woman*, 35)

In fact, Chicana writers often use more bodily images to describe their writing, and their search for the source of that creativity. They also use domestic images that Paz would not have accepted as "poetic." For example, Pat Mora describes her creative well as coming from used furniture.

> As a writer I am most selfishly committed to retrieving my Mexican past because I want all that wonderful used furniture. Whether the artifacts are potshards or myths, they enrich the well from which I draw. The notion of

163

the creative unconscious is most intriguing in the specific. As a writer of Mexican heritage, I want to know about the indigenous peoples in Mexico's history and Mexico's present, about the Toltecs of old as well as the Tarahumaras of today. Their incantations, customs, myths are like discovering strands dyed to a rich hue with natural substances — berries, blossoms, bark — strands that I can then weave into my images, making them distinctive from writers of other ethnic backgrounds, adding a dimension to our collective offering. (*Nepantla,* 39)

For Mora, this source is *chispas* (sparks), popular art, stories. She asks,

Where did the *chispas* come from? Why is *arte popular,* the term in Mexico for folk art, art of the people, as opposed to what can be called elite or academic art, why is it one of the fires burning in some of us? There are psychological explanations, the longing for a quieter life, private inventiveness with a chosen medium, the interest in combining utility and beauty for a community by repeating a process that connects us to our ancestors. . . . Among my personal explanations are my awe at the human ability, in the absence of physical comforts, to bring forth beauty. It's the shiver of delight when we see pansies in hard, cold ground, the blooms delicate in the snow. I think of the women I would see as a child at the *mercado* in Juárez. Their lives were not easy, but they would be laughing and talking to one another, calling out to prospective customers while their hands deftly turned paper into flowers. (*Nepantla,* 27)

Mora's chispas can be compared to *lo rasquache,* defined by Tomás Ybarra-Frausto (and others) as the love for the popular, for the exaggerated. "To be rasquache is to posit a bawdy, spunky consciousness seeking to subvert and turn ruling paradigms upside down — a witty, irreverent and impertinent posture that recodes and moves outside established boundaries" (155). But chispas go beyond rasquache to include all the delicate art embroidered, glued, painted, and crocheted by women who at the same time acknowledge and live life.

The source of creativity is sometimes defined by Chicana writers as the place of the wound. Anzaldúa often articulates this image in her writings, the wound that splits her heart from her mind, the abyss, the dark secret, the split self. The wound shows us that we are abnormal, that we are inadequate; it is an internalization of fear and shame.

The wound can spring from multiple sites and can be the result of extreme anguish and pain. For women who have lived a life of repression, oppression, and the resultant invisibility and silencing, to find the place from which to speak often means going against family, culture, and tradition. At times it can be dangerous, as when writers denounce patriarchy, the dominant culture, and political and social inequality. In her poem "Mirror Image: Womanpoetry," Elba Sánchez describes such a writer.

> this one comes before you
> womb first
> rock bone
> veil foam
> root offspring
> arms hands
> thorns pierce
> her tongue
>
> . . . .
>
> this one
> this one comes
> to give testimony
> to express her pain
> opening the door
> to her reality
> shouting truths
> firmly embracing
> her passion

In terms of giving testimony, Sánchez evokes our now-familiar images of the red blood and white page in "Living Canvas," which she dedicates to the Salvadoran people.

> they will not wipe away the blood
> from the walls
> the streets
> it is there present
> living canvas of spilled reds
> purples magentas
>
> they will not silence the voice
> witness each time
> ever louder
> it is there present

brush in hand
creating images

(48)

Thus she articulates Amy Kaminsky's sense of presence by the giving of testimony and the blood ink on the blank page.

The wound can also mean the disappearance, the working in isolation, and the determination on the part of Chicana writers not to forget. At this time, one of the deepest wounds would be to forget the stories, or not to write them.

Magical Powers and Transformations

Even though the writing causes wounds, the writer also has the power to heal. Alejandra Pizarnik, a contemporary Argentinean poet, wrote that "it has been said that the poet is the great therapist. In this sense the poetic act would imply exorcism, conjuring and moreover healing. To write a poem is to heal the fundamental wound, the rift. For we are all wounded" (20). Chicana poets acknowledge that this can be so, and perhaps none believe so fiercely as Mora in the transformative and curative powers of writing. She often links the writer with the curandera/healer while at the same time linking her to the darker, bruja/witch side. As explored in chapter 2, both the positive and negative sides are powerful.

In *Nepantla,* Mora cites Ruth Behar, who clearly articulates the political stakes of women using witchcraft because their "ultimate aim was to control and change the behavior of the men who dominated them" (125). For Mora, "definitions of illness and wellness are culture bound" (126). Thus many of the elements in her poetry, "learned wisdom, ritual, solutions" spring "from the land. All are essential to curanderas, who listen to voices from the past and the present, who evolve from their culture" (126). It is a psychological healing that cures biological wounds.

Mora emphasizes, too, that the Chicana poet, like the healer, uses "elements of commonality with her listeners: the importance of family, the retelling of familiar tales. . . . Often without formal creative writing training, we struggle to preserve what has given solace in the past. The triumph over cruelty and injustice related in poems and stories can be a shared triumph for an audience, a healing confirmation" (127). Thus holistic, psychological healing is carried out by means of affirmation, identification, confirmation. "In a supportive climate, the listener can confront a reality much as she would an ugly wound and yet experience relief; the known and

named is far more bearable than the unspoken and feared" (128). With the
silence broken, healing can begin. For Mora, the writer heals the historical
neglect by providing the opportunity to "remember the past, to share and
ease bitterness, to describe what has been viewed as unworthy of description, to cure by incantations and rhythms, by listening with her entire being
and responding. She then gathers the tales and myths, weaves them together, and, if lucky, casts spells" (131).

Other authors also understand the power of the curandera as a cultural icon of transformation and writing. Teresa Palomo Acosta writes,

> those curanderas know
> they can heal me
> so they have come to lead me,
> those curanderas
> back to myself
>
> at some point in their plot
> they wanted to put in a part
> a scene
> where they
> lay their hands upon my head
> give me their sacred bundle of magic
> to banish my wounds and fears

The lyric speaker, however, has

> . . . forgotten
> the strength
> of their medicine
>
> (39; Rebolledo and Rivero, 296)

Thus she must pass through the intervention of another healer, a Chicana
poet, to find the way. Given that Palomo Acosta's book is concerned with
finding that which is within "circles," this healing will come as a result of
incorporating the lives of the community with her own, helping her "to see
myself entire" (39; Rebolledo and Rivero, 297). In another poem, "Passing
Time," the poet has punished herself for writing poetry because she has been
told that it is not useful, yet the poems sneak out, and she finds herself
"pounding out more than mere autobiography: ah, salvation itself" (45).

Gaspar de Alba notes that the "bruja," or that frightening, dark, haunting side of writing, is a connection that resides deep within us. "Letters from a Bruja" (*Beggar*, 46–47) are written to her daughter, symbolically visioned as Malinche, and her granddaughter, a Chicana, visioned as the direct descendent of Malinche. The bruja signals her meaning to both women. The healing process will come from the learning, communicative process (that is why it is a letter). The daughter Malinche, "brown woman of tongues and trickery" and mother of a new breed, is the bruja's gift of birth. The bruja sees the granddaughter as even more mixed: "Your tongue was white with that other language." Clearly signaling the granddaughter as a Chicana, the bruja is there to remind her of her ancestry.

> I wind stories in your native
> tongue to frighten you,
> but the only fear here is mine:
> that innocence, that imagination
> brewing me to pieces.
> I am the land you left behind, little girl,
> shadow of my shadow.
> The woman who sold your mother
> for love of Learning.
> We are together only
> to hunt each other down.
> I have waited five hundred years for this.
> In fifty more my bones will rattle
> around your neck. My words will foam
> from your mouth.

The reward that accompanies this healing, once the writer has been able to express and fulfill her subjectivity, is the ability to accept both the dark side and the light side. At that point, the writer becomes the "winged woman" envisioned by Alma Luz Villanueva.

> Winged woman, feathers
> of the peacock you
> stole: you stole
> the rainbow — your
> wings, at once,
> everywhere

. . . . .
You were always
there at the center,
beckoning me to
rise to my feet —

. . . . .
— the air
quivers round
your massive
wings, as
wide as
you are
long. Winged
woman, my
self.

(*Life Span*, 51–52)

In the introduction to *Life Span*, Ordóñez says Villanueva "blends the ethereal and the earthy to create a magical balance of the miraculous and the mundane" (v). This is another aspect of the transformative curation that manifests itself in the healing powers of writing and the text.

It is not unusual for women to portray their joys or their frustration in images of flight. Birds and flight are evident everywhere in Cervantes's *Emplumada,* whose title evokes images of the plumed bird in flight. Uruguayan poet Delmira Agustini foretold her tragic death and described her frustrations in "Las alas" (The wings), and Herrera-Sobek, in a poem where she names herself "María," sees the final letter of her name, the last *a*, as a letter in flight.

And finally
in a coil
again the *a*
with finality
legs outstretched
kicking in the air
ready
to mount

the wind
and fly.

(*Naked Moon*, 73)

Ordóñez connects these "flight" texts to Cixous' theory of the "feminine text" and to "woman's irrepressible penchant toward flight" (67). Cixous sees flying not only as a liberation, but also as a way of "jumbling the order of space, . . . dislocating things and values, . . . and turning propriety upside down" (quoted in Ordóñez, 67). Witches also fly, but they are associated with the earth as well as the sky. Villanueva's flight is connected with the sea. All these images suggest the connection of flight with corporeal as well as textual generation.

In spite of the difficulties and struggle to find a voice and to seize that voice, Chicana writers have been able to give birth to their inner light and to their creativity. They may be wounded by history and society, but the very act of resisting their injuries and healing their wounds through writing becomes an act of triumph. At times the triumph is winged and grand, at times it is quiet and waiting, but always it represents a singing (and its echo) in the snow.

8

The Problematics of Writing in Spanish

Two contemporary Chicana authors who have written narrative texts in Spanish are Margarita Cota-Cárdenas, whose novel *Puppet* was published by Relámpago Books Press in 1985, and Erlinda Gonzales-Berry, whose novel *Paletitas de guayaba* was published in 1991 by El Norte Publications. Both novels were written primarily in Spanish; both were published by small private presses, since the authors were unable to publish them with larger Chicano presses because they were in Spanish; and both have been largely ignored by teachers and critics. Both are also on the cutting edge of the postmodern narrative. In the following discussion, I examine four areas: what it means to be writing in Spanish, and why Spanish was the language choice for these writers; the concept of writing under erasure or the silencing of women's voices; writing as resistance to colonization; and the writing itself in the texts.

According to Juan Bruce-Novoa, "what Chicano literature infuses into the U.S. canon is 'radical dialectics'—it is the language difference . . . that makes U.S. Hispanic literature a radical expression of a more general threat to the pre-dominant canon" (21). In the main, Bruce-Novoa was talking about the way English and Spanish are forced into a linguistic confrontation to form what he calls "a new interlingual product" (50). It was this very language use that, in turn, embodied the search of Chicanos for a distinct literary and cultural identity. It also embodies the historical struggle between "centralizing and decentralizing forces, between majority and minority and between mainstream imposition and peripheral resistance" (23). In addition, Bruce-Novoa points out, Chicano writers, like all writers, tend to use the language they control best (50). However, the reality is that most Chicano writers write in English, whether out of choice or out of necessity. They may nostalgically wish they could write in Spanish, but perhaps they do not control that language well enough, or if they do, they feel unable to write in Spanish because of English-only policies that tend to erase alternative languages. Whatever the reasons, both English and Spanish are "reservoirs of primary material to be molded together as needed" by the authors (50). As Gloria Anzaldúa has so clearly articulated, "ethnic identity is twin skin to linguistic identity — I am my language. Until I can take pride in my language, I cannot take pride in myself. Until I can accept as legitimate Chicano Texas Spanish, Tex-Mex and all the other languages I speak, I cannot accept the legitimacy of myself. Until I am free to write bilingually and to switch codes without having always to translate, while I still have to speak English or Spanish when I would rather speak Spanglish, and as long as I have to accommodate the English speakers rather than having them accommodate me, my tongue will be illegitimate" (*Borderlands*, 59).

Significant to this discussion is the fact that it is not a simple question for writers writing in Spanish to choose this language. It is, in fact, a political act and a declaration of loyalties. It is, particularly for Cota-Cárdenas and Gonzales-Berry, an act of resistance, and one that leads to a separation from mainstream readers and makes it difficult for them to have their work reviewed and published.[1]

Both Cota-Cárdenas and Gonzales-Berry did have a real language choice. They were formally trained in Latin American and Spanish Peninsular literature, and they came from families that spoke Spanish at home. Still, they could (and do) write just as eloquently in English. So, writing in Spanish is a self-conscious political act that offers another dialectic to the language question; even more so because in addition to the basic Spanish texts in both novels, we have the additionally enriching (and subverting) caló, bilingual, and English language levels. And to add an overlay, we have female-language subjects and thoughts.

When I asked why they wrote these texts in Spanish, both authors said that it was the way it came out, that the text chooses what language it wants to be in. For Cota-Cárdenas as well as for Gonzales-Berry, it was the working out of internal conversations, conversations with their Chicana selves. Cota-Cárdenas said that for her there were many things she couldn't say in English, many things she would hear in her mind's eye memory — the joke, the dicho. It was also for her a resistance to what she felt was an annihilation, an aggression, an intrusion, a pushing and pulling. In her essay "Searching for a Voice: Ambiguities and Possibilities," Gonzales-Berry reflects on her own search for a distinct voice that became the voices in her novel.

Uncovering that voice, however, had required the peeling away of layer upon layer of muffling experiences. The problem had been one of not hearing the voice for the noise, the latter disguised as bilingualism, self-consciousness, time, and a deeply entrenched baritone register. . . . My Spanish persona has a certain flair, it's a risk taker, is a game player, is witty. The English me, on the other hand, is more conservative, insecure, highly self-conscious. In Spanish I always felt loved and accepted. In English I always felt like Alejandro Morales' Mateo in *Caras viejas y vino nuevo,* spied upon, on the verge of being judged: Did I, or didn't I measure up? (Rebolledo and Rivero, 26)

And the language issues continue to be debated and discussed within the texts themselves, as when Cota-Cárdenas describes the time her narrator gets head lice.

El español, que era lo que hablábamos todos nosotros excepto los vecinitos americanos como el Brian Roskers, se nos prohibía durante las horas de escuela. . . . Y si te agarraban, pos zas! una *slap,* donde te la pudiera dar la *ticher.* . . . No, no muy fuerte, pero pues, no nos caía muy bien, aunque como les digo, era muy democrático porque a todos nos sonaban igual. . . . Así que nos íbamos a hablar el español . . . había que contarse una de los novios en algún momento, no? . . . debajo de los *oleanders* enormes que estaban en el playground . . . Allí había sombra *besides,* y como Betaville está en el Valle Imperial . . . bueno, usted sabe que hace mucho calor y por allí no importaba impresionar a nadie con un *lawn,* sí un pasto manicurado al estilo corriente. . . . Allí, bajo los oleanders platicábamos todo el español que queríamos, más delicioso porque era a escondidas de la Mees Simpson . . . Y de una manera muy democrático, allí fue donde nos dio a todas nosotras la piojera. . . . (*Puppet,* 18–19)

[Spanish, which was what we all spoke except for our little American neighbors like Brian Roskers, was prohibited during school hours . . . And if they caught you, well zas! a slap wherever the teacher could catch you . . . No, not very hard, but, it didn't make us feel very good, although like I'm telling you it was all very democratic because we were all slapped equally. . . . So we would go to speak Spanish . . . well we had to talk about our boyfriends at some point, isn't that so? . . . underneath the enormous oleanders which were in the playground . . . There was shade there besides, and since Betaville was in the Imperial Valley . . . well, you know that it's very hot there and it didn't make any sense to try to impress anyone with a lawn, yes grass manicured in the current style. . . . There, underneath the oleanders we spoke all the Spanish we wanted, it was even more delicious because it was hidden from Miss Simpson . . . And in a democratic manner, that was where we all caught head lice. . . .]

173

The negative stereotypes imposed by the dominant culture continue to be associated with language use. Both Cota-Cárdenas's and Gonzales-Berry's narrative texts are self- as well as other-referential; they include references to the multiply voiced/multiply cultured influences that have imposed themselves onto the linguistic as well as cultural registers and their representations. The baritone register Gonzales-Berry referred to is the patriarchal silencing and modeling of women. The silencing of the Spanish-speaking children is another silencing register. Puppet, the protagonist of Cota-Cárdenas's novel, embodies that register because he has a speech impediment and therefore rarely speaks.

The concept of writing under erasure comes from Heidegger, Husserl, and Derrida—the idea of a concept that exists but then is erased, and then has another concept superimposed upon it (Torres, 2–17). In terms of Cota-Cárdenas's and Gonzales-Berry's writing, this concept would be one of a quintuple erasure: the English erasure of Spanish, the Anglo erasure of the Chicano, the Mexicano erasure of the Chicano, the patriarchal erasure of the female, and the Chicano erasure of the Chicana. This concept of erasure functions as a metaphor, negative and positive, in *Puppet*; for example, when Puppet dies they cannot afford a grave for him, so he is buried on top of his mother. Indeed the image of mothers dying with their children on top of them is a continuing thread in the novel. Thus Puppet has no space of his own, and neither does his mother. So, too, have women writers had to struggle for their own representational space, and the path toward seizing the language, seizing their voices, has been difficult and painful. And the erasure and silencing continue, exacerbated by the politics of the right.

In order to resist the patriarchal and colonial representations imposed upon them, Chicana writers have had to look to themselves (and each other) to break through the multiply stifling layers. In order to seize the language, it has been necessary to speak through culturally bound perimeters. For Cota-Cárdenas, the paranoia of the linguistic text speaks through the representation of not only Anglo culture but male-dominated Chicano culture as well. Yet speaking out may be as potentially dangerous for Chicana feminists as any overt political act. Cota-Cárdenas's text is an expiation of many social and political boundaries: of those Chicanos who did not immediately support César Chávez, of those Chicanos who do not radically and completely speak out on political issues, of Chicanas who dare to criticize the machista traditions and limitations of Chicano culture. The reprisals for not conforming to a cultural ethic can be great, as Cota-Cárdenas hints in her texts. In "El son de dos caras," she shows that one way to silence the women in the early days was to make them feel that they would be harmed in some way for speaking up.

No solamente
la CIA
usa de las drogas el terror
horror y la muerte
pa' controlar
lo que piensas
pa' chingar
pa' convertir
o por la moda.

Ha habido
manos sabias sucias y morenas
que han suministrado
mariguana
cocaína
heroína
y LSD.

    (*Marchitas,* 23)

[Not only
the CIA
uses drugs, terror
horror and death
to control
what you think
to screw you
so you will convert
or because it's in style.

There have been
knowing hands, dirty and dark skinned
that have administered
marijuana
cocaine
heroin
and LSD.]

    (Translation by Cota-Cárdenas)

As Cota-Cárdenas states in "Serie compraventa" (Buy/sell series),

> No abras la boca
> cuando sea peligroso
> mantén el silencio
> y aguántate.
>
> (*Marchitas*, 11)

> [Don't open your mouth
> when there's danger
> keep silent
> and endure it.]

Gonzales-Berry understands this paranoia and contextualizes it.

> Venía pensando también que nosotros, los chicanos, representamos una especie de síntesis y de sincretismo. Allá estamos tan constantemente conscientes de nuestra posición marginada, de nuestra relación defensiva con ese espacio que nos es extraño y por lo tanto caótico, que nos vemos forzados a mantenernos en un estado de tensión constante con esa otredad. Nos sentimos permanentemente amenazados; a cada paso anticipamos que alguien nos meta traba, ya sea literal o figurativamente. Es este constante estado de alerta lo que he bautizado la neurosis chicana — en realidad la neurosis, o sea, la doble consciencia, a que aflige a todo ser marginado — y fíjate que no utilizo el término en su sentido negativo porque es precisamente esta neurosis, este estado exaltado de auto-conciencia lo que nos impulsa a afirmarnos y a superar los obstáculos de esa sociedad que nos rechaza. (*Paletitas de guayaba*, 36)

> [I have been thinking also that we, Chicanos, represent a sort of synthesis and syncretism. There we are so constantly conscious of our position in the margin, of our defensive relationship with that space that for us is strange and therefore chaotic, that we are forced to maintain ourselves in a state of constant tension with that otherness. We feel permanently threatened; at every step we anticipate that someone will screw us over, either literally or figuratively. It is this constant state of alertness that I have baptized Chicano neurosis — in reality that neurosis, or a double consciousness which afflicts all marginal beings, note that I don't use the term in its negative sense because it is precisely this neurosis, this heightened state of self-consciousness that pushes us to affirm ourselves and to overcome the obstacles of that society that rejects us.]

Gonzales-Berry takes possession of the speaking subject in various ways. To begin, although the speaking subject in her novel appears to be having conversations with various people, we never hear them speak. In particular, in her conversations with Sergio, we only hear him filtered through the perspective of the speaking subject. Marina, the protagonist of the novel, goes beyond merely telling her story: she seizes the language by appropriating male public language and imposing on that language the alterity, or otherness, of speaking the female body, of speaking female sexuality. In addition, she subverts the mythology of male language by using irony to make fun of male sexual body parts and by laughing at the mythology. By so doing, Gonzales-Berry not only has seized the language but has undermined and overturned it, thus controlling the power of this language. She continues to demythify masculine power, in particular as seen in the penis, by articulating and speaking out female desires and needs.

> After all is said and done, todo lo que les interesa es encontrarse un hoyito húmedo donde reposar (cómo que reposar, más bien escribir agitar) su infame y precaria masculinidad. (Andale, no te hagas la delicada; no me andes con eufemismos; dale nombre a ese instrumento sagrado, vehículo y portador del ego masculino, el verbo echo carne, extensión obsena, motivo de nuestro pavor, objeto de nuestro deseo, la cosa del hombre, la picha, la chora, la verga, la manguera, la tripa, la estaca, la pinga, la moronga, la herramienta, la cara de papa, la trompeta, la menina, el pájaro, el pollo, el palo, el chichote, el chile, el chorizo, el bicho, el pepino, el pipote, el pitito. ¿No ves lo mejor que se siente una al haberla-lo llamado por sus nombres? ¿Verdad que el nombrar las cosas es encontrarle un hilito a la libertad?)
> (*Paletitas de guayaba*, 52)

> [After all is said and done, all that interests them is to find a moist hole in which to rest (what do you mean rest, better to write agitate) their infamous and precarious masculinity. (Go on, don't play the delicate role; don't forget the euphemisms; give name to that sacred instrument, vehicle and bearer of the masculine ego, the word made flesh, obscene extension, catalyst of our fear, object of our desire, the man's thing, the cock, the dick, the pecker, the magic wand, the tool, the pope's nose, the trumpet, the bird, the dipstick, the bush beater, the whip, the prick, the mouse, the chile, the sausage, the hambone, the drumstick, the big banana, the lollypop, the cucumber, the percolator, the peewee. Don't you see how much better one feels about calling it by its names. Isn't it true that in naming things one discovers one of liberty's tiny threads?)]

To name the unnameable, to speak the unsayable, to articulate clearly without euphemisms the female sexual experience is to find freedom. As Mari says,

Pero sabes que también me gusta cuando no nos vemos por algún tiempo porque siempre son mucho más intensos mis orgasmos. No sé, duran más. Hoy por ejemplo fue increíble, como una torrente de ola tras ola de espasmos eléctricos. Creí que nunca iba a terminar. Te imaginas lo que sería quedarse uno atrascado en un orgasmo perpetuo? Sería algo así como las personas que no pueden dejar de estornudar placer y agonía. En términos puramente biológicos, el estornudar es semejante al orgasmo, ¿no te parece? A mí por ejemplo, me encanta estornudar. Siento gran satisfacción y placer al hacerlo. (*Paletitas de guayaba*, 63)

[But you know that I also like it when we don't see each other for some time because then my orgasms are always much more intense. I don't know, they last longer. Today for example it was incredible, like a crashing of wave after wave of electric spasms. I thought it would never end. Can you imagine what it would be like to be trapped in a perpetual orgasm? It would be something like those people who can't stop sneezing, pleasure and agony. In purely biological terms, sneezes are similar to orgasms, don't you think? I, for example, love to sneeze. I feel great satisfaction and pleasure when I do.]

In the linking of orgasm with the more mundane pleasure of sneezing, Gonzales-Berry elevates and makes ordinary both experiences: surely it is a uniquely creative female experience that makes the nexus between these two acts. Yet this articulation of female sexuality is also ideology, against the repression and ownership of women. This linguistic articulation of woman's sexuality, the subversion of the masculine myth within the text, are all forms of resistance against erasure and silencing.

The final area I would like to discuss is how these two texts fit within the postmodern. One characteristic of postmodern text that does not fit within the context of ethnic female literature is what has been called the death or absence of the speaking subject. The speaking subject within these texts is not dead. On the contrary, Chicana writers are just beginning to seize their voices, to articulate their identities. It is true, however, that a single work can contain multiple voices that shift positions in a self-conscious conversation with themselves. If we could characterize the postmodern as a stance that looks back on tradition while self-consciously reflecting on one's positionality in reference to that tradition, simultaneously referencing and recognizing one's voice without that tradition, then both these novels are vigorously postmodern.

In an extremely naive review of Gonzales-Berry's novel, one critic stated that the narration was jumpy and hard to understand (Claremón, *Albuquerque Journal*, 17 Nov. 1991). Certainly the same could be said about Cota-Cárdenas's novel. Both novels articulate a female experience that is not linear, and they include narrative techniques such as shifts of voice and time; erasure of clear demarcations between popular culture, oral literature, and written literature; and incorporation of terms common in popular speech. If you add to these techniques a collusion with the reader and a playfulness within the text, you have many of the elements of a postmodern text. For me, the outstanding characteristic of these texts is how the self-ironizing, self-referential, social and political (and certainly feminist) modern consciousness leaps out of the text in collusion with the reader and with herself.

In Gonzales-Berry's *Paletitas de guayaba,* the speaking subject often gives directions to herself as to what should be going on in the text.

> Ay cielo olvídate ya de ser tan histriónica, ahíncate en el análisis objetivo porque si no jamás saldrás de ese enmarañamiento de subjetividad que te ofusca la realidad material. Ya, ya sé, pero no entiendes que yo no tengo control sobre este aspecto de mi ser; quizá surjan del hemisferio del lado derecho del cerebro, qué te parece? (56)

> [Oh my love, forget about being so hysterical, stick to an objective analysis because if you don't you will never get out of that mire of subjectivity that obscures material reality. I know, I know but don't you understand that I don't have control over that aspect of my being; perhaps they spring from the right hemisphere of my brain, what do you think?]

Later, in Marina's discussions with Sergio, the subject and the object become confused as the subject positions and repositions herself as a thinking, writing, and seeing subject, one who has come to consciousness within and about the sociopolitical text and context. As Mari begins to assimilate and control the object, or "the Other," the subject becomes confused. "¿Sabes algo? No te (me) entiendo" (53). (You know something? I don't understand you [me].) Later, the subject and object melt into each other. This "Other," personified as Sergio, is a postmodern object of speculation. As Elizabeth Meese explains, "the question of 'the Other' remains one of feminism's most pressing interests, as it seems to come to us from within—what we understand as different, but nonetheless part of 'us'—and it strikes us from without—what we understand to be something or someone else and therefore not part of or like us, the intentional and unwitting exclusions Feminism commits in the interest of consolidating and asserting its identity" (78). That this is clear also for Gonzales-Berry is illustrated when she tells us,

> Se habrán preguntado más de una vez por qué es que no le he dado ni voz ni corporeidad a él. De eso no estoy totalmente segura. No obstante, les

ofrezco algunas posibilidades que se me ocurren a medida que voy poniendo los dedos en las techas: 1) la técnica la vi en la novela de un escritor mexicano y me dejó muy impresionada; 2) no lo recuerdo bien, o lo recuerdo muy bien pero es tan dulce el dolor de ese recuerdo que no quiero compartirlo; 3) él realmente es el/la lector/a con quien desea Mari entrar en una íntima relación; 4) habrá entre ustedes quienes dirán que él nunca existió, que no es otra cosa que la proyección de su/mi/nuestra visión particular del varón ideal, o sea, el Segundo Sexo inventando al Primero tal como quisiera que fuera. (*Paletitas de guayaba,* 39)

[You must have asked yourselves more than once why it is that I have given him neither voice nor body. I'm not totally sure about that. Nevertheless, I offer some possibilities that occur to me as my fingers press the keyboard: 1) I saw the technique in a novel of a Mexican writer and I was duly impressed; 2) I don't remember him well, or I remember him very well but the pain of that memory is so sweet I don't want to share it; 3) he is really the reader with whom I wish to have an intimate relationship; 4) there will be some of you who will say that he never existed, that he is nothing more that the projection of her/my/our personal vision of the ideal male, that is, the Second Sex inventing the First as it wishes it were.]

Thus, in good postmodern style, Gonzales-Berry leaves it up to us, the readers, to position ourselves.

This self-referential voice is apparent also in Cota-Cárdenas. It is a voice that comments on the writing as it is happening, and positions itself as necessary, but it is also a voice that cannot necessarily control what is happening. For example, in a scene where the speaking subject imagines an unbelievably romantic episode with her lover, the voice interpolates,

"Ja, ja, de veras les vas a contar de Vittorio? Oh, tú no tienes vergüenza, vas sacando las garritas poco a poco y verás que cuando menos lo esperes . . . lo que no querías . . . ja . . . Bueno, adelante, burrita, but I don't think I want to stick around for this . . . Chale . . ." (*Puppet,* 41)

["Ha, Ha . . .are you really going to tell them about Vittorio? Oh, you have no shame, you stick out your claws little by little and you'll see when you least expect it . . . just what you didn't want . . . ha . . . Well, go ahead, little donkey, but I don't think I want to stick around for this . . . Bye . . ."]

This ironic commentator shifts from inside to outside, calls the main speaking subject *tuerta, burrita,* and often warns her, "Cuidado, te estás saliendo fuera del papel" (Careful, you're getting off the page [your role]). These warnings are both metaphorical and about the actual writing.

Both novels also constantly refer to other writings of both the Latin

American and Chicano traditions, and sometimes to their own writings. For example, it is significant that the presence in both these texts of Malinche and her "discursos" emphasizes the authors' final seizing of power. For both Cota-Cárdenas and Gonzales-Berry, Malinche appears as "la lengua" (the tongue) and represents an appropriation of the language, the power to write, and female subjectivity as well as female sexuality. That they have chosen to write in Spanish is a politically conscious act as well as a social one. They write to affirm their culture and their traditions, even though writing in Spanish may mean being more marginalized and unrecognized as writers. Margarita Cota-Cárdenas and Erlinda Gonzales-Berry, as well as all the Chicana writers mentioned here, have seized for themselves as well as for their readers a sociopolitical sexual expression that represents for all of us.

9

Mujeres Andariegas: Good Girls and Bad

Mujeres andariegas, mujeres callejeras, women who wander and roam, women who walk around, women who journey: the terms imply restlessness, wickedness. These are women who don't stay at home tending to their husbands, children, parents. The terms suggest women without respect for other people. Perhaps they cross boundaries, like Gloria Anzaldúa's *atravesadas.* They are not bound by societally construed morals, nor cultural practices. They must, therefore, be those wicked, sexual women seen as *putas,* or prostitutes. The negative cultural stereotypes placed on mujeres andariegas result from a patriarchal culture that wills women to be passive, self-denying, and nurturing to others. And women who walk the streets can be demanding, self-satisfying, and worse, perhaps they don't need a man. For contemporary Chicana writers, these mujeres andariegas are quite appealing; they are women who go into male spaces such as the cantina, and appropriate them. They are the *mujeres de fuerza* — strong, independent women. They are women who are self-sufficient and build their own houses with their own hands. And they do more than survive — they thrive and prosper, in spite of the dire consequences that society has predicted for them.

For Chicana writers, sexual politics in all of its forms, hetero- and homosexual, has been an important step towards healing the wounds of racism, homophobia, and marginalization. The ability to write the body and to write sexuality has been instrumental in giving Chicana writers an empowered voice. To become whole, they must be able to seize the voices that articulate the shame, the secrets. Clearly there has been nothing more oppressed than women's sexuality, the lips that cannot speak. Thus Chicana writers seize upon the notion of mujeres andariegas as symbols of empowering the body, sexuality, and the self.

This form of writing the body is one that writes the sexual body, and the lesbian body. The writers discuss menstruation, lactation, and the reality of childbirth. They explore the love of and for women, and women's symbolic physiognomy. As Amy Kaminsky acknowledges, "the human body is not just a physical phenomenon in the natural world, it is one of the most heavily burdened bearers of meaning in culture" (98). Lesbian Chicana writers have been at the forefront of sexual politics, articulating sexual oppression as well as the love and attention of women towards other women. These are the *mujeres escandalosas,* and their writings find a place for an oppressed and marginalized subjectivity. These atravesadas, escandalosa troublemakers, are figures that are both enormously appealing and problematic for Chicano culture. They are at times even problematic for Chicana writers. Moreover, these women are not new arrivals as images in Mexicano/Chicano literature. They emerge as early as Nahuatl literature and stand out throughout the centuries as our brash, rasquache peladas, malcriadas, and pachucas.

Mujeres Andariegas in Pre-Columbian Literature

The image of the mujer andariega is seen in Mexican literature as early as pre-Columbian times. In the *Historia general de las cosas de Nueva España* (the *Florentine Codex*), we see the image of the *ahuianas,* or *las alegradoras,* the happiness givers (pre-Columbian prostitutes). The *Florentine Codex* was a remarkable document recorded by Fray Bernardino de Sahagún from native informants. The vivid portrait of a "happiness giver, one who lives from pleasure," is even more noteworthy when one considers the rigid moral code that governed behavior in Nahuatl/Aztec society. It was a code that repressed any sort of extravagant or deviant behavior in all people, but which was particularly repressive towards the social conduct of women.

The all-pervasive sense of religiosity and the blending of the church and the autocratic state (all Aztec rulers were also priests) created a society with fairly rigid ideals. At birth, children were ritually addressed and the ideal conduct of their lives outlined. The ritual address given when a girl was born (quoted in chapter 3) presents a rather gloomy picture of life for women as drudges who were restricted to the home. It also warns them away from "bad predispositions"; girls were educated in special schools and taught at an early age to be circumspect about their behavior. They were warned not to be flirtatious, not to dally in the streets, nor speak to young men — and they were severely punished for minor infractions. When a young girl was of marriageable age, she exchanged bondage to her father

184

for bondage to her husband. If she were caught committing adultery, her punishment was death.

Life among women of the nobility was not as difficult. Even they, however, are mentioned only briefly in the chronicles — mostly they are referred to as important economic and social links to royal lineage: as wives, daughters, and concubines of rulers, traded for political power and influence. Several wives and concubines who are mentioned in the chronicles as having committed adultery were put to death (Ixtlilxóchitl, 169–72).

Sadly, as Iris Blanco comments, the knowledge we have of pre-Columbian Mexican women comes to us through an upper-class male perspective: male native informants of the Indian nobility either wrote the accounts themselves or told their stories to Catholic missionaries who inserted their own viewpoints and prejudices into the histories. Almost nothing comes to us through the words of the women themselves.[1] As one cacique said, "women like children, don't know how to speak" (Blanco, 252).

Nevertheless, within this rigid system, some women were able to live their lives in comparative freedom. Midwives, priestesses, healers, merchants, and prostitutes were in one way or another outside the strict rules of society. Although prostitutes were not socially condoned, it seems likely they were tolerated. We know that young men in school slept with prostitutes, as did warriors. We also know that at certain times of the year (the feast to Tlaxochimaco, for example) ritualistic dances were held after which the warriors copulated with women as a kind of "conjuration of fertility" (Anton, 56). Yet when a young man married, he was warned, "Of course you must now as a man adopt other habits than those you have had before now. You are a man and have not any more the soul of a boy. It is no longer seemly for you to be like a high spirited youth and to take part in the entertainment and pleasures of the bachelors, or in buffoonery, and most of all you must not go to the brothels; for you are a married man" (Anton, 24). Thus while prostitution was tolerated, it was at the same time condemned.

Nevertheless, the double standard of other male-dominant societies was evident in pre-Columbian Mexico. "It was not the man who made use of it, however, who was despised, but the woman who took it up as a job, since for the Mexicans the body did not hide the inner soul but laid it bare. . . . Self restraint was thought the chief virtue of women as well as of men. There was in the everyday relations of men and women much restraint, ceremonial reserve and modesty, based on a sense of shame with regard to one's own as well as to other people's nakedness" (Anton, 46).

We have in Aztec/Nahuatl literature at least three excellent examples of texts that personify and even exalt the prostitute and sexuality: "La alegradora: La que vive del placer" (The happiness giver: She who lives from pleasure) text from the *Florentine Codex,* the "Chalca cihuaciucatl" (Song of the women of Chalco) from *Cantares mexicanos,* and a poem written by Tlaltecatzin, also from *Cantares mexicanos.* Aside from the ritual admonitions, these texts are almost the only surviving poetic texts that refer to women. It is difficult to say whether this indicates a complete absence of texts about women and that these are atypical, or if these are a few that somehow escaped censorship from the Nahuas themselves, as well as the Catholic priests.

For the priests who recorded them, these poems served as an example of the scandalous conduct of people they considered primitive, and it was justification for indoctrinating them into Christianity. On the other hand, perhaps Nahuatl society was not as rigid as we have been led to believe, as these are only a few examples of a genre called buffoon songs or *cantos traviesos.* The "Song of the women of Chalco" was remembered because it was clever and appealing, if not outright shocking. In the years since the initial collection of these texts in the sixteenth century, few have seen fit to translate and publish them. It was just in 1967 that Father Angel Garibay first translated the "Song of the women of Chalco," the more erotic and outrageous of the texts.

In Nahuatl poetry, there are two distinct philosophical perspectives. One is pessimistic, lamenting the brevity of life and questioning its meaning. These poems exhort men to leave temporary pleasure and to create a more lasting self that should be manifested in a true heart and a true face (Nicholson, 8). The other is an epicurean perspective, believing likewise that life is brief and uncertain, but exhorting people to pleasure, to enjoy all that God has given, including nature in all its sensory aspects: flowers, wine, friendship, and poetry. It is into this area that the *cantos traviesos,* which were meant to amuse, and the erotic poems and the poems of the ahuianas fall.

Who were these happiness givers and what were they like? One critic has gone so far as to say that they were women from other tribes, not the Aztec, because Aztec society would not have allowed its women to be prostitutes (Quirarte, 805–6). Although this may have been true, it seems more probable that the happiness givers were women who were sexually disgraced (a danger if the admonitions to young girls are an indication), divorced, or widowed. For some women, it also could have been a way of escape.

The text of the happiness giver is an ambivalent one. On one hand, it shows how this woman is wicked and withered up, and on the other hand,

it is a remarkable portrait of a vivid, vibrant woman — a woman full of life
and of her own beauty and power. However, the text begins with a negative
image, whose undercurrents run throughout the poem.

> The happiness giver: a woman already lost,
> with her body she gives pleasure, she sells her body,
> she always walks around offering her body,
> Drunk, outside of herself,
> In her insides definitely drunk,
> like a victim of sacrifice, like the flowery victim,
> like the slave that has been bathed, like a divine victim,
> like those who die to honor the gods,
> like he who must die.
>
> (León-Portilla, "Las alegradoras," 708, translation mine)

This woman does away with all restraint. She is, to say the least, immodest.
Sexual excess is compared to alcoholic excess, and she acts drunk. (It is
interesting that those who were close to god, the warriors, and those about
to be sacrificed to the gods are also described as intoxicated.) She wanders
the streets, particularly the market, where she sells herself just as goods are
sold. The text continues to describe her as a woman who moves around in a
vain manner. She watches her face, she has a sexual appetite, she makes
herself desirable; "without shame she gives herself to sleep with anyone, she
loans herself. She is a flower who cohabits, she is lascivious, she has itchy
hips" (708). Yet the appeal of this woman is also undeniable.

> She makes herself beautiful, she shows off her clothes . . .
> she looks at herself in a mirror, she has a mirror in her hand.
> She bathes frequently and incessantly puts on perfume . . .
> She paints her face, with many colors she paints it, . . .
> She chews gum, she makes noise with it.
> She walks along the canals, she knows the roads,
> she frequents the market.
> She goes from here to there, she pushes people,
> she pinches them,
> she laughs, she makes fun of people.
> She is always smiling . . .
> With her hand she beckons,
> with her eyes she calls,

she winks, she calls with her hands,
she arches her eyebrows, she laughs, she goes around laughing,
she shows her attractions.
She shows her appetite, she makes herself desirable,
she goes around making herself desirable, she makes men seek her out.

(León-Portilla, "Las alegradoras," 708, translation mine)

The fact that this woman is able to travel and leave her home, that she knows the roads outside her village, is interesting indeed. She is vain, she is bathed, she is perfumed. She has money to purchase what she needs. She wears makeup, she chews and snaps her gum. She is also smiling and laughing. Above all, she is restless. This poem, though meant to be condemnatory, elicits admiration from the modern reader for its attention to detail, the vivid description of the woman's hair, mannerisms, energy, and her fiercely independent air.

In the "Song of the Women of Chalco" (in León-Portilla, *The Chalco*), the women of Chalco (a town conquered and subjugated by the great Aztec king Axayácatl [1469–1481]) seduce and sexually exhaust the king, thereby metaphorically conquering him. The poem is a challenge from the women of Chalco to the king to a sexual battle. Although in his analysis, León-Portilla believes the king wins the battle, throughout the poem it is clearly the women who are actively and threateningly sexually aggressive, belittling the king and taunting him with the diminutive of his name "Axayacatito," also a reference to his sexual prowess. The poem is an erotic satire, meant to be sung, danced, and melodramatically acted out. It is the collective song of the women of Chalco, in which one woman invites her sisters to help with the battle. Thus we have a group of women who in their various and multiple sexual aspects have come to challenge Axayácatl. If Axayácatl is to win, he must prove his sexual prowess with them one by one. The speakers (it seems there are at least eight) taunt him in turn. The last woman (and this was hilarious to the Nahuatl audience) is an old hag, dried out, and perhaps representing the goddess Coatlicue. She is the final conquest, and if Axayácatl can conquer his revulsion, he will have won. However, the women have worn him out and he falls asleep. The woman says, triumphantly, "slowly, slowly surrender to sleep, rest my little son, you, Lord Axayácatl" (258, translation mine).

These texts make clear that eroticism and sexuality were an integral part of Nahuatl life. Although not condoned by moralistic society, they must have been prevalent enough to require constant admonitions against excessive behavior. It is also clear that women bore the brunt of societal criticism while men were more or less free to behave as they pleased. The texts that have come down to us, however, were not free from the religious strictures of this society. The texts were also offerings to divine beings: to Tlatzonil, Xochiquetzal, and to the other, dark side of the deity, probably Coatlicue or Huitzilopochtli. And perhaps the texts have remained because the temptress signifies an aspect of woman in her freedom and power. It was one aspect that could not be controlled by religion nor dominated by men. If the moody goddess could destroy the emerging maize crop with deluges of water, she could also destroy man by death. It was men's hidden fear that caused them, as always, to be alternately attracted to and repelled by the ahuiana, the happiness giver. And although the portraits were meant to condemn her, we see an attractive, strong woman coming to us through, and in spite of, ideological stereotyping.

The early texts that come down to us from the Nahuatl tradition are examples of the continuing questioning of the systems that would control and regulate women's behavior. Chicana writers explore these traditions and continue to question.

Escandalosas: Troublemakers

The moralistic ideal of the good girl who will stay at home, be self-sacrificing, and let others control her body, and its opposite, the image of the woman who desires to control her own destiny and sexuality, and to establish another way to be, are both part of the cultural heritage that enriches Chicana literature. Chicanas, in their texts, propose alternative parameters. In fact, the literature abounds with women who grow up to be self-sufficient, self-nurturing, troublemaking mujeres de fuerza. As discussed in chapter 2, the Catholic heritage that many Chicanas share would have us be other-oriented, pure, and "good." The alternative is to be "bad," and bad girls are wicked.

This aspect of being urged to be good while simultaneously knowing that you are "bad" is explored constantly by Chicana writers in an attempt to break out of the either/or syndrome that says if you are not the Virgin then you must be the prostitute. Chicana writers attempt to create a more realistic image of what women are, in all their aspects. As Bernice Zamora has said, "My divisions are infinite" (52; Rebolledo and Rivero, 78).

There is a series of texts that discuss women's desire to break through the barriers, including Pat Mora's poem "Aztec Princess" (*Chants*, 28; Rebolledo and Rivero, 195–96), discussed in chapter 3, which illustrates the dichotomy seen in the *discursos* of the *ancianos* of the Nahuatl tradition. Mora explores the socialization process that limited a girl's life—exemplified by the ritual of burying the girl's umbilical cord inside the house. For Mora, such traditions need readjustment so that they free, rather than cage, her heroine, who carries what is left of the umbilical cord outside, whispering "breathe."

While Mora's heroine whispers, Demetria Martínez's heroine shouts out loud, "I'm going to be a troublemaker / when I grow up" (110; Rebolledo and Rivero, 317). But in her poem "Hail Mary," Martínez also defines the Virgin Mary as a witch and bitch, who

> made love with
> life instead of a man,
> birthed a troublemaker,
> you asked for it.
>
> (111)

Women who dare to speak out on public issues are also defined as troublemakers, a label many of us have received. Margarita Cota-Cárdenas describes such an experience in "Malinche's Discourse" (discussed in chapter 3). ". . . she's a menace to our cause that's it only learned to say crazy things to say accuse with HER EYES and they didn't want then troublemakers in their country" (204). Many women are labeled troublemakers for actively seeking change, seeking justice, a common theme throughout Chicana literature.[2]

Beyond being a troublemaker is the next exaggerated step, that of being an escandalosa. As defined by Alma Luz Villanueva, this type of woman is not only condemned by men but is especially condemned by women.

> I heard my grandmother, the
> other women mutter
>   "Escandalosa" —
> a woman who says too
> much, too loudly —
> abrasive, furious,
>   "Escandalosa" —
> She is me.
>
> (*Life Span*, 30)

Although this name is a negative one, Villanueva accepts the connotations, but expands the meaning of the word: "escandalosa" is also a rainbow-colored sail, which waits for the creative (furious, she says) wind to fill her (31).

Among the various representations of troublemakers in Chicano culture are the pachucas, the rebellious, tough, with-it women seen in Inés Hernandez's poem "Para Teresa" (*Siete poetas,* 31–32; Rebolledo and Rivero, 330–33), and the peladas, who live out life on the margin sustained by "laughter and a cosmic will to be" (Ybarra-Frausto, 156). Gina Valdés captures this attitude in "Weeping With Laughter."

> Slapping our thighs and weeping
> with laughter at the worm
> in Eve's apple . . .
>
> .   .   .   .   .   .
>
> at the red stains on our underwear
>
> .   .   .   .
>
> . . . giggling
> at the Pope with a rubber on
> his nose, at Mother Teresa clutching
> a red rose in her teeth, laughing
> at our mother's guilt pounding
> our ovaries
>
> .   .   .   .
>
> two females
> shaking our butts
> at a very serious world
>
> (368–69)

Another example is the daring act of Clotilde in Portillo Trambley's "The Paris Gown" (*Rain of Scorpions,* 1–9; Rebolledo and Rivero, 360–68). In this story, Clotilde does not want to be married off to an old man, so on the day of her engagement party, instead of wearing the beautiful gown especially ordered for her from Paris, she comes down the stairs of her house, in front of a huge crowd, stark naked. This scandalous act earns her exile from her family and town, and freedom for herself as she goes to live in Paris.

Las Malcriadas: Wicked Women

In addition to troublemaking, some Chicana writers define themselves as being just plain bad. Often this badness is associated with the body and a growing awareness of sexuality, which is also associated with guilt. The desire to understand their sexual selves and capabilities clashes with the norms of a strongly traditional family, the church, and a male-oriented society. As the editors of *Third Woman: The Sexuality of Latinas* wrote, "Our sexuality has been hidden, subverted, distorted within the 'sacred' walls of the 'familia' — be it myth or reality — and within the even more privatized walls of the bedrooms. Like many women, our understanding of our sexual desire too often comes through the reality of sexual violence. In the journey to the love of female self and each other we are ultimately forced to confront father, brother, and god (and mother as his agent)" (Alarcón, Castillo, and Moraga, 9).

The narrative or lyric voice in Chicana writing often reflects the guilt felt in rebelling against established cultural institutions. In Patricia Santana-Béjar's "In the Toolshed" (discussed in chapter 5), for example, the young narrator agonizes over her growing sexuality. Her sin is autoeroticism, and although she tries to stop, she cannot because her "bad angel" is in control. In a carefully constructed moralistic world, the child is taught that her body is bad and that her left side is evil. As her sexuality emerges, she even hates her pubic hairs, at one point trying to cut them off, and she knows with great certainty that she is "going to go to the Devil" (2).

Everyone knows that if you are wicked, it is because you were *malcriada,* that is, you were not brought up in the right way. Therefore, the responsibility for being malcriada rests on your parents and your immediate family. Of course, this attitude then places double pressure on your parents and family, who then pressure you not to transgress. Any Chicana could speak of the constant admonitions placed on all children, but particularly female children, "pórtate bien, no te portes mal, debes mostrar respeto" (behave yourself, don't behave badly, you must show respect).

The bad girl grows up to be the wicked woman, so clearly articulated in Sandra Cisneros's *My Wicked, Wicked Ways.* This collection of several sets of poems illustrates the progression of wickedness, and it acquires added dimensions of freedom and power that include sexuality, but go even beyond it. The section titled "My Wicked, Wicked Ways" begins with a quote by Maxine Hong Kingston, "Isn't a bad girl almost like a boy?" (21). This insight into bad girls does not mean that they want to be boys but is rather an acknowledgment that bad girls transgress the realm of propriety for females by acting outside the rules and by desiring completion and freedom for themselves. For Cisneros, the transgression is represented by the girl who moved away from the protection of her family, the girl who lived alone, the girl who writes. "My Wicked, Wicked Ways" is a search for guidance, a quest for direction. She asks, "What does a woman inherit / that tells her how / to go?" (x). The answer is that once you "chuck" the life your parents have picked for you, you have to immerse yourself in the process: the loneliness, the fears, the silences. The poet is "wicked" because she wants to be a writer and "invent herself." But for many women writers, there are no role models, no how-to guides to tell them how to behave, and "nothing in the texts to tell me" (xii).

To be wicked, then, is to know that you have sinned — against the church, against your parents, against the norms of society. To sin is to expose your body, to have unauthorized sexual relations, to expose your private self in a public way. To sin is to be the mistress or lover instead of the wife. To sin is not to be a nun. To sin is to love another woman. To sin is to go into spaces reserved for men: politics, writing, and bars. Yet, throughout Chicana literature, admiration for the wicked sinners is evident. For Cisneros, in her own family there is a tradition of sinners, of wicked women, that Cisneros's lyric speakers can identify with. In "His Story," the lyric speaker explains that to begin with, she was "born under a crooked star," but that,

It is an ancient fate.
A family trait we trace back
to a great aunt no one mentions.

Her sin was beauty.
She lived mistress.
Died solitary.

There is as well
the cousin with the famous
how shall I put it?
profession. . . .
And of course,
grandmother's mother
she died a death of voodoo.
There are others.

(*My Wicked, Wicked Ways*, 38)

The worst of all is that

> a girl with both my names
> was arrested for audacious crimes
> that began by disobeying fathers.
>
> (39)

In Cisneros's *Mango Street,* a young girl risks censure by defying convention. "I have begun my own quiet war. Simple. Sure. I am one who leaves the table like a man, without putting back the chair or picking up the plate" (82). When she is grown, she is beautiful and cruel, "the one who drives the men crazy and laughs them all away. Her power is her own. She will not give it away" (82). Clearly, however, this idealized desire is not real; the real woman suffers from love even when being wicked. She is abandoned, at times alone.

As the speaker matures, the "wicked ways" begin to assault cultural icons of morality, art, and the body. In the powerful poem "Los desnudos: A Triptych" (*Loose Woman,* 86–90), Cisneros describes three paintings by Chicana artist Terry Ybáñez, who has taken famous paintings of nude women and turned the women/objects into men/objects. Instead of the male gazing upon the female object, Cisneros and Ybáñez image themselves the gazers. Considering replacing the female of "The Naked Maja" with a male, Cisneros says,

> Instead of the erotic breasts,
> we'll have the male eggs to look at
> and the pretty sex.
>
> (*Loose Woman,* 86)

Her gaze transposes the garment of the Renaissance painting to her eye.

> My velvet and ruffled eye will linger,
> precise as brushstrokes,
> take pleasure in the looking and look long.
>
> (86)

Her gaze thus becomes the process of desire for an object that is not only trivialized (she calls him "my petty mischief"), but mute.

The second nude is of a man painted a la Diego Rivera holding calla lilies. "What you get a good view of is his famous backside" (87). This nude is associated with a man she shares with another woman, just as Frida shared

Diego with her sister (and other women). The third nude is "like a Mexican Venus at his toilet" (89). Again the lyric speaker objectifies him, saying,

> You're very
> pretty primped and pretty proud as
> any man is wont to be.
>
> (89)

The irony arises from the fact that the object is held and made permanent through both her gaze and her poem. The mischief, the wickedness here, is the transformation of the male gaze into a female gaze and desire. At this point, the wickedness delights in itself, free from Catholic and social guilt, able to relish its joke and its own wittiness.

From being singled out, by herself and others, as wicked, the lyric speaker in Cisneros's "Loose Woman" accepts the "Other" designation as self-designation.

> They say I'm a macha, hell on wheels
> viva-la-vulva, fire and brimstone,
> man-hating, devastating,
> boogey-woman lesbian.
> Not necessarily so,
> but I like the compliment.
>
> (112)

She has created herself in her own image. "I am the woman of myth and bullshit. (True I authored some of it.)" (113). Her self-image becomes so exaggerated, so rasquache, that she becomes "a danger to society," a desperada whose "happy picture" grins from the wall. As she celebrates the terror she strikes in the hearts of men, her qualities include those that transcend sexuality, namely her ability to think and to articulate. With a sly admission, "I break things" (114), she joins the long line of free-wheeling, liberated, and perhaps angry women slinging crockery at their men, at the world. So does this "loose" woman let herself, her mind, and her tongue hurl themselves at control, order, and limitations.

D/escribiendo el Cuerpo: Writing the Body

According to Rosalyn Jones, French feminists agree that women have been "prevented from expressing their sexuality in itself or for themselves. If they can do this, and if they can speak about it in the new language it calls for, they will establish a point of view (a site of *différence*) from which male concepts and controls can be seen through and taken apart, not only in theory but also in practice" (87). For Luce Irigaray, the facts of women's bodies and women's sexual pleasures are the starting points for female self-consciousness. Clearly one aspect in the game of sexual politics is breaking the taboos. It is only by "opening the wound" and breaking the silences that the wound can be healed, says Anzaldúa (*Borderlands*, 51).

One of the taboos is talking about the fluids and functions of a woman's body. A woman's body objectified and romanticized, even eroticized by the male gaze, is accepted (in varying degrees) by society. The reality of the female body often is not. As Alicia Ostriker has pointed out, "one of the ways we recognize that a woman writer has taken some kind of liberating jump is that her muted parts begin to explain themselves" (92). Ostriker points out that in the last two (now three) decades, "American women poets have been writing about their bodies with decreasing embarrassment and increasing enthusiasm. They write about the sensation of making love. They write about eating and sitting on the toilet. They write about their faces, their arms, their breasts, their wombs, their menstrual periods. Necks and throats, knees and teeth. They write about giving birth, giving suck, growing old. Poems about abortion, poems about breast surgery, poems about rape have become part of women's poetic repertoire. . . . the issue reaches deeply into the question of what our bodies mean to us" (93).

Given their largely Catholic education, Chicanas were often taught to be extremely prudish about their bodies. There has been such sexual repression that it was taboo to even talk about underwear, which was never supposed to be seen. Often one of life's most embarrassing moments had been when your underpants showed, as in "Los calzones de la piña" by Mary Helen Ponce (Rebolledo, *Las mujeres hablan*, 52–58). Thus even the mention of underwear, menstruation, or articles used to stop the flow of menstruation, not to mention actual descriptions of the genitalia, are all taboos in writing. To break through this body of silence, women writers in general, and Chicana writers here in particular, have felt the need to speak the body even though it may mean speaking it through a language that negates it.

As we have seen in Gonzales-Berry's naming of male genitalia, saying the words gives freedom, and even, some would say, power over it. For Chicana writers, it has been extraordinarily liberating to write about the body, and many of them are engaged in a battle of sexual politics of naming and representing that female power and that female space of the body. It is a sexual naming that comes from female experience itself, not from an outside objectified experience, and of course, in Chicana writing, it comes from the specificity of Chicana sexual politics, however that may manifest itself. In 1989 and 1991, two important collections about sexuality were published by Third Woman Press, *The Sexuality of Latinas* (Alarcón, Castillo, and Moraga) and *Chicana Lesbians: The Girls Our Mothers Warned Us About* (Trujillo). The published work of Chicanas and Latinas in these collections constitutes a dynamic representation of sexual politics that seeks to unmask that "secret self."

Menstruation, Tampax, and Other Bodily Things

For centuries, the fact that women menstruated was hidden, and stories abound of the shock that young women suffered when they first menstruated without knowing anything about it. Girls thought they were dying, sick, or had done something disastrous to themselves. These "secrets" were sometimes told from mother to daughter, and young girls were often helped by older sisters or friends who had already experienced menarche. Frequently, however, girls lived through the terror by themselves, too ashamed to mention it to anyone. As Helena Michie has shown, Victorian women writers worked their body functions into the text in a most oblique way: female bleeding was hinted at by the pin pricks that Victorian women experienced while sewing, and at the same time, that very "work" was a displacement of sexual desire (39). Nothing of the sort is ever mentioned, even in the most oblique way, in early Chicana writing. Thus one of the first taboos to be broken was that of beginning to articulate the menstruation experience and to turn it into a celebratory one. Ana Castillo was one of the first writers to discuss a "tampon experience." In "A Letter to Alicia" (1984), she writes,

> i covered for you at the ruins of monte albán
> while you changed your tampon
> before the eyes of gods and ghosts
> and scorpions.

(*Women Are Not Roses*, 19; Rebolledo and Rivero, 105–6)

For Natasha López, the fact that women menstruate locates her within a community of Latinas of the Third World. Her First-World privilege, the

"Walgreens 'feminine hygiene' aisle," is contrasted with the woman washing her panties in the river; they are linked because "everywhere / somewhere / we bleed" (156).

Cisneros's poem "Down There" (22–23) is a contestatory poem to all the male poems that exult masculine sexuality, her menstruation's "transparent drop of light / to the fifth day chocolate paste." In terms of smell, it is "sweet exotic stuff." The taboo becomes celebration when the instrument used to stop the flow becomes the instrument of writing the poem of womanhood,

> in fact, I'd like to dab my fingers
> or a swab of tampax
> in my inkwell
> and write a poem across the wall.

The naming of the unspeakable is a creative coming to voice that, as Julie Watson says, can create new subjects "precisely because women's marginality may be nameable within the terms or parameters of the dominant culture" (139).

Lesbian Topographies

Chicana lesbian writers have, from an early stage, directly and creatively confronted the issues of homophobia and oppression, and the many lesbian voices to be found currently in Chicana literature are as varied as the women themselves. Veronica Cunningham was writing about lesbian consciousness in the early 1970s, and in 1983, the remarkable *This Bridge Called My Back*, edited by Cherríe Moraga and Gloria Anzaldúa, appeared. In *Bridge*, as Norma Alarcón has so clearly pointed out, an understanding and acceptance, indeed a thrusting forth, of multiple voices and split subjectivities was articulated ("Theoretical Subjects," 358). The sexual and political voices of lesbians were defined and uncompromised in *Bridge*. This landmark book, which contained writings by women of color besides Chicanas, was followed by Cherríe Moraga's equally remarkable *Loving in the War Years*, which continues to be fresh in its reading today.

In *Loving*, Moraga articulated issues central to her lesbian consciousness and at the same time engaged in a form of genre blending, forcing a mediation between literature and her social reality. It is a book about voice and silence as well as about body. "I had known for years that I was a lesbian, had felt it in my bones, had ached with the knowledge, gone crazed with the knowledge, wallowed in the silence of it. Silence *is* like starvation" (52). In addition, *Loving* is the search for the brown mother as the speaker examines her ability to pass as white and also her fear of passing. In the end, Moraga argues for her "right to passion" (136). This desire is not only artic-ulated in the genitalia but also in the tongue, both as metaphor and as real-ity. The mother tongue that has been taken from her is the desire for accep-tance as a Mestiza, a desire for the culture of her mother, a desire for the mother herself. For Moraga, this right implies both celebration and fear. At the moment she is about to celebrate her liberation, she hesitates, and it is in that silence of anticipation that her fear (internalized to be sure) steps in.

Moraga's central image for this contradictory metaphor is the mouth. "In recent months I have had a recurring dream that my mouth is too big to close, that is the *outside* of my mouth, my lips, cannot contain the inside — teeth, tongue, gums, throat. I am coming out of my mouth, so to speak. . . My mouth cannot be controlled. It will flap in the wind like legs in sex, not driven by the mind. It's as if la boca were centered on el centro del corazón not in the head at all. The same place where the cunt beats" (142). In "Linguistic Terrorism," Anzaldúa associates the tongue in a related manner, echoing the French feminist analysis of the lips that never speak.

The genre blending mingled with social critique found in *Loving* is also manifest in Anzaldúa's *Borderlands*. With these landmark works, the body of lesbian literature and criticism is adding to a rich legacy of counter-hegemonic thought. In addition to *The Sexuality of Latinas* and the many short stories, essays, and poems in *Chicana Lesbians,* the 1990s has brought forth a variety of lesbian novels and other creative materials about lesbian consciousness, including *Margins* by Terri de la Peña.

How then does the lesbian body and lesbian consciousness begin to map itself in Chicana literature? Certainly, as Kaminsky has explained, "sex-uality remains the constant of women's subordination" (225). In a culture that so heavily relies on male definition, women can be terrorized by even the threat of the mark of deviance, and lesbian critics and writers have noted that they are "faced with a set of problems that make our work particularly delicate and problematic, requiring caution, sensitivity, and flexibility as well as imagination and risk" (Zimmerman, 137). Thus lesbian writers not only have had to forge their own identity, but they have also had to try to come to terms with their past (and to forge a sexual meaning to the past). This forging of a sexual meaning to the past is relatively new to Chicana literature because it means giving meaning to a body that has been seen as culturally meaningless (or considered atravesada). Part of the challenge in this construction is to discover or to create a female-centered image. This may involve exercising lesbian separatism, that is, removal from a hetero-sexist world. It may mean searching for clues to a lesbian history. And it means resisting heterosexual meanings and images and forcing oneself not to be absorbed by them.

If heterosexual women are estranged from language, then women-centered women see language as doubly or triply removed, which makes finding the path to self-understanding through language, and consequently through the body, even more difficult. Carmen Abrego states, "i do not know how to dress my words of desire" (63). Anzaldúa sees the border as her body, and constructs a protective covering, a skin, around the image of the formless "Other." This is parallel to images created by Latin American lesbian writer Sylvia Molloy in her novel *En breve cárcel* (Certificate of absence). For Molloy, the search for form and psychic wholeness begins with a separation from heterosexist society so that her protagonist can begin that painful investigation of self in order to create the center of her being. Molloy is not writing the body, Kaminsky claims, "but rather spin-ning it a protective covering—weaving a skin, creating order, giving shape. Feminists have called this naming, coming out, finding a voice. When she has completed the text, the writer emerges from her room/cocoon, which had been a temporary and only partially protective covering, and she is no longer vulnerable and formless, but rather defiant" (106). Julia Kristeva would concur about that painful wounding of the lesbian body, seeing women as estranged from language but then becoming visionaries, "danc-ers who suffer as they speak" (166).

Zimmerman and other lesbian critics have examined the difficulties in forging a lesbian body of literature, and they see an absence of lesbian material and certainly an absence of lesbian literary antecedents. If Anglo-European writers have been able to establish a lesbian tradition in literature pointing to such notable women as Virginia Woolf, Gertrude Stein, Emily Dickinson, and others, Chicana writers have been unable to establish such a tradition, particularly given that it has been difficult to find early writers at all. Some writers may turn to the Latin American tradition and appropriate such women-identified women as Sor Juana Inés de la Cruz. In "Juana Inés," Alicia Gaspar de Alba has written about Sor Juana, incorporating her into the lesbian tradition (1). Others point to Gabriela Mistral, who in fact remains encoded as a lesbian writer even today. Nevertheless, it has been almost impossible for Chicana lesbian writers to refer to the past to find a tradition with which they can identify, although it may be noted that in the oral tradition we find "hints" of women-identified women. Chicana lesbians must look to their contemporaries for support in this field.

Notwithstanding the difficulties they have encountered, Chicana writers within this realm have contributed to what Zimmerman sees as an important struggle to eliminate the stigma historically attached to lesbianism by associating lesbianism with positive and desirable attributes, and diverting women's attention away from male values (120). Barbara Smith, writing about Black lesbians, states that positive and realistic portrayals of Black lesbians are needed, although "by positive I do not mean characters without problems, contradictions, or flaws, mere uplift literature for Lesbians, but instead, writing that is sufficiently sensitive and complex, which places Black Lesbian experience and struggle squarely within the realm of recognizable human experience and concerns" (58). Certainly this desire for authentic lesbian images is shared by Chicana lesbian writers also.

Among lesbian topographies, lesbians are creating new myths for themselves, such as Monica Palacios's reinvention of La Llorona in "La Llorona Loca" (see chapter 3) and Anzaldúa's creation of a lesbian Chicana mythos in "La historia de una marimacho." In "La historia," Anzaldúa enters into the timeless, mythic world of archetypes when she creates the romance of two women in some mythic/historic time in Mexico. These women have no names, but their physical descriptions are clear. One is "chaparrita" (short) with "manos delgaditas, esquisitas" (thin, exquisite hands) (64). The narrator, on the other hand, is strong, forceful, and rides a horse well. She declares, "A mí no me manda nadie" (No one tells me what to do) (66). The narrator wants to marry her true love, but the girl's father refuses, so the two women take their lives into their own hands: they run away and make a life for themselves. After several years, the girl's father catches up with them and is beating his daughter when the narrator returns home. She forces him to stop, cutting off the fingers of his hand and one of his ears as a punishment. The story ends with the father changing his ways and helping the women (after he recovers). The narration is not only a romance, after the tragic romances of Spain, it is also a corrido of life and vengeance. Written in Spanish, Anzaldúa uses colloquial language to situate the tale in a mythic time. That the women win is certainly an event, since women hardly ever have the upper hand in these tales.

The lesbian articulation of the female body in Chicana literature has been surprisingly culture specific. The graphic and symbolic description of female genitalia as chiles, flowers, and the Southwestern landscape is poetic and shocking at the same time. Angela Arellano, for example, compares the genitalia to "red rock canyon walls" that crumble

like

biscochitos dunked in hot creamy coffee

(62)

The sense, smell, and taste of the female body has never been so lovingly described in male literature. In addition, the association of the female body with Chicano foods — enchiladas, salsas, and chiles — serves further to inscribe a Chicana lesbian identity.

The cultural critique by lesbian writers is not only a resistant text but also visionary since it exemplifies disobedience, a metaphor for disruption of the social construction, and points towards social change. As Kaminsky has stated, "a feminist textual theory cannot simply move from text to world; it must be able to account for the levels of mediation between literary and social domains, in particular the diverse and often contradictory ideological and cultural forces which shape processes of literary production and reception. In other words, a feminist literary theory is dependent upon a feminist social theory, which can relate texts to changing ideological structures as they affect women as social subjects" (8). Zimmerman would concur, saying that lesbian criticism provides "cutting edge" and radical energy, a positive way of viewing the world (198). For Zimmerman, critics who maintain a "consciously chosen position on the boundaries (and not one imposed by a hostile society) help keep lesbian and feminist criticism radical and provocative" (198). This is intimately connected to Anzaldúa's vision of Mestiza consciousness in which she emphasizes that those positioned on the boundaries are often able to have a clearer vision of their surroundings (*Borderlands,* 77–91).

From the Cocina to the Cantina: Transgressing Spaces

In the chapter 6 discussion of Chicana writers as cooks, I examined the importance of kitchens to Chicanas' self-image and creativity. The cocina is generally acknowledged to be a place of and for women. It is a haven in the house, a separate space where nourishment and creativity take place. However, there is an acknowledged opposite space, that of the street, the cantina, and the highway, which signals a different kind of freedom, the invasion of public space. As María Herrera-Sobek has pointed out in an extremely perceptive article on the work of Evangelina Vigil and Beverly Silva, "The Street Scene: Metamorphic Strategies," the street scene "implies a complex of images associated with the public domain of the city: bars, street language, street people, street happenings, the pachuco, the bato loco, the bag lady, winos and so forth." For Herrera-Sobek, the street serves as a metaphor for Chicanas' "going-out-into the world." She sees the street as serving as a bridge between the house (and women's roles as mother, ama de casa, and wife) and the cantina, expressive of the male domain.

In regard to the cantina, previously only "bad girls" inhabited them, yet Vigil's lyric speaker seizes the cantina space for all women, and after a while, the customers get used to her presence. As Herrera-Sobek points out, Vigil not only inhabits the cantina with her physical presence (the cover of *Thirty an' Seen a Lot* shows Vigil beckoning toward the bar and a sign saying "Ladies Welcome"), but she also uses violent and graphic male expletives as a contestation to that use of "male" language in the bar. The invasion of the male domain takes place both physically and linguistically. Herrera-Sobek also analyzes Silva's intrusion into this male space in *The Second St. Poems.*

For other Chicana writers, public spaces of all sorts signal both their having arrived at a confident sense of themselves and of being able to manage public spaces and to maneuver in them. Just as Lorna Dee Cervantes understands that she is the "Translator of Foreign Mail" (*Emplumada,* 11; Rebolledo and Rivero, 116) between the public and private worlds of her grandmother, and between the female space and traditional patriarchal culture, Vigil and Silva, among others, understand that they need to seize both the public space and public language. From those first women seizing spaces, the 1990s bring women with a sure sense of who they are: "black lace bra kind of woman," says Cisneros.

> Ruin your clothes, she will.
> Get you home way after hours.
> Drive her '59 seventy-five on 35
> like there is no tomorrow.
>
> (*Loose Woman,* 78)

It is no longer a single woman venturing out on her own, it is "Las Girl-friends" who have been so bad they are no longer welcome in the bars.

> Girlfriend, I believe in Gandhi.
> But some nights nothing says it
> quite precise like a Lone Star
> cracked on someone's head.

Last week in this same bar,
kicked a cowboy in the butt
who made a grab for Terry's ass.
How do I explain, it was all
of Texas I was kicking,
and all our asses on the line.

      (*Loose Woman*, 105)

But even though they are declared "wicked mean," the response reveals a sense of high adventure.

Naw, not mean. Shit
Been to hell and back again.
Girl, me too.

      (106)

    In addition to seizing the cantina, other Chicana writers write about the freedom of seizing the highways, moving outside of their enclosed and limited areas. Beyond that, we have the world of the journey: to Mexico, to Europe, to the Far East. These experiences are not only transformations but also amplifications of sexual experiences. Cisneros, Ana Castillo, and Er-linda Gonzales-Berry have all written about sexual experiences as part of their journeys abroad. As Herrera-Sobek acknowledges, "these literary texts present a dynamic vision of the Chicana's struggle into a meaningful, restraint-free dialectic with the world at large. Both the Vigil and the Silva texts [the same could be said of the others] can be perceived as manifestos or declarations of independence: they forcefully point to the complete liberation of the Chicana when she will be free from the outside imposed bondage of gender" ("The Street Scene," n.p.).

And Finally the Good Girls:
Do Chicana Writers Want To Be Like Them?

    The cultural expectation for women, as stated repeatedly here, is the ideological model of being good: selfless, nourishing, steady, circumspect, respectful, and passive. The role models are the Virgin Mary, the mother, the teacher, the nurse. These are all ideals that we admire and respect in Chicana culture, but for most women they are not only limiting, they are impossible. The idea that one can be a mother and a virgin at the same time sends completely contradictory messages to Catholic Chicanas. The notion of self-denial (in favor of one's children, husband, and parents), while perhaps noteworthy, is not realistic. There are, however, many such female images in Chicano literature (especially men's romantic, nostalgic views of mother, such as in "La jefita" by José Montoya).

Contemporary Chicana writers, however, explicitly reject the limitations that these ideological (and patriarchal) standards have placed on women. Cisneros, for example, paints the pictures in *Mango Street* of all the women who spent their lives staring out the window, and waiting, waiting for something to happen. Like frozen fairy-tale heroines, they await the kiss, the arrival of the prince, to wake them up. As Esperanza says, speaking of her grandmother, "She looked out the window all her life, the way so many women sit their sadness on an elbow. I wonder if she made the best with what she got or was she sorry because she couldn't be all the things she wanted to be. Esperanza. I have inherited her name, but I don't want to inherit her place by the window" (12; Rebolledo and Rivero, 79). As Chicana writers try to understand the lives of their female forbearers and trace their accomplishments and their abilities, they admire their ability to survive and even flourish under cultural and social constraints, but they don't want to be like them.

Perhaps an accommodation to being "good girls" can be seen in the short story "Federico y Elfiria" by Carmen Tafolla. The story is told from the point of view of Federico, a young man imbued with all the stereotypes of women, especially the sexual ones. For him, a woman is virgin or puta, and his wife is a good girl. After the birth of their first child, Elfiria comes to him "real suavecito" and says,

> . . . Hace mucho tiempo. I'm healed now, tú sabes, down there . . ." Federico was touched, but muy caballero, comforts, "That's O.K. honey. I don't need it. I can wait some more." The dam burst, and Elfiria, tired and glad the baby was finally asleep, burst too. "But I need it! I can't wait some more!"
>
> Federico was stunned. " . . . But . . . you . . . hombre! I always thought you were . . .," he gulped and said it directo, " . . . a good girl." (111; Rebolledo and Rivero, 29)

Thus even sexuality within marriage is acceptable only if initiated by the male. Any assertion of desire on the part of the female would have her crossing the line of what was proper behavior. Yet Elfiria addresses the problem directly, saying, "Of course I'm a good girl. I'm more than that!"

As Federico thinks about the situation, he accepts the idea of someone "being a good girl plus more" (111; Rebolledo and Rivero, 29). And yet this is all within the framework of being a mother and a wife.

If Chicanas can gain acceptance of being complex figures, of being good girls and more, they might be satisfied. They could be portrayed in the work of both women and men in a realistic way as women of infinite divisions, or infinite dimensions. At the same time, the figure of the wicked woman, the troublemaker, the woman who speaks and writes, is a very appealing one. It is an image that Chicana writers are not only willing to accept and to integrate, but one that they enthusiastically and passionately embrace.

Epilogue

What I have tried to do in this book is to situate Chicana writers and their writings within a social, cultural, and historical context. In this way I have visualized Chicana texts as a continuum of creative and social impetus. From the early days in the oral tradition, women told stories and represented their lives. They were always the subjects of their own discourse, and there was cognizance of that. If women's stories were marginal to mainstream culture, however that may be defined (patriarchal, Anglo, American), they were not marginal nor silenced in their own. Women imprinted themselves, their lives, and their representation in their own unique forms of art: embroidery, dress, the dressing of saints, their homes, their gardens, food preparation and serving, ritual, sayings, oral stories, "estorias," and finally, their writings. Thus the image of women singing, painting, and embroidering in the snow is central to this phenomenon. There have always been strong women who have survived and even thrived in hostile environments, just as these women have been able to represent themselves in ways that live beyond the life span of an individual person.

I have also tried to show how Chicana writers have struggled to become the subjects of their own discourse, how they have created not only a dialogue of resistance to the dominant culture in multiple subversive ways, but also a dialogue of affirmation that sees the positive sides of self, family, culture, and community. In spite of the difficulties we are faced with every day in terms of finding the time and space in which to write, in spite of the painful wounding that permeates our literature, Chicanas have been able to articulate their subjectivities and their subsequent healings. All Chicana writing is political because we are surrounded by politics, ideology, and gender inequities. What is remarkable is that Chicana writers, even the early ones, have been acutely aware of this and have grappled with it in

.1ave dialogued, they have subverted, they have resisted, .1 in Spanish, they have invented and re-created. And al-ιear knowledge of what they were doing.

emonstrated how Chicanas have bonded with and looked to .1 for role models and heroines. These heroines may be family .r friends, or they might be the traditional female icons of Chi-cano are: the Virgin of Guadalupe, Coatlicue, La Llorona, La Ma-linche, Sor Juana Inés de la Cruz. The writers have not been afraid to recast these images in ways that are more useful to them; they have incorporated them into contemporary life, dressing them in karate suits, making them talk-show hostesses, making them active and wise. In their struggles to represent, they have evolved other ways of knowing and of authority. The courage and creativity of these writers are exemplary for all of us.

Chicana writers have struggled with the dilemma of the relationship between individual and collective representation, and they have been able, because of their consciousness of gender as well as identity politics, to strike a balance between the two. It seems to me that with every individual repre-sentation, with every individual voice, we see the collective that formed it, the collective that shaped it and whose roots permeate its very heart. Thus one woman can sing, but she is always conscious of her echoes, the re-verberations that play off the multiple voices. As they have nurtured and named themselves individually, so have they inscribed themselves into the collectivity. And it is from multiple voices and multiple perspectives that Chicana writers find themselves singing in the now-melting snow.

Chicana writers, in their desire to represent their totality, have thrown off the taboos of the past and have written their sexuality, written their bodies. These liberating texts engage in dialogue with each other as Chi-canas strive to represent who they are in all of their aspects and posi-tions. Liberating themselves from the teachings of the church, from Anglo-Victorianism, from mothers, and from lovers, the celebration of the body in all its natural functions allows for a fruition of self and creativity.

A clear message from Chicana writers is that we must learn to accept ourselves as we are: our history, our culture, our positive and negative aspects. It is only as we learn to be whole that we can also become free. We must recognize the underworld and its power if we are to understand and become all that we are. Certainly these welcome insights will expand as Chicana writers continue the exploration of their bodies, their conscious-ness, their history, and their culture.

As more and more Chicanas become empowered to write, I believe there will be an expansion of what we have already seen. In the next few years, several books will be published that continue to examine the growing-up period of Chicanas. *Canícula: Snapshots of a Girlhood on La Frontera* by Norma Cantú, and Gloria López-Stafford's *A Place in El Paso* are two such books that will contribute to our growing understanding of how social and cultural factors influence young women. In *Canícula,* Cantú explores the social significance of moments in her life caught by photographs. Her exploration involves the analysis of such things as the dress she is wearing, who made it and why, the interweaving of relationships of various members of her family, how wars in faraway places impacted her community, and other moments of import in the life of a young Chicana. This creative work allows us to analyze the greater society and how Chicanos interface with it. And there will be an outpouring of autobiographies as Chicana writers reach an age of maturity that allows them to reflect on their lives. These autobiographies will continue to be testimonios about politics and social events as well as of individual lives.

Previously unknown or forgotten texts will be discovered, printed, or reprinted. Thus they will begin to more fully influence our thinking about how, historically, women impacted the community. So, too, as more and more oral histories are collected, these stories of ordinary (and extraordinary) women will show how Chicanas have interacted with the world at large.

As more Chicanas begin to write, we will see an increase in fiction, novels, and short stories. So, too, will we see an increase in the essay form. The essay has always seemed a very male way of writing, but encouraged by books such as Pat Mora's *Nepantla,* Gloria Anzaldúa's *Borderlands,* and Ana Castillo's *Massacre of the Dreamers,* more and more Chicanas will begin to explore that form. However, the form will become transformed, as it has been in the texts mentioned, as various genres are blended. Thus not only the content but also the structure of Chicano literature will be changed.

I also expect to see many more children's books written by Chicanas. There has been a realization for some time now that we need to provide positive images in literature so that young Chicanas/os can see themselves represented from an early age, and young non-Chicanos/as can also see Chicanas/os represented in a positive way. Many Chicana writers, such as Mora and Mary Helen Ponce, are engaged in this transformative work.

Another positive development has been the coming together of Chicana artists and writers in a common struggle, and there will be increasing collaboration between the two groups as they represent their perspectives on culture and society. At two recent conferences, "Las mujeres hablan" in Lubbock, Texas, and "Communities in Dialogue" at Irvine, California, writers and artists met and discussed common concerns. Evident also is the collaboration of writers and artists in the publishing of books: *Paletitas de guayaba* (Erlinda Gonzales-Berry and Soledad Marjon), *From the Cables of Genocide* (Lorna Dee Cervantes and Diana Rodríguez Cárdenas), *My Wicked, Wicked Ways* (Sandra Cisneros and Terry Ybáñez), *Las mujeres hablan* (Rebolledo, Gonzales-Berry, Teresa Márquez, and Tina Fuentes), and even *Infinite Divisions* (Rebolledo, Eliana Rivero, and Celia Alvarez).

In this book, it has been impossible to cover every aspect of Chicana literature. I leave it for other critics to expand and explore the many other facets of language and writing that Chicanas journey into. And perhaps, just perhaps, Chicana literature and criticism will take its rightful place in American literature.

What I have done in this book is just begin to suggest some of the myriad ways and strategies that Chicana writers have used to explore their world, to find their sexual and textual self-fulfillment. Chicana writers and artists are engaged in an empowering process that cuts through the silences and the erasures — through the snow. They have affirmed their identities as writers and artists, found their voices, and represented their multiple subjectivities in words — words that find an echo in all of us.

Notes

Chapter 1

1. The Federal Writers' Project was part of Franklin D. Roosevelt's New Deal program in the 1930s, and guides were assembled to the forty-eight states. The Arizona Federal Writers' Project will be referred to as AZFWP and identified by interviewee and collector. The project's papers are part of the State History Archives in Phoenix. The New Mexico Federal Writers' Project will be referred to as NMFWP. Following Marta Weigle's "Readers Guide" in *New Mexicans in Cameo and Camera,* each NMFWP item is identified, if possible, by title, informant, collector, date of writing, and the location of the document at the History Library of the Museum of New Mexico in Santa Fe.

2. There is, of course, written material that chronicles the lives of early pioneer women, including biographies of Spanish-speaking women from well-to-do families who became civic leaders. Evelyn M. Carrington, who edited *Women in Early Texas* (1975), is one such source. The education and lives of these well-known women were very different from the lives chronicled in other oral histories: "From an early age the children were carefully trained: in the meticulous practice of their Catholic faith, in love, respect and implicit obedience to their parents: in the knowledge of, and strict adherence to family background and traditions; and in the elegant courtesy and social graces of the times" (Parker, in Carrington, 51). These girls were carefully sheltered, never leaving the home without a chaperone or older companion, but some were well educated because "women could own, inherit, administer, buy and sell property" (51).

3. Romelia Gómez's interviews are particularly interesting for their attention to detail. When Hispanic women interviewed older Hispanic women, the interviewees seem to have been more forthcoming about their lives.

4. The cuento/"estoria" tradition is not just a female tradition but is also incorporated into the writings of male authors such as Sabine Ulibarrí, Rudolfo Anaya, and Miguel Méndez.

5. Marta Weigle's *New Mexicans in Cameo and Camera* is extremely useful in

documenting the lives of the collectors of the NMFWP as well as those of the people interviewed.

6. NMFWP, collected by Bright Lynn, 29 Apr. 1939, 5-5-7 #4.

7. This is the argument expressed in Rosan A. Jordan and Susan J. Kalcik's *Women's Folklore, Women's Culture* in talking about Mexican American women's tales about La Llorona and the vaginal serpent. In addition to questioning women's roles, the tales may also express sexual anxiety, fears of sexual vulnerability and pregnancy, and rejection of the traditional Mexican American image of women as selfless and nurturing.

8. This tradition of strong female figures who portray positive as well as negative aspects of the female archetype has provided a rich mother lode for many contemporary Chicana writers, in particular Pat Mora and Carmen Tafolla. See chapters 3 and 4.

9. NMFWP, 5-5-49 #45.

10. NMFWP, collected by Lou Sage Batchen, 17 Sept. 1938.

11. NMFWP, collected by Simon Tejada, 3 Jan. 1939, 5-5-29 #2.

12. For an in-depth analysis of these novels, see Rosaura Sánchez and Beatrice Pita's introduction to *The Squatter and the Don*.

13. Some Chicano critics argue that writers such as Niggli who were not of Mexican parentage do not fall within the purview of Chicano writers. They acknowledge these writers' interest in things Mexican and Mexican American, and agree that through context and perspective they may adhere to Chicano values, but because the writers are not Chicanos, some critics believe their work should fall within a category called "Chicanesque." Nevertheless, it could be argued that Niggli was born in Mexico and had a lifelong interest in things Mexican, and her subsequent studies and interests allowed her to develop a perceptive understanding of Mexican American relations.

Chapter 2

1. In recent years, several more books by New Mexican women have added to our knowledge of oral traditions. Moreover, they follow many of the structures of the writers mentioned here. *Enchanted Temples of Taos* by Dora Ortiz Vásquez is an account of the history and people of Taos as told by her mother and by a Navajo Indian woman simply called "Rosario." Of interest here is the author's intent to capture truthfully the nature of these cuentos. "Rosario always spoke a broken Spanish and when she told stories about Luardo, a character she hated, she used her worst Spanish to tell them. When she told the Padre's stories (Father Antonio José Martínez) she called him Tata-Padre, then she used her best Spanish. It was all very interesting to me. If I could only write them as told! I think this has been my discouragement first in translation and my way of writing might lack or change some of their deep feelings. I wrote those stories for my children in the late 30's and put them away" (xi).

Josephine M. Córdova's *No lloro pero me acuerdo* was published in 1976. Córdova was a school teacher in Taos for many years, and her book is a collection of local color, literature, customs, and personal memoirs. She proudly points out that she has used no references in her book and that "all the material presented here has come to me by tradition" (6).

A Beautiful, Cruel Country, written by an Arizona woman, Eva Wilbur-Cruce, describes her life growing up with the Pima Indians on a large ranch in Arizona and also sheds much light on life in the early Arizona territory.

2. There is, in addition, the theoretical issue of which texts should be included in the literary canon. Whereas all explorers, conquistadores, priests, military officers, etc. (Cabeza de Vaca, Marcos de Niza, Juan de Oñate et al.) are touted as the Aztlanense literature pioneers with their nonliterary texts, the distinctly female nonfictional texts are dismissed. As we think about women's creativity, we must include oral forms such as songs, recipes, and sayings as well as new popular culture such as romances and fotonovelas. Women used all of these forms of expression, which are also being incorporated into Chicana writing today.

3. Although she was sympathetic to the Hispano loss of land to Anglos, there is no corresponding sympathy about the Indian plight after the Spanish conquest. This is true also of the other writers (such as Otero-Warren) who viewed the Indians before the conquest (and for some time after) as savages.

Chapter 3

1. For a fuller description of religious hierarchy as patriarchy, see W. A. Visser't Hooft's *The Fatherhood of God in an Age of Emancipation.*

2. Stories concerning the Virgin's true power were told when an earlier version of this chapter was read at a conference and many of the Chicanas attending protested that the Virgin was much more complex and powerful than the way in which she had been presented. Nevertheless, some of them admitted that she was linked with many mixed messages and that she was often problematic for them.

3. Through the years, the NFWA shouted, "¡Que siga la huelga! ¡Que viva la causa! ¡Que viva la Virgen de Guadalupe!" (Let the strike continue! Long live the cause! Long live the Virgin of Guadalupe!) As a matter of fact, what many consider the birth of La Causa took place on 16 Sept. 1965 in Guadalupe Church Hall in Delano, California, when the NFWA voted to join the Filipino grape pickers who were on strike. Later they called their march to Sacramento a "pilgrimage," and the Plan of Delano says, "At the head of the Pilgrimage we carry La Virgen de Guadalupe because she is ours, all ours, patroness of the Mexican People." For the men, Guadalupe was a comfortable symbol, the mother who could save and protect them.

4. See also a short story by Mary Helen Ponce, "El mes de mayo" (*Hoyt Street,* 162–68), which deals with this same issue.

5. See also Herrera-Sobek's study on archetypal heroines in the corrido, *The Mexican Corrido: A Feminist Analysis,* which examines the mythology of women in these popular songs.

6. For short, informative accounts in English of Sor Juana's life and works and the controversy still surrounding her figure, see Dorothy Sehons, "Some Obscure Points in the Life of Sor Juana Inés de la Cruz," and Electa Arenal, "Comment on Paz's 'Juana Ramírez.'"

7. For more information on La Malinche, see Adelaida R. Del Castillo, "Malintzín Tenepal: A Preliminary Look into a New Perspective"; Rachel Phillips, "Marina / Malinche: Masks and Shadows"; and Sandra Messinger Cypress, *La Malinche in Mexican Literature: From History to Myth.*

8. As Norma Alarcón states, "Moraga, while recognizing the problem of any questioning of patriarchal tradition being labeled Malinchismo feels that she, as a Lesbian, must take control of her own sexual identity and destiny . . . for Moraga lesbianism in our culture is the ultimate trope for the pursuit of new gender identities, for anything that smacks of differences in the face of traditional gender values. Rather than try to revise the myths of Malintzín, Moraga accepts them and in a sense labels them male myths whose purpose is to exercise social control over women. To escape the double bind, Moraga has no choice but to declare that, indeed, she comes 'from a long line of vendidas'" ("Traddutora, Traditora," 81).

9. Norma Alarcón, in her excellent article on Malintzín, argues that Corpi's use of her Spanish name Marina "inserts Marina into Biblical discourses rather than prepatriarchal ones" ("Traddutora, Traditora," 79). I would argue that this only occurs on a superficial level with the pre-Columbian text paralleling and undermining the biblical one. Alarcón also disputes Marta Sánchez's analysis of these poems. Sánchez sees "Corpi's cultural paradigm" as a passive Marina. And while Sánchez sees the sacrificed Marina as left behind waiting to "reinscribe herself," Alarcón sees Sánchez as having "in part" missed "the point and trajectory of the poems which end with the promise of a recreated female self who will shed the ancestral burdens that Marina symbolically and experientially may represent for today's Chicanas" ("Traddutora, Traditora," 79).

10. Although Marta Sánchez's extensive analysis of the poem (*Chicana Poetry,* 183–95) is suggestive, some aspects of my interpretation vary greatly from hers.

11. Other women, as already noted, also have dialogues with the "official" version. Rosario Castellanos, in particular, speaks in the voice of La Malinche presenting a personal version of her history in *Poesía no eres tú.*

Chapter 4

1. See chapter 1 for a discussion of the oral stories on curanderas and brujas collected by the WPA Federal Writers' Project.

2. Of course, Coatlicue is also represented by the head of a bird, and thus

the pairing with snake images symbolizes her duality—of sky and earth, upper and lower.

Chapter 5

1. In this article, Chabrám (formerly Chabrám-Dernersesian) says that "La Loca" was written by Marta Cotera. In a recent conversation with Cotera, she stated that she did not write the poem, although she wished she had.

Chapter 6

1. That a recipe is a very loose construction can be illustrated by Susan J. Leonardi, who in giving a recipe for summer pasta begins by giving a long list of ingredients for the dish but finishes by saying, "You can leave anything out of this recipe except the pasta and the olive oil" (340).

Chapter 7

1. One can also think of the universal metaphor that only men can write in the snow, as in the old adage not to eat yellow snow. This metaphor is also linked to the idea of the difficulty of writing for women because they do not possess the proper equipment—i.e., phallocentric power—to do so.

2. I am indebted to Elizabeth J. Ordóñez's article "Body, Spirit, and the Text: Alma Villanueva's *Life Span*," in which I first encountered Villanueva's poem "Siren," and for Ordóñez's elucidating article and its cultural context.

3. The use of caló and bilingual texts has been the object of much study in linguistics and literature. It has often been a distinguishing feature in many Chicana/o texts. Some scholars have studied individual authors in order to determine why particular words are used in Spanish and others in English. Since this field of sociolinguistics is so extensive, I will not elaborate further since I am not a linguistic expert. However, I do mention it as it is important in the cultural positioning of specific authors. For more information, see: Otto Santa Ana, *Toward a More Adequate Characterization of the Chicano Language Setting*; Federico Peñalosa, *Chicano Sociolinguistics: A Brief Introduction*; and Rosaura Sánchez, *Chicano Discourse: Sociohistoric Perspectives*.

Chapter 8

1. Other Chicanas who, at least at the beginning, published in Spanish are Lucha Corpi and Angela de Hoyos. Nonetheless, in their latest writings, they have written almost exclusively in English (Corpi) or bilingually; that is, with the translation of the Spanish published simultaneously on the facing page (de Hoyos). These are the decisions made in order to find a publisher and a reading public.

Chapter 9

   1. There are a few exceptions: a poem written by Macuilxóchitl Cinco Flor; an anonymous cradle song written by a young Aztec girl; and speeches of the elders, ritualistic discourses proclaimed at times of importance in a girl's life. Even these, however, were re-narrated or recorded by men. See Miguel León-Portilla, *Trece poetas del mundo azteca*, 155–69, and Rebolledo, "Comience la danza."

   2. For an intriguing analysis of the bad woman in Sandra Cisneros's "La Fabulosa: A Texas Operetta", see Laura Gutiérrez Spencer's "Fairy Tales and Opera: The Fate of the Heroine in the Work of Sandra Cisneros." Gutiérrez Spencer sees "La Fabulosa" as a transformation of the opera *Carmen* in which the bad woman is allowed to "live and thrive."

Bibliography

Abrego, Carmen. "A Conversation." In Trujillo, 63.

Agustini, Delmira. *Poesías*. Montevideo: Claudio García y Cia., 1940.

Alarcón, Norma. "Making 'Familia' from Scratch: Split Subjectivities in the Work of Helena María Viramontes and Cherríe Moraga." *The Americas Review* 15 (fall–winter 1987): 147–59.

———. "The Sardonic Powers of the Erotic in the Work of Ana Castillo." In Horno-Delgado et al., 94–107.

———. "The Theoretical Subject(s) in *This Bridge Called My Back* and Anglo-American Feminism." In Anzaldúa, *Making Face,* 356–69.

———. "Traddutora, Traditora: A Paradigmatic Figure of Chicana Feminism." *Cultural Critique* (fall 1989): 57–87.

———. "What Kind of Lover Have You Made Me Mother?" In *Women of Color: Perspectives on Feminism and Identity,* edited by Audrey T. McCluskey, Occasional Papers Series 1:1. Bloomington: Women's Studies Program, Indiana University, 1985.

Alarcón, Norma, Ana Castillo, and Cherríe Moraga, eds. *Third Woman: The Sexuality of Latinas.* Berkeley, Calif.: Third Woman Press, 1989.

Alarcón, Norma, Rafaela Castro, Emma Pérez, Beatriz Pesquera, Adaljiza Sosa Riddell, and Patricia Zavella. *Chicana Critical Issues.* Berkeley, Calif.: Third Woman Press, 1993.

Alvarez, M. "La enchilada." In Trujillo, 71–72.

Anaya, Rudolfo. *Bless Me, Ultima.* Berkeley, Calif.: Tonatiuh-Quinto Sol International Inc., 1972.

———. *The Legend of La Llorona.* Berkeley, Calif.: Tonatiuh-Quinto Sol International Inc., 1984.

Anton, Ferdinand. *Women in Pre-Columbian America.* New York: Abner Schram, 1973.

Anzaldúa, Gloria. "La historia de una marimacho." In Alarcón, Castillo, and Moraga, 64–68.

———. *Borderlands/La frontera: The New Mestiza.* San Francisco: Spinsters/Aunt Lute, 1987.

———, ed. *Making Face, Making Soul: Haciendo caras.* San Francisco: Aunt Lute, 1990.

Arellano, Angela. "Untitled." In Trujillo, 62.

Arellano, Anselmo F. *Los pobladores nuevo mexicanos y su poesía, 1889–1950.* Albuquerque, N.M.: Pajarito Press, 1976.

Arellano, Esteban. "La poesía nuevo mexicana: Su desarrollo y su transición durante los fines del siglo diez y nueve." Unpublished paper (1985).

Arellano, Margarita. "Día de campo." *El Nuevo Mexicano* (June 1932).

Arenal, Electra. "Comment on Paz's 'Juana Ramírez.'" *Signs* (spring 1980): 552–55.

Arizona Federal Writers' Project (AZFWP). State History Archives, Phoenix, Ariz. "Martina Diaz," "Isabel Hernández," "Apolonia Mendoza," "Lola Romero," "Casimira Valenzuela": collected by Romelia Gómez.

Bachelard, Gaston. *The Poetics of Space.* Translated by María Jolas. Boston: Beacon Press, 1969.

Baker, Houston A., Jr. *Three American Literatures.* New York: Modern Language Association, 1982.

Bchar, Ruth. "Sexual Witchcraft, Colonialism, and Women's Powers: Views From the Mexican Inquisition." In Lavrin, 197–226.

Beltrán, Carmen Celia. "La cuna vacía." Unpublished play.

———. *Remanso lírico.* Published privately, 1983.

Beverly, John. "The Margin at the Center: On Testimonio (Testimonial Narrative)." In Smith and Watson, 91–114.

Blanco, Iris. "La mujer en los albores de la conquista de México." *Aztlán II* 11 (1980): 251–63.

Bornstein-Somoza, Miriam. *Bajo cubierta.* Tucson, Ariz.: Scorpion Press, 1976.

———. *Siete poetas.* Tucson, Ariz.: Scorpion Press, 1978.

Brinson-Piñeda, Barbara. "Poets on Poetry: Dialogue with Lucha Corpi." *Prisma* (spring 1979): 4–9. (*See also* Curiel, Barbara Brinson)

Broyles Gonzáles, Yolanda. "Toward a Re-Vision of Chicano Theater History: The Women of El Teatro Campesino." In Hart, 209–38.

———. "Women in El Teatro Campesino: '¿Apoco estaba molacha la Virgen de Guadalupe?'" In Córdova et al., 162–87.

Bruce-Novoa, Juan. *Chicano Poetry: A Response to Chaos.* Austin: University of Texas Press, 1982.

———. *Retrospace: Collected Essays on Chicano Literature.* Houston, Tex.: Arte Público Press, 1990.

Burland, C. A. *The Gods of Mexico.* New York: G. P. Putnam's Sons, 1967.

Cabeza de Baca, Fabiola. *See* Gilbert, Fabiola Cabeza de Baca.

Calderón, Hector. "At the Crossroads of History, On the Borders of Change: Chicano Literary Studies Past, Present and Future." *Left Politics and the Literary Profession,* edited by Leonard J. Davis and M. Bella Mirabella, 211–35. New York: Columbia University Press, 1990.

Calderón, Hector, and José David Saldívar, eds. *Criticism in the Borderlands: Studies in Chicano Literature, Culture, and Ideology.* Durham, N.C.: Duke University Press, 1991.

Calvillo-Craig, Lorenza. "Soy hija de mis padres." *El Grito* 7 (1973): 1.

Camarillo, Lydia. "Mi reflejo." *La palabra* 2 (1980): 2.

Candelaria, Cordelia. *Ojo de la cueva/Cave springs.* Colorado Springs: Maize Press, 1984.

———. "The 'Wild Zone' Thesis as Gloss in Chicana Literary Study." In Alarcón et al., *Chicana Critical Issues,* 21–31.

———, ed. *The Wild Zone: Essays in Multi-Ethnic Literature.* Boulder: University of Colorado, 1989.

Cantares mexicanos: Songs of the Aztecs. Translation, introduction, and commentary by John Bierhorst. Palo Alto, Calif.: Stanford University Press, 1985.

Cantú, Norma. *Canícula: Snapshots of a Girlhood on La Frontera.* Albuquerque: University of New Mexico Press, forthcoming (1995).

Carrington, Evelyn M. *Women in Early Texas.* Austin, Tex.: Jenkins Publishing Co., 1975.

Castañeda, Antonia. "Memory, Language, and Voice of Mestiza Women on the Northern Frontier: Historical Documents as Literary Text." In Gutiérrez and Padilla, 265–77.

———. "The Political Economy of Nineteenth Century Stereotypes of Californianas." In Del Castillo, 213–36.

Castellanos, Rosario. *Album de familia.* 2d ed. México: J. Mortiz, 1975.

———. *Poesía no eres tú.* México: Fondo de Cultura Económica, 1972.

Castillo, Ana. *Massacre of the Dreamers.* Albuquerque: University of New Mexico Press, 1994.

———. *The Mixquiahuala Letters.* Binghamton, N.Y.: Bilingual Press, 1986.

———. *My Father Was a Toltec.* Novato, Calif.: West End Press, 1988.

———. *Sapogonia.* Tempe, Ariz.: Bilingual Press, 1989.

———. *So Far From God.* New York: W. W. Norton and Co., 1993.

———. *Women Are Not Roses.* Houston, Tex.: Arte Público Press, 1984.

Castillo, Debra A. *Talking Back: Toward a Latin American Feminist Literary Criticism.* Ithaca, N.Y.: Cornell University Press, 1992.

Castro, Carrie. "The Night Filled With Faint Cries." In Lomelí, 22–23.

Cather, Willa. *Death Comes to the Archbishop.* New York: Alfred A. Knopf, 1927.

Cervantes, Lorna Dee. "Para un revolucionario." In Fisher, 381–82.

———. *Emplumada.* Pittsburgh, Pa.: University of Pittsburgh Press, 1981.

———. *From the Cables of Genocide: Poems on Love and Hunger.* Houston, Tex.: Arte Público, 1991.

———. "Grandma." *Revista Chicana-Riqueña* 3 (winter 1975): 23.

———. "You Cramp My Style, Baby." *Fuego de Aztlán* 1 (summer 1977): 39.

Chabrám-Dernersesian, Angie. "'I Throw Punches for My Race, but I Don't Want to Be a Man' Writing Us–Chica-nos (Girl, Us) /Chicanas–Into the Movement Script." In *Cultural Studies,* edited by Grossberg, Nelson, and Treichler, 81–95. New York: Routledge, 1992.

Chávez, Denise. "Hecho en Mexico." Unpublished play.

———. *The Last of the Menu Girls.* Houston, Tex.: Arte Público Press, 1986.

———. "Tilt-a-Whirl." Unpublished poem.

Cisneros, Sandra. "Down There." In Alarcón, Castillo, and Moraga, 19–23.

———. *The House on Mango Street.* Houston, Tex.: Arte Público Press, 1983.

———. *Loose Woman.* New York: Prager, 1994.

———. *My Wicked, Wicked Ways.* Berkeley, Calif.: Third Woman Press, 1987. Reprinted, New York: Turtle Bay, 1992.

———. *Woman Hollering Creek and Other Stories.* New York: Random House, 1991.

Cixous, Hélène. "The Laugh of the Medusa." In Marks and de Courtivron, 245–64.

Conn, Joann Wolski. *Women's Spirituality: Resources for Christian Development.* New York: Paulist Press, 1986.

Córdova, Josephine M. *No lloro pero me acuerdo.* Dallas, Tex.: Mockingbird Pub. Co., 1976.

Córdova, Teresa, Norma Cantú, Gilberto Cárdenas, Juan García, and Christine M. Sierra, eds. *Chicana Voices: Intersections of Class, Race, and Gender.* Austin, Tex.: Center for Mexican American Studies, 1986.

Corpi, Lucha. *Delia's Song.* Houston, Tex.: Arte Público Press, 1989.

———. *Eulogy for a Brown Angel.* Houston, Tex.: Arte Público Press, 1992.

———. *Fireflight: Three Latin American Poets.* Oakland, Calif.: Oyez, 1975.

———. *Palabras de mediodía: Noon words.* Berkeley, Calif.: El Fuego de Aztlán Publications, 1980.

———. "Protocolo de verduras" (The Protocol of Vegetables). *Prisma* (spring 1979): 12. Translation by Catherine Rodríguez-Nieto.

———. *Variaciones sobre una tempestad/Variations on a storm.* Berkeley, Calif.: Third Woman Press, 1990.

Cota-Cárdenas, Margarita. "Aay Cucuy . . . !" In Rebolledo, "The Bittersweet Nostalgia of Childhood," 33–34.

———. "The Chicana in the City as Seen in Her Literature." *Frontiers: A Journal of Women Studies* 11 (1991): 13–18.

———. "The Faith of Activists: Barrios, Cities, and the Chicana Feminist Response." *Frontiers: A Journal of Women Studies* 14 (1991): 51–80.

———. "Malinche's Discourse." In Rebolledo and Rivero, 203–7.

———. "Lírica fanática." In Rebolledo and Rivero, 299.

———. "To a Little Blond Girl of Heber, Califas." In Rebolledo, "The Bittersweet Nostalgia of Childhood," 33.

——. *Marchitas de Mayo (Sones pa'l pueblo)*. Austin, Tex.: Relámpago Books Press, 1989.

——. *Noches despertando inConciencias*. Tucson, Ariz.: Scorpion Press, 1977.

——. *Puppet*. Austin, Tex.: Relámpago Books Press, 1985.

——. "Whimpy's Wake." In Rebolledo and Rivero, 132–34.

Crumm, Stella M., ed. *Down the Santa Fe Trail and Into Mexico: The Diary of Susan Shelby Magoffin, 1846–1847*. New Haven, Conn.: Yale University Press, 1926.

Cunningham, Veronica. "ever since." *Capirotada*. Los Angeles: Fronteras, 1976.

Curiel, Barbara Brinson. *Speak To Me From Dreams*. Berkeley, Calif.: Third Woman Press, 1989. (Formerly Brinson-Piñeda)

Del Castillo, Adelaida R. "Malintzín Tenepal: A Preliminary Look Into a New Perspective." In Sánchez and Martínez Cruz, 124–49.

——, ed. *Between Borders: Essays on Mexicana/Chicana History*. Encino, Calif.: Floricanto Press, 1990.

Díaz del Castillo, Bernal. *Conquest of New Spain*. Translated by J. M. Cohen. London: Penguin Books, 1963.

Esquivel, Laura. *Como agua para chocolate*. México: Planeta, 1989.

Fisher, Dexter, ed. *The Third Woman: Minority Women Writers of the United States*. Boston: Houghton Mifflin, 1980.

García, John A., Theresa Córdova, and Juan R. García, eds. *The Chicano Struggle: Analyses of Past and Present Efforts*. Binghamton, N.Y.: Bilingual Press, 1984.

García, Nasario. *Abuelitos: Stories of the Rio Puerco Valley*. Albuquerque: University of New Mexico Press, 1992.

——. *Recuerdos de los viejitos: Tales of the Rio Puerco*. Albuquerque: University of New Mexico Press, 1987.

Garibay K., Angel María. *Historia de la literatura náhuatl*. Mexico: Editorial Porrua, 1953–54.

Gaspar de Alba, Alicia. *Beggar on the Córdoba Bridge* in *Three Times a Woman, Chicana Poetry*. Tempe, Ariz.: Bilingual Review/Press, 1989.

——. "Caldo de pollo." Unpublished poem.

——. "Juana Inés." In Tatum, *New Chicana 1*, 1–15.

——. "Literary Wetback." *The Massachusetts Review* 29 (2): 242–46.

——. *The Mystery of Survival*. Tempe, Ariz.: Bilingual Press, 1993.

——. "The Philosophy of Frijoles." Unpublished poem.

Gilbert, Fabiola Cabeza de Baca. *The Good Life*. Santa Fe: Museum of New Mexico Press, 1982.

——. *Historic Cookery*. 1949. Las Vegas, N.M.: La Galeria de los Artesanos, 1970.

——. *We Fed Them Cactus*. Albuquerque: University of New Mexico Press, 1954. Reprinted with an introduction by Tey Diana Rebolledo, 1994.

Goldman, Anne. "'I Yam What I Yam': Cooking, Culture, and Colonialism." In Smith and Watson, 169–95.

Gómez, Alma, Cherríe Moraga, and Mariana Romo-Carmona, eds. *Cuentos: Stories by Latinas*. New York: Kitchen Table Press, 1983.

Gonzales, Gloria. "There is Nothing." In Rebolledo, Gonzales-Berry, and Márquez, 184.

Gonzales, María Dolores. "María." In Rebolledo, Gonzales-Berry, and Márquez, 186.

Gonzales, Rudolfo. *Yo soy Joaquín (I am Joaquin): An Epic Poem.* New York: Bantam Books, 1972.

Gonzales-Berry, Erlinda. "Carlota Gonzales." In Rebolledo, *Nuestras mujeres,* 35–36.

———. "Malinche Past: Selection from *Paletitas de guayaba.*" In Rebolledo and Rivero, 107–21.

———. *Paletitas de guayaba.* Albuquerque, N.M.: El Norte Publications, 1991.

———. "Rosebud." In Rebolledo, Gonzales-Berry, and Márquez, 27–31.

———. "Searching For a Voice: Ambiguities and Possibilities." Unpublished paper.

———, ed. *Pasó por aquí: Critical Essays on the New Mexican Literary Tradition, 1542–1988.* Albuquerque: University of New Mexico Press, 1989.

Gonzales-Berry, Erlinda, and Tey Diana Rebolledo. "Growing Up Chicano: Tomás Rivera and Sandra Cisneros." In Olivares, *International Studies,* 109–19.

González, Jovita. "America Invades the Border Towns." *Southwest Review* 15 (summer 1930): 469–77.

———. "Folk-lore of the Texas-Mexican Vaquero." *Texas and Southwestern Lore* 6 (1927): 1.

———. "Tales and Songs of the Texas-Mexicans." *Man, Bird, and Beast* 8 (1930): 97.

———. "Among My People." *Southwest Review* 17 (1932): 182–86.

Gubar, Susan. "'The Blank Page' and the Issues of Female Creativity." *Critical Inquiry* 8 (1981): 243–63.

Gutiérrez, Ramón A. "Marriage and Seduction in Colonial New Mexico." In Del Castillo, 448–58.

Gutiérrez, Ramón, and Genaro Padilla, eds. *Recovering the U.S. Hispanic Literary Heritage.* Houston, Tex.: Arte Público Press, 1993.

Gutiérrez Spencer, Laura. "Cactus Flowers and Other Floral Images in Pat Mora." Unpublished paper.

———. "Fairy Tales and Opera: The Fate of the Heroine in the Work of Sandra Cisneros." *Bilingual Review,* forthcoming.

Hammond, George P., and Agapito Rey. *The Rediscovery of New Mexico, 1580–1594.* Albuquerque: University of New Mexico Press, 1987.

Hart, Lynda, ed. *Making a Spectacle: Feminist Essays on Contemporary Women's Theater.* Ann Arbor: University of Michigan Press, 1989.

Hernandez, Inés. "Testimonio de memoria." In Tatum, *New Chicana 2,* 17. (Formerly Hernandez-Tovar)

Hernandez-Tovar, Inés. *Con razón, Corazón.* San Antonio: Caracol, 1977.

———. "Para Teresa." In *Siete poetas,* 31–32.

———. "Untitled." *Caracol* 4 (November 1977): N. pag.

Herrera-Sobek, María. "Canon Formation and Chicano Literature." In Gutiérrez and Padilla, 209–19.

——. *The Mexican Corrido: A Feminist Analysis.* Bloomington: Indiana University Press, 1990.

——. "Mi poesía." *Chasqui,* (Feb.–May 1980): 114.

——. *Naked Moon/Luna desnuda* in *Three Times a Woman, Chicana Poetry.* Tempe, Ariz.: Bilingual Review/Press, 1989.

——. "Poema inédito." In Rebolledo and Rivero, 297.

——. "The Street Scene: Metamorphic Strategies in Two Contemporary Chicana Poets." In Herrera-Sobek and Viramontes, *Chicana (W)rites,* forthcoming.

——, ed. *Beyond Stereotypes: The Critical Analysis of Chicana Literature.* Binghamton, N.Y.: Bilingual Press, 1985.

——. *Reconstructing a Chicano/a Literary Heritage: Hispanic Colonial Literature of the Southwest.* Tucson: University of Arizona Press, 1993.

Herrera-Sobek, María, and Helena María Viramontes, eds. *Chicana Creativity and Criticism: Charting New Frontiers in American Literature. The Americas Review* 15 (1987): 3–4.

——. *Chicana (W)rites: On Word and Film.* Berkeley, Calif.: Third Woman Press, forthcoming.

Horno-Delgado, Asunción, et al., eds. *Breaking Boundaries: Latina Writing and Critical Readings.* Amherst: University of Massachusetts Press, 1989.

Hooft, W. A. Visser't. *The Fatherhood of God in an Age of Emancipation.* Geneva: World Council of Churches, 1982.

Hoyos, Angela de. *Arise, Chicano! and Other Poems.* San Antonio, Tex.: M & A Editions, 1975.

——. *Chicano Poems for the Barrio.* San Antonio, Tex.: M & A Editions, 1975.

——. *Selected Poems/Selecciones.* San Antonio, Tex.: Dezkalzo Press, 1979.

——. *Woman, Woman.* Houston, Tex.: Arte Público Press, 1985.

Irigaray, Luce. "This Sex Which is Not One." In Marks and de Courtivron, 99–106.

Ixtlilxóchitl, Fernando de Alba. *Obras históricas.* México: UNAM, 1975.

Jara, René, and Hernán Vidal. *Testimonio y literatura.* Minneapolis, Minn.: Institute for the Study of Ideologies and Literature, 1986.

Jaramillo, Cleofas. *Cuentos del hogar.* El Campo, Tex.: Citizen Press, 1939.

——. *The Genuine New Mexico Tasty Recipes.* 1939. Rev. ed., Santa Fe, N.M.: Seton Village, 1942.

——. *Romance of a Little Village Girl.* San Antonio, Tex.: Naylor, Co., 1955. Reprinted with an introduction by Genaro Padilla, Albuquerque: University of New Mexico Press, forthcoming (1995).

——. *Shadows of the Past (Sombras del pasado).* Santa Fe, N.M.: Seton Village, 1941.

Jensen, Joan M., and Darlis A. Miller, eds. *New Mexico Women: Intercultural Perspectives.* Albuquerque: University of New Mexico Press, 1986.

Johnson, Elizabeth A. "The Incomprehensibility of God and the Image of God Male and Female." In Conn, 245–60.

Jones, Rosalyn. "Writing the Body." In Rosenfelt, 86–95.

Jordan, Rosan A., and Susan J. Kalcick, eds. *Women's Folklore, Women's Culture.* Philadelphia: University of Pennsylvania Press, 1985.

Juana Inés de la Cruz, sor. *Obras escogidas.* 10th ed., México: Espasa-Calpe Mexicana, 1959.

——. *Respuesta a sor Filotea de la Cruz. A Woman of Genius: The Intellectual Autobiography of Sor Juana Inés de la Cruz.* Translated by Margaret Sayers Peden. Salisbury, Conn.: Lime Rock Press, 1982.

Kaminsky, Amy K. Reading the Body Politic: Feminist Criticism and Latin American Women Writers. Minneapolis, Minn.: University of Minnesota Press, 1993.

Kristeva, Julia. "Creations." In Marks and de Courtivron, 165–66.

La Chrisx. "La Loca de la Raza Cósmica." *Comadre 2* (1978): 5–9.

La Peña, Terri de. *Margins.* Seattle, Wash.: Seal Press, 1992.

Lavrin, Asunción, ed. *Sexuality and Marriage in Colonial Latin America.* Lincoln: University of Nebraska Press, 1989.

Lawhn, Juanita Luna. *"El Regidor* and *La Prensa*: Impediments to Women's Self Definition." In Alarcón, Castillo, and Moraga, 134–42.

——. "Women Publishing in *La Prensa,* 1913–1920." Unpublished paper, 1985.

Lecompte, Janet. "The Independent Women of Hispanic New Mexico, 1821–1846." In Jensen and Miller, 71–93.

León-Portilla, Miguel. "Afrodite y Tlazolteotl," *Vuelta* (Oct. 1982): 71.

——. "Las alegradoras de tiempos pre-hispánicos." *Cuadernos del Viento* 45–46 (1964): 708.

——. "The Chalco Cihuacuicatl of Aquiauhtzin: Erotic Poetry of the Nahuas." *New Scholar* 5 (1978): 256–62.

——. *Trece poetas del mundo azteca.* México: UNAM, 1967.

Leonardi, Susan J. "Recipes for Reading: Summer Pasta, Lobster a la Riseholme, and Key Lime Pie." *PMLA* 104 (1989): 340–47.

Lizárraga, Sylvia. "The Gift?" In Rebolledo and Rivero, 91. First published in Spanish in *Caracol* (1973): N. pag.

——. "Monarquía." In R. Sánchez, *Requisa,* 133–34.

Lomas, Clara. "The Articulation of Gender in the Mexican Borderlands, 1900–1915." In Gutiérrez and Padilla, 293–308.

——. "Libertad de no procrear: La voz de la mujer en 'A una madre de nuestros tiempos' de Margarita Cota–Cárdenas." In Córdova et al., 195–201.

——. "Mexican Precursors of Chicana Feminist Writing." In Candelaria, *The Wild Zone,* 21–33.

Lomelí, Francisco. "Chicana Novelists in the Process of Creating Fictive Voices." In Herrera-Sobek, *Beyond Stereotypes,* 29–46.

——. "Isabella Ríos and the Chicano Psychic Novel." *Minority Voices: An Interdisciplinary Journal of Literature and the Arts* 4 (1): 49–61.

——, ed. *Morena.* Santa Barbara, Calif.: N.p., 1980.

López, Natasha. "From Between Our Legs." In Trujillo, 156.

López de Padilla, Esperanza. "María Esperanza." In Anselmo Arellano, 147.

———. "Simplicidades." In Anselmo Arellano, 146.

López-Medina, Sylvia. *Cantora*. Albuquerque: University of New Mexico Press, 1992.

López-Stafford, Gloria. *A Place in El Paso*. Albuquerque: University of New Mexico Press, forthcoming.

Lorenzana, Apolonia. "Memorias de la Beata." 1878. Manuscript. Bancroft Library, University of California, Berkeley.

Lummis, Charles F. *The Land of Poco Tiempo*. 1893. Reprinted, Albuquerque: University of New Mexico Press, 1973.

Marks, Elaine, and Isabelle de Coutivron, eds. *New French Feminisms*. New York: Schoken Books, 1981.

Martínez, Demetria. *Turning* in *Three Times a Woman, Chicana Poetry*. Tempe, Ariz.: Bilingual Review/Press, 1989.

McKenna, Teresa. "On Chicano Poetry and the Political Age: Corridos as Social Drama." In Calderón and Saldívar, 188–202.

Meese, Elizabeth A. *(Ex)Tensions: Re-figuring Feminist Criticism*. Urbana: University of Illinois Press, 1990.

Mena, María Cristina. "The Emotions of María Concepción." *Century Magazine* 7 (January 1914): 358.

———. "Marriage By Miracle." *Century Magazine* 19 (February 1916): 732–34.

Michie, Helena. *The Flesh Made Word: Female Figures and Women's Bodies*. New York: Oxford University Press, 1987.

Miguélez, Armando. *Antología histórica del cuento literario chicano, 1877–1950*. Ann Arbor: University Microfilms, 1981.

Miller, Beth, ed. *Women in Hispanic Literature: Icons and Fallen Idols*. Berkeley: University of California Press, 1984.

Mirandé, Alfredo, and Evangelina Enríquez. *La Chicana: The Mexican-American Woman*. Chicago: University of Chicago Press, 1979.

Mistral, Gabriela. *Poesías completas*. Madrid: Aguilar, 1966.

Molloy, Sylvia. *En breve cárcel*. Barcelona: Seix Barral, 1981.

Montes, Ana. "Adelita." *Comadre* 2 (1978): 23.

Montoya, José. "La jefita." In Romano and Ríos, 232–33.

Mora, Pat. *A Birthday Basket for Tía*. New York: MacMillan, 1992.

———. *Borders*. Houston, Tex.: Arte Público Press, 1986.

———. *Chants*. Houston, Tex.: Arte Público Press, 1984.

———. "Coatlicue Rules: Advice From an Aztec Goddess." Unpublished poem.

———. *Communion*. Houston, Tex.: Arte Público Press, 1991.

———. "Hands." *Revista Chicano-Riqueña* 10 (1982): 33–36.

———. *Listen to the Desert: Oye al desierto*. New York: Clarion Books, 1994.

———. "The Named, the Namer, the Naming." *Cuentos del Zaguán*. Unpublished book.

———. *Nepantla: Essays from the Land in the Middle*. Albuquerque: University of New Mexico Press, 1993.

Moraga, Cherríe. *Giving Up the Ghost*. Los Angeles: West End Press, 1986.

———. *Loving in the War Years*. Boston: South End Press, 1983.

Moraga, Cherríe, and Gloria Anzaldúa, eds. *This Bridge Called My Back*. Watertown, Mass.: Persephone Press, 1981.

Munt, Sally, ed. *New Lesbian Criticism: Literary and Cultural Readings*. New York: Columbia University Press, 1992.

New Mexico Federal Writers' Project (NMFWP). "An Old Native Custom: La Curandera," 5-5-49 #45. "Las Tres Gangozas," collected by Bright Lynn from Guadalupe Gallegos, 5-5-7 #4. "Placitas Witch Stories," collected by Lou Sage Batchen from Rumaldita Gurulé, 17 Sept. 1938. "The Tale of the Sick Woman," collected by Simon Tejada from Senaida Sebastian, 5-5-29 #2.

Nicolson, Irene. *A Guide to Mexican Poetry, Ancient and Modern*. México: Editorial Minutae Mexicana, 1968.

Niggli, Josephina. *Mexican Folk Plays*. Chapel Hill: University of North Carolina Press, 1938.

———. *Mexican Village*. Chapel Hill: University of North Carolina Press, 1945; Reprint, with a foreward by María Herrera-Sobek, Albuquerque: University of New Mexico Press, 1994.

———. *New Pointers on Playwriting*. Boston: The Writer, Inc., 1967.

———. *Pointers on Radio Writing*. Boston: The Writer, Inc., 1946.

Norwood, Vera, and Janice Monk, eds. *The Desert Is No Lady*. New Haven: Yale University Press, 1987.

Ohanneson, Joan. *Woman: Survivor in the Church*. Minneapolis, Minn.: Winston Press, 1980.

Olivares, Julián, ed. "International Studies in Honor of Tomás Rivera." *Revista Chicano-Riqueña* 13: 3–4.

———. "Sandra Cisneros' *The House on Mango Street* and the Poetics of Space." In Herrera-Sobek and Viramontes, 160–70.

———. "Seeing and Becoming: Evangelina Vigil, *Thirty an' Seen a Lot*." In García, Córdova, and García, eds., 152–65.

Ordóñez, Elizabeth J. "Body, Spirit and the Text: Alma Villanueva's *Life Span*." In Calderón and Saldívar, 61–71.

———. "Sexual Politics and the Theme of Sexuality in Chicana Poetry." In Miller, 7–16.

Ostriker, Alicia. *Stealing the Language: The Emergence of Women's Poetry in America*. Boston: Beacon, 1986.

Otero, Nina. *Old Spain in Our Southwest*. New York: Harcourt Brace and Co., 1936.

Padilla, Genaro M. "Imprisoned Narrative? Or Lies, Secrets, and Silence in New Mexico Women's Autobiography." In Calderón and Saldívar, 43–60.

———. "Recovering Mexican-American Autobiography." In Gutiérrez and Padilla, 153–78.

———. "The Recovery of Chicano Nineteenth-Century Autobiography." *The American Quarterly* 42 (1988): 287–98.

————. *My History, Not Yours: The Formation of Mexican American Autobiography*. Madison: University of Wisconsin Press, 1994.

Palacios, Monica. "La Llorona Loca: The Other Side." In Trujillo, 49–51.

Palomo Acosta, Teresa. *Passing Time*. Austin, Tex.: Published privately, 1984.

Paredes, Raymond. "The Evolution of Chicano Literature." In Baker, 33–79.

Parker, Edith Olbrich. "María Gertrudis Pérez Cordero Cassiano (1790–1832)." In Carrington, 49–57.

Paz, Octavio. *The Bow and the Lyre*. New York: McGraw Hill, 1973. Translation by Ruth L. C. Simms.

Peñalosa, Federico. *Chicano Sociolinguisitics: A Brief Introduction*. Rowley, Mass.: Newbury, 1980.

Pérez, Emma. "Sexuality and Discourse: Notes from a Chicana Survivor." In Trujillo, 159–84.

Pérez, Eulalia. "Una vieja y sus recuerdos." 1877. Manuscript. Bancroft Library, University of California, Berkeley. Translated by Ruth Rodríguez. (C-D 139)

Pescatello, Ann M. *Female and Male in Latin America*. Pittsburgh, Pa.: University of Pittsburgh Press, 1973.

Phillips, Rachel. "Marina/Malinche: Masks and Shadows." In Miller, 97–114.

Pico, María Inocenta. "Reminiscences of California." 1878. Manuscript. Bancroft Library, University of California, Berkeley. (C-D 34)

Pineda, Cecile. *Face*. New York: Viking, 1985.

Pizarnik, Alejandra. *La tierra más ajena*. Buenos Aires: Ediciones Botella al Mar, 1955.

Ponce, Mary Helen. *Hoyt Street: An Autobiography*. Albuquerque: University of New Mexico Press, 1993.

————. "Los calzones de la piña." In Rebolledo, Gonzales-Berry, and Márquez, 52–54.

————. *Taking Control*. Houston, Tex.: Arte Público Press, 1987.

————. *The Wedding*. Houston, Tex.: Arte Público Press, 1990.

Portillo Trambley, Estela. *Rain of Scorpions*. Berkeley, Calif.: Tonatiuh International, 1975.

————. *Sor Juana and Other Plays*. Ypsilanti, Mich.: Bilingual Press, 1983.

————. *Trini*. Binghamton, N.Y.: Bilingual Press, 1986.

Pratt, Annis. *Archetypal Patterns in Women's Fiction*. Bloomington: Indiana University Press, 1981.

Pratt, Mary Louise. *Imperial Eyes: Travel Writing and Transculturation*. New York: Routledge, 1992.

Preciado Martin, Patricia. *Del rancho al barrio: The Mexican Legacy of Tucson*. Tucson: Arizona Historical Society, 1983.

————. *Images and Conversations: Mexican Americans Recall a Southwestern Past*. Tucson: University of Arizona Press, 1983.

————. *Songs My Mother Sang to Me: An Oral History of Mexican-American Women*. Tucson: University of Arizona Press, 1992.

Quezada, Noemí. *Amor y magia amorosa entre los Aztecas.* México: UNAM, 1975.

Quintana, Alvina E. "Ana Castillo's *The Mixquiahuala Letters:* The Novelist as Ethnographer." In Calderón and Saldívar, 72–83.

———. "Politics, Representation, and the Emergence of a Chicana Aesthetics." *Cultural Studies* 4 (October 1990): 257–63.

———. "Women: Prisoners of the Word." In Córdova et al., 208–19.

Quiñónez, Naomi. "The Confession." In Rebolledo and Rivero, 300–302.

———. *Sueño de colibrí/Hummingbird dream.* Los Angeles: West End Press, 1985.

Quirarte, Josefina Lomelí. "Condición social de la mujer." In *México prehispánico.* México: Editorial Emma Hurtado, 1946.

Rebolledo, Tey Diana. "The Bittersweet Nostalgia of Childhood in the Poetry of Margarita Cota-Cárdenas." *Frontiers* 5 (1980): 31–35.

———. "Comience la danza: La poesía nahuatl de Macuilxóchitl, 5 Flor." *Revista interamericana de bibliografía* 27 (1978): 283–89.

———. "From Coatlicue to Doña Luz: Mitotes in Chicana Literature." In *To Speak or Be Silent,* edited by Lina Ross, 210–25. Wilamette, Ill.: Chiron Publications, 1993.

———. "Las escritoras: Romances and Realities." In Gonzales-Berry, *Pasó por aquí,* 199–214.

———. "The Maturing of Chicana Poetry: The Quiet Revolution of the 1980s." In Treichler, Kramarae, and Stafford, 143–58.

———. "Narrative Strategies of Resistance in Hispana Writing." *The Journal of Narrative Technique* 20 (1990): 134–46.

———. "The Politics of Poetics: Or, What Am I, a Critic, Doing in This Text Anyhow?" In Herrera-Sobek and Viramontes, 129–38.

———. "Tradition and Mythology: Signatures of Landscape in Chicana Literature." In Norwood and Monk, 98–124.

———. "Walking the Thin Line: Humor in Chicana Literature." In Herrera-Sobek, *Beyond Stereotypes,* 91–105.

———. "Witches, Bitches, and Midwives: The Shaping of Poetic Consciousness in Chicana Literature." In García, Córdova, and García, 166–77.

———, ed. *Nuestras mujeres: Hispanas of New Mexico: Their Images and Their Lives, 1582–1992.* Albuquerque, N.M.: El Norte Publications, 1993.

Rebolledo, Tey Diana, Erlinda Gonzales-Berry, and Teresa Márquez, eds. *Las mujeres hablan: An Anthology of Nuevo Mexicana Writers.* Albuquerque, N.M.: El Norte Publications, 1988.

Rebolledo, Tey Diana, and Eliana S. Rivero, eds. *Infinite Divisions: An Anthology of Chicana Literature.* Tucson: University of Arizona Press, 1993.

Rendón, Armando. *The Chicano Manifesto.* New York: Collier, 1972.

Reyna, Dorotea. "Voice." In Tatum, *New Chicana 1,* 172–74.

Riker, Kathryn. "Alejandra Pizarnik: Between the Languages of Dis-Order." Dissertation. Albuquerque: University of New Mexico, 1992.

Ríos, Isabella. *Victuum.* Ventura, Calif.: Diana-Etna Inc., 1976.

Rivera, Marina. "Mestiza." English translation in Rebolledo and Rivero, 97–101.

———. *Mestiza*. Tucson, Ariz.: Grilled Flowers, 1977.

———. *Sobra*. San Francisco: Casa Editorial, 1977.

Rivero, Eliana. "Escritoras chicanas: Fronteras de la lengua y la cultura." *Anales del Pacífico* (forthcoming).

———. "Escritura chicana: Introducción y contexto." *Areíto* 5 (18): 38–52.

———. "Escritura chicana: La mujer." *La Palabra* 2 (2): 2–9.

———. "Poesía en Arizona: Las voces de *Mestiza*." *La Palabra* 1 (1): 26–33.

———. "*The House on Mango Street:* Tales of Growing Up Female and Hispanic." *SIROW Working Paper Series,* no. 21 (1986): 2–19 (University of Arizona Southwest Institute for Research on Women).

Rocha, Rina García. *Eluder.* Chicago: Alexander Books, 1980.

Rodoreda, Mercé. *Camelia Street.* Translated by David H. Rosenthal. New York: Graywolf, 1993.

Rodríguez, Elena Guadalupe. "Tu canto." In Lomelí, *Morena,* 66.

Romano-V., Octavio Ignacio, and Herminio Ríos-C., eds. *El Espejo–The Mirror: Selected Chicano Literature.* Berkeley, Calif.: Quinto Sol Publications, Inc., 1969.

Rosenfelt, Navton. *Feminist Criticism.* New York: Methuen, 1985.

Ruiz de Burton, María Amparo. *The Squatter and the Don.* Edited and introduced by Rosaura Sánchez and Beatrice Pita. Houston, Tex.: Arte Público Press, 1992.

Rule, Janice. *Lesbian Images.* London: Peter Davies, 1975.

Sahagún, Bernardino de. *Historia general de las cosas de Nueva España.* México: Porrua, 1956. (*Florentine Codex*)

Saldívar, Ramón. *Chicano Narrative: The Dialectics of Difference.* Madison: University of Wisconsin Press, 1990.

Saldívar-Hull, Sonia. "Feminism on the Border: From Gender Politics to Geopolitics." In Calderón and Saldívar, 203–20.

Sánchez, Elba. "Living Canvas." In Tatum, *New Chicana 1,* 47.

———. "Mirror Image: Womanpoetry." In Tatum, *New Chicana 1,* 50.

Sánchez, Margarita V. "Acróstico: Al dulcísimo nombre de Jesús." *La Bandera Americana,* Feb. 4, 1921.

Sánchez, Marta. *Contemporary Chicana Poetry: A Critical Approach to an Emerging Literature.* Berkeley: University of California Press, 1984.

———. "Chicana Prose Writers: The Case of Gina Valdés and Sylvia Lizárraga." In Herrera-Sobek, *Beyond Stereotypes,* 61–70.

Sánchez, Rosaura. *Chicano Discourse: Sociolinguistic Perspectives.* Rowley, Mass.: Newbury, 1983.

———. "Nineteenth-Century California Narratives: The Hubert H. Bancroft Collection." In Gutiérrez and Padilla, 279–92.

———. *Requisa treinta y dos.* La Jolla, Calif.: Chicano Research Publications, 1979.

Sanchez, Rosaura, and Rosa Martínez Cruz. *Essays of La Mujer.* Los Angeles: Chicano Studies Center Publications, 1977.

Santa-Ana, Otto. *Toward a More Adequate Characterization of the Chicano Language Setting.* Albuquerque: University of New Mexico Southwest Research Institute, 1993.

Santana-Béjar, Patricia. "In the Toolshed." *Maize* 4 (1981): 1–2.

Santillanes, Millie. "Flossie Córdova." In Rebolledo, *Nuestras mujeres,* 107–8.

Schneiders, Sandra. M. *Woman and the Word: The Gender of God in the New Testament and the Spirituality of Women.* New York: Paulist Press, 1986.

Sehons, Dorothy. "Some Obscure Points in the Life of Sor Juana Inés de la Cruz." *Modern Philology* 14 (November 1926): 141–62.

Shirley, Paula W. "Josefina Niggli." *Dictionary of Literary Biography Yearbook,* 279–86.

Siete poetas. Tucson, Ariz.: Scorpion Press, 1979.

Silva, Beverly. *The Cat and Other Stories.* Tempe, Ariz.: Bilingual Press, 1986.

———. *The Second St. Poems.* Ypsilanti, Mich.: Bilingual Press, 1983.

Smith, Barbara. "The Truth That Never Hurts: Black Lesbians in Fiction in the 1980s." In Warhol and Herndl, 690–712.

Smith, Sidonie, and Julia Watson, eds. *De/Colonizing the Subject: The Politics of Gender in Women's Autobiography.* Minneapolis: University of Minnesota Press, 1992.

Stephens, Sandra L. "The Women of the Amador Family, 1860–1940." In Jensen and Miller, 257–77.

Stevens, Evelyn P. "Marianismo: The Other Face of Machismo." In Pescatello, 89–101.

Tafolla, Carmen. *Curandera.* San Antonio, Tex.: M & A Editions, 1983.

———. "Federico y Elfiria." In Alarcón, Castillo, and Moraga, 105–12.

———. *Get Your Tortillas Together.* N.p.: 1976.

———. "La Malinche." *Encuentro artístico feminil* (Austin, 1978): 41–42.

Tatum, Charles. "Some Considerations on Genres and Chronology for Nineteenth Century Hispanic Literature." In Gutiérrez and Padilla, 199–208.

———, ed. *New Chicana/Chicano Writing 1.* Tucson: University of Arizona Press, 1992.

———. *New Chicana/Chicano Writing 2.* Tucson: University of Arizona Press, 1993.

———. *New Chicana/Chicano Writing 3.* Tucson: University of Arizona Press, 1993.

Tinajero, Sara G. "The Role of a Mexican American Woman Poet in the Southwestern United States." M.A. thesis. Laredo State University, 1988.

Torres, Hector. "Postmodernism and Contemporary Chicano/a Narrative." Unpublished paper.

Torres, Olga Beatrice. *Memorias de mi viaje.* Introduction and translation by Juanita Luna Lawhn. Albuquerque: University of New Mexico Press, 1994.

Treichler, Paula A., Cheris Kramarae, and Beth Stafford, eds. *For Alma Mater: Theory and Practice in Feminist Scholarship.* Chicago: University of Illinois Press, 1985.

Treviño, Gloria. "Early Chicana Prose Fiction Writers: In Search of a Female Space." Paper presented to the Modern Language Association, December 1985.

Trujillo, Carla, ed. *Chicana Lesbians: The Girls Our Mothers Warned Us About.* Berkeley, Calif.: Third Woman Press, 1991.

Valdés, Gina. *Comiendo lumbre/Eating fire.* Colorado Springs: Maize Press, 1986.

———. "Josefina's Chickens." *Caracol* (March 1979): 15–20.

———. *Puentes y fronteras.* Los Angeles: Castle Lithograph, 1982.

———. *There Are No Madmen Here.* San Diego, Calif.: Maize Press, 1981.

———. "Weeping With Laughter." In Rebolledo and Rivero, 368–69.

Vasconselos, José. *La raza cósmica: Misión de la raza iberoamericana, argentina, y brasil.* Paris: Agencia Mundial de Librería. 5th ed., México: Espasa-Calpe Mexicana, 1977.

Vásquez, Dora Ortiz. *Enchanted Temples of Taos: My Story of Rosario.* Santa Fe, N.M.: Rydel Press, 1975.

Vigil, Evangelina. *The Computer is Down.* Houston, Tex.: Arte Público Press, 1987.

———. *Nade y nade.* San Antonio, Tex.: M & A Editions, 1978.

———. *Thirty an' Seen a Lot.* Houston, Tex.: Arte Público Press, 1982.

———, ed. *Woman of Her Word: Hispanic Women Write.* Houston, Tex.: Arte Público Press, 1984.

Villanueva, Alma Luz. *Bloodroot.* Austin, Tex.: Place of Herons Press, 1982.

———. *Life Span.* Austin, Tex.: Place of Herons Press, 1985.

———. *Mother, May I?* Pittsburgh, Pa.: Motheroot, 1978.

———. *Naked Ladies.* Tempe, Ariz.: Bilingual Press, 1994.

———. *Planet.* Tempe, Ariz.: Bilingual Press, 1993.

———. *The Ultraviolet Sky.* Tempe, Ariz.: Bilingual Press, 1988.

Viramontes, Helena María. *The Moths and Other Stories.* Houston, Tex.: Arte Público Press, 1985.

Warhol, Robyn R., and Diane Price Herndl. *Feminisms: An Anthology of Literary Theory and Criticism.* New Brunswick, N.J.: Rutgers University Press, 1991.

Warner, Marina. *Alone of All Her Sex: The Myth and Cult of the Virgin Mary.* New York: Knopf, 1976.

Watson, Julia. "Unspeakable Differences: The Politics of Gender in Lesbian and Heterosexual Women's Autobiographies." In Smith and Watson, 139–68.

Weed, Elizabeth. *Coming to Terms: Feminism, Theory, Politics.* New York: Routledge, 1989.

Weigle, Marta. *New Mexicans in Cameo and Camera.* Albuquerque: University of New Mexico Press, 1985.

Wilbur-Cruce, Eva Antonia. *A Beautiful, Cruel Country.* Tucson: University of Arizona Press, 1987.

Xelina. *KU.* San Antonio, Tex.: Caracol, 1977.

Yarbro-Bejarano, Yvonne. "Chicana Literature From a Chicana Feminist Perspective." In Warhol and Herndl, 731–37.

———. "De-constructing the Lesbian Body: Cherríe Moraga's *Loving in the War Years*." In Trujillo, 143–55.

———. "Insider/Outsider: Multiple Cultural Critiques in Chicana Art and Literature." Unpublished paper.

Ybarra-Frausto, Tomás. "Rasquachismo: A Chicano Sensibility." Chicano Art: Resistance and Affirmation, 1965–1985. Los Angeles: Wight Art Gallery UCLA, 1991.

Zamora, Bernice. *Restless Serpents*. Menlo Park, Calif.: Diseños Literarios, 1974. Reprinted in *Releasing Serpents,* Arizona State University, Tempe: Bilingual Press/Editorial Bilingüe, 1994.

Zimmerman, Bonnie. "Lesbians Like This and That: Some Notes on Lesbian Criticism for the Nineties." In Munt, 1–16.

———. "What Has Never Been: An Overview of Lesbian Feminist Literary Criticism." In Warhol and Herndl, 117–37.

Source Acknowledgments

Anzaldúa, Gloria. "My Black Angelos" from *Borderlands/La frontera: The New Mestiza,* copyright © 1987 by Gloria Anzaldúa. Reprinted with permission from Aunt Lute Books (415) 826-1300.

Candelaria, Cordelia. "Go 'Way From My Window, La Llorona" and "Haciendo tamales" from *Ojo de la cueva/Cave Springs* (Colorado Springs: Maize Press, 1984). Reprinted by permission of the author.

Cisneros, Sandra. From *The House on Mango Street,* copyright © 1984 by Sandra Cisneros. Published by Vintage Books, a division of Random House, Inc., New York, and in hardcover by Alfred A. Knopf. Reprinted by permission of Susan Bergholz Literary Services, New York. From *My Wicked, Wicked Ways,* copyright © 1987 by Sandra Cisneros. Published by Third Woman Press and in hardcover by Alfred A. Knopf. Reprinted by permission of Third Woman Press. From *Loose Woman,* copyright © 1994 by Sandra Cisneros. Published by Alfred A. Knopf, New York. Reprinted by permission of Susan Bergholz Literary Services, New York.

Corpi, Lucha. The "Marina" poems, translated by Catherine Rodríguez-Nieto, appeared in *Fireflight: Three Latin American Poets* (Oakland, Calif.: Oyez, 1975); "Protocolo de verduras/The Protocol of Vegetables" appeared in *Palabras mediodía/Noon Words* (Berkeley, Calif.: Fuego de Aztlán, 1980). They are reprinted here with permission from Lucha Corpi, the poet, and Catherine Rodríguez-Nieto, the translator.

Cota-Cárdenas, Margarita. "Crisis de identidad" from *Noches despertando inConciencias* (Tucson, Ariz.: Scorpion Press, 1978). "Marchitas de Mayo," "Dedicated to American Atomics II," "Watercolors," and "El son de dos caras," from *Marchitas de Mayo* (Austin, Tex.: Relámpago Books Press, 1989). "Malinche's Discourse" and "Lírica fanática" from *Infinite Divisions: An Anthology of Chicana Literature,* eds. Tey Diana Rebolledo and Eliana S. Rivero (Tucson: University of Arizona Press, 1993). Selections from *Puppet* (Austin,

Tex.: Relámpago Books Press, 1985). Reprinted by permission of the author.

Curiel, Barbara Brinson. "Recipe" from *Speak To Me From Dreams* (Berkeley, Calif.: Third Woman Press, 1989). Reprinted by permission of the author.

Gaspar de Alba, Alicia. Selections from *Beggar on the Córdoba Bridge* in *Three Times a Woman, Chicana Poetry* (Arizona State University, Tempe: Bilingual Press/Editorial Bilingüe, 1989). Reprinted by permission of Bilingual Press/Editorial Bilingüe.

Gonzales, Gloria. "There Is Nothing" from *Las mujeres hablan,* eds. Tey Diana Rebolledo, Erlinda Gonzales-Berry, and Teresa Márquez (Albuquerque, N.M.: El Norte Publications, 1988). Reprinted by permission of the author.

Gonzales, María Dolores. "María" from *Las mujeres hablan,* eds. Tey Diana Rebolledo, Erlinda Gonzales-Berry, and Teresa Márquez (Albuquerque, N.M.: El Norte Publications, 1988). Reprinted by permission of the author.

Gonzales-Berry, Erlinda. Selections from *Paletitas de guayaba* (Albuquerque, N.M.: El Norte Publications, 1991). Reprinted by permission of the author.

Hernandez-Tovar, Inés. "Guerillera soy" from *Con razón, Corazón* (San Antonio, Tex.: Caracol, 1977). Reprinted by permission of the author.

Herrera-Sobek, María. Selections from *Naked Moon/Luna desnuda* in *Three Times a Woman, Chicana Poetry* (Arizona State University, Tempe: Bilingual Press/Editorial Bilingüe, 1989). Reprinted by permission of Bilingual Press/Editorial Bilingüe. "Poema inédito" from *Infinite Divisions* (Tucson, Ariz.: University of Arizona Press, 1993). Reprinted by permission of the author.

Martínez, Demetria. Selections from *Turning* in *Three Times a Woman, Chicana Poetry* (Arizona State University, Tempe: Bilingual Press/Editorial Bilingüe, 1989). Reprinted by permission of Bilingual Press/Editorial Bilingüe.

Mora, Pat. "Aztec Princess," "Bruja-Witch," "Curandera," "Legal Alien," and "1910" from *Chants* (1984); "To Big Mary From an Ex-Catholic" and "Maybe a Nun After All" from *Borders* (1986); and "The Young Sor Juana" and "Mothers and Daughters" from *Communion* (1991) are reprinted with permission of the publisher, Arte Público Press—University of Houston, Tex.

Sánchez, Elba R. "Living Canvas" and "Mirror Image: Womanpoetry" from *Chicana/Chicano Writing 1,* ed. Charles M. Tatum (Tucson: University of Arizona Press, 1992). Reprinted by permission of the author.

Tafolla, Carmen. "curandera" from *Curandera* (San Antonio, Tex.: M & A Editions, 1983). Reprinted by permission of the author.

Valdés, Gina. "Weeping With Laughter" from *Infinite Divisions: An Anthology of Chicana Literature,* eds. Tey Diana Rebolledo and Eliana S. Rivero (Tucson: University of Arizona Press, 1993). Reprinted by permission of the author.

Villanueva, Alma Luz. "Siren," "Winged Woman," and "Escandalosa," from *Life Span* (Austin, Tex.: Place of Herons Press, 1985). Reprinted by permission of the author.

Zamora, Bernice. "Pueblo, 1950" from *Restless Serpents* (Menlo Park, Calif.: Diseños Literarios, 1974). Reprinted in *Releasing Serpents* (Arizona State University, Tempe: Bilingual Press/Editorial Bilingüe, 1994). Reprinted by permission of Bilingual Press/Editorial Bilingüe.

Index

About the Author

Tey Diana Rebolledo is an associate professor of Spanish at the University of New Mexico, where she teaches Latin American and Chicano literature. She was born in Las Vegas, New Mexico, in 1937. Rebolledo is the author of numerous articles on Chicana writers, and the editor of *Nuestras mujeres: Hispanas in New Mexico: Their Images and Their Lives, 1582–1992* and *Las mujeres hablan: An Anthology of Nuevo Mexicana Writers*. She is also coeditor (with Eliana Rivero) of *Infinite Divisions: An Anthology of Chicana Literature*. Rebolledo has been a New Mexico Eminent Scholar and a Faculty Scholar at the University of New Mexico, and she has served as Chair of the National Association for Chicano Studies. Her current project is a cultural history of Spanish / Mexicanas in the Southwest. Rebolledo lives in Albuquerque with her compañero, Michael Passi, two spaniels, Fina and Gus, and a cat, Esperanza.